Landmarks
of Canadian Art

EDITORIAL BOARD

Landmarks
of Canadian Art

Peter Mellen

McCLELLAND AND STEWART

Dedicated to my wife, Frances,
and to my son, Peter William

CANADIAN CATALOGUING IN PUBLICATION DATA

Mellen, Peter.
  Landmarks

Bibliography: p.
Includes index.

ISBN 0-7710-5828-4

1. Art, Canadian - History. 2. Art, Modern -
Canada - History. 3. Artists - Canada - Biography.
I. Title.

N6540.M44   709'.71   C78-001240-2

Illustrated Books Division
McClelland and Stewart Limited
The Canadian Publishers
25 Hollinger Road, Toronto M4B 3G2

Printed and bound in Canada

PAGE 5 PLATE 1
Cornelius Krieghoff (1815-1872)
Merrymaking 1860
oil on canvas 88.0 x 122.0 cm
Beaverbrook Canadian Foundation

PAGE 6 PLATE 2
Paul Peel (1860-1892)
After the Bath 1890
oil on canvas 147.3 x 110.5 cm
Art Gallery of Ontario

PAGE 7 PLATE 3
William Brymner (1855-1925)
A Wreath of Flowers 1884
oil on canvas 120.7 x 139.7 cm
National Gallery of Canada

PAGE 8 PLATE 4
Lawren Harris (1885-1970)
Mt. Lefroy 1930
oil on canvas 132.7 x 152.3 cm
McMichael Canadian Collection

PAGE 9 PLATE 5
Tom Thomson (1877-1917)
The Jack Pine 1917
oil on canvas 127.7 x 139.7 cm
National Gallery of Canada

PAGE 10 PLATE 6
Joseph Légaré (1795-1960)
L'incendie du Quartier Saint-Jean c. 1845
oil on canvas 151.1 x 220.3 cm
Art Gallery of Ontario

PAGE 11 PLATE 7
Jack Chambers (1931-1978)
Lake Huron No. 4 1970-76
oil on wood 121.9 x 121.9 cm
Private Collection

PAGE 12 PLATE 8
Paul-Emile Borduas (1905-1960)
Le chant de la pierre 1956
oil on canvas 113.0 x 114.5 cm
The Toronto Dominion Bank

PLATE 1

PLATE 2

PLATE 3

7

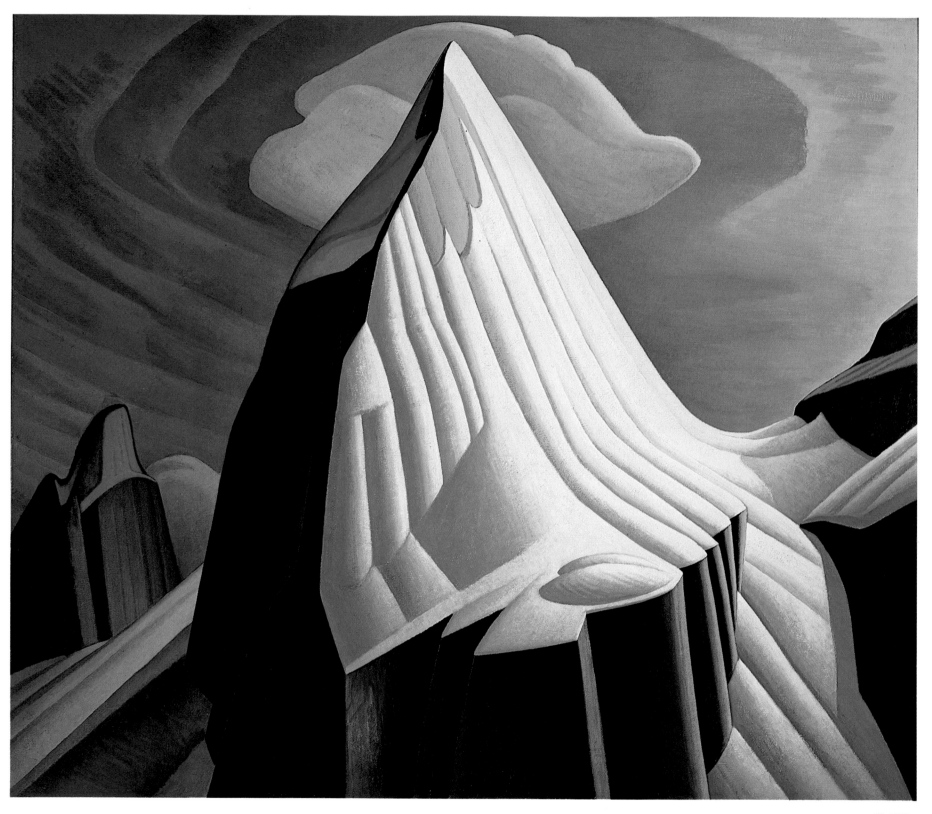

PLATE 4

PLATE 5

PLATE 6

PLATE 7

PLATE 8

CONTENTS

Preface by Jean Sutherland Boggs   14

Introduction   15

1   This Sacred Land:
    Art of the Native Peoples   17
    THE PLATES   53

2   Art for the Glory of God:
    The Early Explorers and the French Regime   23
    THE PLATES   85

3   The Garrison and the Frontier:
    Documenting the New Society   27
    THE PLATES   103

4   Contradictions and Change:
    Art in the Victorian Era   32
    THE PLATES   135

5   The Canadian Spirit in Art:
    The Group of Seven and Their Contemporaries   37
    THE PLATES   167

6   The Search Within:
    Contemporary Art   43
    THE PLATES   203

New Ways of Seeing   248
    THE PLATES   251

Bibliography   257
Acknowledgements   258
Index   259

PREFACE

This book contains one hundred and sixteen works that are landmarks in the development of art in Canada.

For the purposes of selection here, the Canadian artist has been defined as one who is a permanent resident of the geographic entity known as Canada; this includes the Inuit, the Indians, and those who have emigrated, or have descended from those who have emigrated, from countries over the surface of the earth. Most of the works reproduced are from the nineteenth and twentieth centuries, but also included are the prehistoric art of the Inuit and Indian, and religious works from Quebec in the sixteenth, seventeenth, and eighteenth centuries.

Although cultural, historic, and geographic considerations were not ignored in making the selection, the objects reproduced were chosen as works of art and not as anthropological evidence of the state of Canadian society at any given time. (Some works are, however, admittedly both art and documentation.) The intention is to reproduce the landmarks in Canadian art, the treasures of our heritage. This has meant reproducing such familiar and beloved works as Tom Thomson's *Jack Pine*, as well as lesser-known works that are a further revelation of the vitality of Canadian art.

The choice was made by an editorial board of distinguished scholars: James Houston, one of the first to acknowledge the greatness of Inuit art; Jean Trudel, Director of The Montreal Museum of Fine Arts and author of works on the silver, sculpture, and painting of pre-Conquest Quebec; J. Russell Harper, author of many monographs on individual Canadian artists and the invaluable book, *Painting in Canada*; Joan Murray, Director of The Robert McLaughlin Gallery in Oshawa and former Curator of Canadian Art at The Art Gallery of Ontario, who has organized eleven exhibitions on Canadian art, including those on Tom Thomson and Canadian Impressionism; and Luke Rombout, Director of The Vancouver Art Gallery and first director of the Canada Council's Art Bank who, through official acquisitions and exhibitions, has a comprehensive knowledge of what is being produced in Canada now. I attended the board meetings, presumably because as a former director of The National Gallery of Canada (from 1966 to 1976) I might act as a catalyst. Peter Mellen, the coordinator and chairman, had already discussed the project with, and been given advice by, a variety of other experts on Canadian art, including curators, gallery owners, critics, other historians, and the living artists themselves.

At board meetings, individual members proposed works from their fields of expertise. These were discussed, and alternatives suggested, until a final list was drawn up. The selection represents the convictions of a group of Canadians who possess a particularly intimate knowledge of our art. Included in this book are the works that they believe represent landmarks in creative achievement in the visual arts in Canada.

Besides acting as coordinator, Peter Mellen prepared the text for the book. A Montreal-born graduate of McGill, he studied art history in Paris and London. His books include *Jean Clouet* (published by Phaidon Press in London and Flammarian in Paris) and *The Group of Seven* (McClelland and Stewart), now in its seventh printing. He has taught the history of Canadian art at Toronto and York universities, and now devotes all of his time to writing and film-making. His text for *Landmarks of Canadian Art* describes the circumstances under which these works were produced, and establishes their importance in Canadian art history.

Jean Sutherland Boggs

INTRODUCTION

The purpose of this book is to bring together the most exceptional works created in the history of Canadian art, reproducing them in full colour and in large format. Each one of them is a major landmark, charting the dramatic course of art in Canada over a period of twenty centuries. They form part of an immensely rich artistic heritage, and help to provide a deeper understanding of our culture and ourselves.

Compressing three thousand years into a few pages has been an awesome challenge. What I hoped to communicate was the way the artists of each era expressed the dynamics of their culture, as well as their own personal vision. I have tried to tell this story simply and directly, with as little jargon as possible.

The selection of Canada's artistic landmarks was an agonizing experience — not because of what has been included, but because of what has been left out. Our aim was simple: to find the best works by the most important artists in Canadian art. The committee felt that it was important to include the great classics of Canadian art that were accessible to the general public, rather than to search for esoteric examples hidden in private collections. Those plates included here represent the collective experience of the members of the editorial board, which amounts to over one hundred and fifty years of involvement in the art world. I am immensely indebted to the board members, who all gave generous support to the project. They patiently answered my endless questions, and their insights and expertise shaped not only the selection, but the text as well. I am particularly grateful to Joan Murray, who wrote many of the captions for the book, including nearly all those in Chapter Four, and many in Chapters Five and Six.

Other experts have provided invaluable assistance. In preparing the chapter on art of the native peoples, I received guidance from George Swinton, Jack and Sheila Butler, Jeanne Pattison, Peter Macnair, Selwyn Dewdney, Hugh Dempsey, Helga Goetz, Jean Blodgett, and William Taylor, Jr. For insights on other Canadian art, Dennis Reid was a tremendous inspiration, generously giving of his time and knowledge. Many others helped along the way: Pierre Théberge, Charles Hill, Mayo Graham, Rosemarie Tovell — all of the National Gallery — and Mary Allodi, Doris Shadbolt, Nancy Dillow, David Silcox, Jeffrey Spalding, and Ken Carpenter. To all these individuals and the institutions they represent, my heartfelt thanks. Many gallery owners, especially Avrom Isaacs, Carmen Lamanna, and Jack Pollock, tracked down works and provided information on the artists they represent. The artists themselves were enlightening and informative in their responses to my queries.

Much of the original research for the book was done with the assistance of a Senior Arts Grant from the Canada Council. My sincere thanks to them for their support.

The book demanded enormous efforts on the part of all those involved in its production. I am grateful to Denise Avery and Bob Young at McClelland and Stewart for their support. The photographers — Michael Neill in particular — produced transparencies of unfailing high quality. Audrey Armstrong proved to be a capable and delightfully cheerful research assistant. Judy Sachs did all the typing with the same enthusiasm.

My deepest thanks go to my wife Fran, who provided not only loving support and encouragement, but also invaluable criticism. She insisted on a strong conceptual framework, helped with research, and kept me on the track when I became too flowery or pedantic. I dedicate the book to her and my son Peter William, who patiently put up with a father who for a long period couldn't do the things that dads usually do.

Peter Mellen

1
This Sacred Land:
Art of the Native Peoples

By the time the white man arrived in North America, there were over 240,000 native peoples living in what is now Canada. It was a time when the land was sacred and there was no word for art: "Art was a part of life, like hunting, gathering, or growing food, marrying and having children."[1]

Three thousand years ago the forerunners of the Northwest Coast Indian were living along the beautiful western coastline. Very few works have survived from prehistoric times, but a number of larger stone sculptures have been found that reveal a vital and powerful culture. These include the striking *Twin Mask* (p. 60), *The Death Bringer Club* (p. 59), and *The Sechelt Image* (p. 59). All these images show a preoccupation with the basic instincts of survival, on an immensely sophisticated level. Nothing is known of the people who made them, other than what can be deduced from the works themselves.

On the Prairies, the culture of the early Indian centred on the buffalo. Just prior to the arrival of the white man, there were several tribes living on the Prairies, including the Cree, the Blackfoot, the Assiniboin, and the Sarcee. These nomadic people followed herds of buffalo, and several prehistoric stone buffalo images suggest that they may have worshipped them. The period following the introduction of horses (after 1700) is known as the Plains culture, which lasted until the virtual disappearance of the buffalo in the late nineteenth century. It was a period of great chivalry and splendour, when Indians rode across the Prairies in colourful regalia. These were the native peoples Paul Kane depicted in paintings such as *Assiniboin Hunting Buffalo* (p. 131), shortly before this way of life disappeared forever.

The lakes and forests of the Eastern Woodlands had been inhabited from the time the last glaciers retreated about seven thousand years ago. The most important tribes (from west to east) were the Cree, Ojibwa, Iroquois, Algonkin, Montagnais, Naskapi, Malecite, Micmac, and Beothuk. These tribes included about 100,000 people when the white man arrived.

The Woodland Indians had a rich and varied range of creative art forms, intimately tied to their culture and religion. Their extant works include the extraordinary petroglyphs of the Algonkins, carved into huge exposed rocks; the sacred rock paintings of the Ojibwa, representing powerful mythic figures such as *Mishipeshu* (p. 70); the grotesque masks of the Iroquois, carved directly out of living trees (p. 69); the unique painted skins of the Naskapi; and the exquisitely decorated baskets of the Micmac.

The first known people to live in the far North belonged to the Pre-Dorset culture (2,500 BC – 800 BC); the subsequent Dorset culture lasted until about 1300 AD. The few objects that survive from this period reveal a people of imagination and intelligence. Works such as the *Shaman's Mask* (p. 55) were almost certainly carved by the shaman or medicine man, and were intended to serve some sacred function.

Around 900 AD another people, known as the Thule culture, began to move eastward from northern Alaska, replacing the Dorset people. They were far more advanced in tools and technology than their predecessors. The Thule people developed new techniques for whaling and invented the dog sled, the bow drill, and the open-skinned boat. Thule artifacts seem more elegant and playful than those of the Dorset culture, which were weighty and serious. Thule works consist mainly of small figurines representing women and birds, or graceful combs carved in ivory. Unlike the Dorset objects, which were often incised with deep lines, Thule pieces were usually drilled with rows of decorative dots. The Thule people also created a new graphic style by engraving pictographs of whaling and hunting scenes on objects such as bow-drill handles or pipestems.

The Thule culture thrived as late as the sixteenth century, when Martin Frobisher journeyed to Baffin Island. Shortly afterwards, this culture declined and was replaced by the predecessors of the contemporary Eskimo. They called themselves the Inuit, meaning the "real people" or the "human ones."

For the native peoples, art formed an integral part of the fabric of society, and was not admired for its own sake. In some cases it had a specific religious function, in others a definite social or utilitarian purpose. Many objects, such as masks and ceremonial regalia, were seen only in sacred ceremonies and kept hidden the rest of the time. They were part of a total experience involving music, dance, and song. Whether it was the Dorset *Shaman's Mask* (p. 55), the Tsimshian *Sea Monster Headdress* (p. 66), or the *Crooked Nose Mask* of the Iroquois (p. 69), they were all meant to be experienced within the context of their original sacred purpose. As contemporary Indian artist Bill Reid has said, "When we look at a particular work . . . and see the shape of it, we are only looking at its after-life. Its real life is the movement by which it got to be that shape."[2]

Most of the ceremonies central to the life of the native peoples revolved around the rites of passage of birth, marriage, or death. Others marked the passing of the seasons or events of social importance. They were usually highly structured, with long and complex rituals. For the Northwest Coast Indians it was the Potlach; for the Plains Indians it was the dramatic Sun Dance; for the Iroquois it was the Feast of the Dead; and for the Eskimo it was the Feast of Sedna.

Both the Indian and the Eskimo lived in close harmony with nature and its seasons. Everything in nature was thought to be alive and filled with spirits, whether it was the trees, the animals, or even the rocks. There was usually little distinction between man and nature or man and animals. A man could transform himself into a bear or vice versa; there was an affinity between the hunter and the hunted. Whether it was the grizzly bear of the West Coast, the black bear of the Eastern Woodlands, or the great polar bear of the North, the bear was usually revered as the most sacred of all animals.

Nearly all the native peoples have images of bears in their art. One of the earliest is the prehistoric ivory *Bear* (National Museum of Man) from the Dorset culture, with "x-ray" incisions on its back. This bear was probably carved by the shaman and used for magico-religious purposes. The shaman possessed special powers that enabled him to make contact with the world of the spirits, which were sometimes friendly, sometimes hostile, and sometimes neutral. They inhabited a world similar to that of humans on earth, but they could transform themselves into an

Dorset *Bear* 0-500 AD

animal or another person – and they could also reside in a variety of inanimate objects. The shaman contacted these spirits through fasting, meditation, or dreams: "I have been on the other side of the world, I, the great supernatural being. There I obtained all the supernatural power."[3] One of the shaman's roles was to create objects that possessed magical power. He had the ability to travel through the spirit world, and to "see himself as a skeleton . . . divesting himself of his flesh and blood, so that nothing remains but his bones."[4]

After the arrival of Europeans in the seventeenth century, new materials and tools were introduced to the Indian and Eskimo. The earlier art forms continued, but additional objects were now produced for trade with the white man. Although there were significant changes in each culture, most of the native peoples did not lose their traditional way of life for years to come.

The Northwest Coast Indian culture reached the height of its expression during the nineteenth century. The Indians of the Prairies remained relatively undisturbed until the building of the railroad and the disappearance of the buffalo. The Eskimos preserved their way of life well into the twentieth century. In the East, the changes were more immediate and drastic. It was not long before disease and warfare destroyed most of the population.

The first white people showed a total disregard for native traditions, and were determined to impose their own values. But anthropologists and ethnologists such as Franz Boas, Knud Rasmussen, and Marius Barbeau came to study the life and culture of the native peoples. Paul Kane and others documented it in their paintings; Edward Curtis created a striking photographic record of both the Indian and the Eskimo; and Robert Flaherty produced the unique documentary film, *Nanook of the North.*

Perhaps the most impressive art of the native people is that of the Northwest Coast Indian. Late in the nineteenth century there were about fifty thousand Indians living along the West Coast. With a temperate climate and a plentiful supply of food from the sea, the coastal Indians had more time to devote to social and religious activities, and to their art. Although these Indians had many things in common, they were divided into at least six different nations, each with its own society and culture. In the north, there were the Haida, Tlingit, and Tsimshian; in the central province, the Kwakiutl and Nootkan; and in the south, the Coast Salish.

For the West Coast people, art encompassed the entire environment, and their creativity can be found in every aspect of human endeavour. The fisherman went to sea in a large wooden canoe with a brightly painted prow carved in the form of an animal; he used a harpoon that not only was a highly functional weapon, but also was beautiful. His catch was cooked in an elaborately carved box and was served on wooden plates carved in the form of a beaver or a seal. Even the spoons had intricately carved handles and graceful shapes. When there was a Potlach, or ceremonial feast, the chief wore a chilkat blanket and a ceremonial frontlet as an expression of his social importance.

Most Northwest Coast Indian art demonstrated the social status of the chief of the clan. By far the most impressive expression of prestige was the totem pole, which contained the "essential spirit" of the chief or family who had commissioned it. In front of every large wooden house a majestic pole towered high into the air, tracing the family's ancestry back to its mythological beginnings. Carved on the pole were all the people, animals, and supernatural beings involved in each family's history, which could be read like a story.

There were many different kinds of poles – house poles, which told the lineage of the chief who lived inside; memorial poles, which were built to commemorate a special event, and mortuary poles, which were erected as a chief's or shaman's grave post. One of the most remarkable is the *Hole-in-the-Sky* pole, which still stands in its original location in Kitwancool, B.C.. The large oval opening was used as an entranceway to the house on ceremonial occasions, and symbolizes the "hole-in-the-sky" that the shaman passes through on his ascent to the spirit world. The pole itself reflects the ancient concept of the cosmic Tree of Life, and shows

that totem poles may once have had sacred significance, before they became symbols of wealth and prestige.

Late in the nineteenth century, the West Coast people became more and more preoccupied with demonstrating social status through art and ceremony, primarily through the Potlach, where the chief and his guests attempted to out-do each other in gift-giving. Missionaries viewed the Potlach as a pagan activity and had it banned by the government. The increasing influence of missionaries, as well as contact with other white men, caused the once vital culture to fall apart from the centre.

Only recently was the Potlach ban lifted, coincidental with an enormous revitalization of the culture. Artists such as Bill Reid (p. 82), Henry Hunt, and Robert Davidson revived the old craft traditions. Through their art, they helped many Indians rediscover their heritage. A group named Ksan established a craft centre, a museum, and an innovative work program in Hazelton, BC. Craftsmen such as Walter Harris, Earl Muldoe, and Vernon Stephens emerged as highly talented and accomplished artists.

In other parts of Canada, contemporary Indian artists are also reinterpreting their ancient traditions in a new and vital way. They include Daphne Odjig, Alex Janvier, Jackson Beardy, Clifford Maracle, and Carl Ray. The father of them all is Norval Morriseau (p. 81), an Ojibwa artist who began painting in the 1950s. These artists face the challenge of trying to balance a reaffirmation of their ancestry with an awareness of their present position in a predominantly white culture, as well as their own personal search for self-expression.

In 1948, artist James Houston made a momentous trip to the east coast of Hudson Bay. While at Port Harrison he was impressed by the high quality of the carvings he saw. He brought some back to the Canadian Handicrafts Guild in Montreal. With the guild's encouragement, he purchased about a thousand pieces on his next trip. These were exhibited at the guild in November, and within three days every work had been sold. This astounding success led

to other Arctic expeditions, and to much-needed government support. The Inuit had been trading carvings with the *kablunait* (the people with the heavy eyebrows) ever since the arrival of the first explorers, but they had never been given any direction or encouragement. With the help of Houston and others, the production of art rapidly became a major new development, just at a time when the Inuit way of life was declining. It meant that they had a new means of supporting themselves and a new way of keeping their heritage alive.

When the Eskimo first began recording their impressions in carvings and prints, often the elders in the community produced the art. These people knew the old ways and were intimately familiar with the early legends, which had been handed down to them through many generations. With a fondness for storytelling, they translated these stories into graphic art. As artist Pitseolak said of herself, "I draw the things I have never seen, the monsters and the spirits, and I draw the old ways, the things we did long ago before there were many white men."[5] Pitseolak and other artists, such as Kiakshuk, Davidialuk, and Jessie Oonark (p. 77), have recorded the Eskimo way of life with originality and imagination.

A new generation of Eskimo artists has grown up, one that has lived through the acculturation process and at the same time has come to a deeper understanding of its past. Karoo Ashevak was one such artist. Before his death in 1974, he carved many fantastic images representing his own dreams from the spirit world. Some, such as *Spirit* (Rothman's Collection), reflect the traditional preoccupation with the shaman's flight through the spirit world. Other Inuit artists continue to assert their powerful individuality with an exceptional facility for adopting outside influences and transforming them into their own unique vision. They create images that not only reflect their own culture, but also express a message of universal significance.

Inuit art has changed radically in the past thirty years, along with the culture. But the changes — mostly in terms of size and

Hoesem-hliyawn *Hole-in-the-Sky* nineteenth century Kitwancool, BC material – are more astonishing for their inventiveness and originality than for any decline in traditional values. Works have become larger, and carved primarily in stone, instead of ivory, bone or antler. In 1957 James Houston introduced print-making to the North, starting a vigorous new tradition. Inuit artists also have explored drawing, wall hangings, ceramics, batik, and painting. New subject matter has appeared, including Christian imagery and scenes of skidoos and airplanes. Artists have achieved a sense of independence by running their own cooperatives and taking an active part in all phases of production. Different regional styles have developed, reflecting the diversity of communities spread over two million square miles. The most important centres are Cape Dorset, Baker Lake, Inouckjouac, Pangnirtung, Rankin Inlet, Eskimo Point, and Holman Island.

Even with the intense acculturation process, important contemporary Inuit artists have managed to preserve their own integrity and traditions. They still draw upon past legends, the spirit world, and scenes from their daily lives. Despite all these changes, they have not adopted the white man's concept of art. *Sananguaq* is the term used for carving, referring to the "making of a likeness," or more literally, "a little likeness we have achieved." The emphasis is on the quality of craftsmanship rather than beauty; a good carving is one that has most successfully embodied its own abstract, or spiritual, reality. As printmaker Kenojuak (p. 78) once said, "There is no word for art. We say it is to transfer something from the real to the unreal."[6]

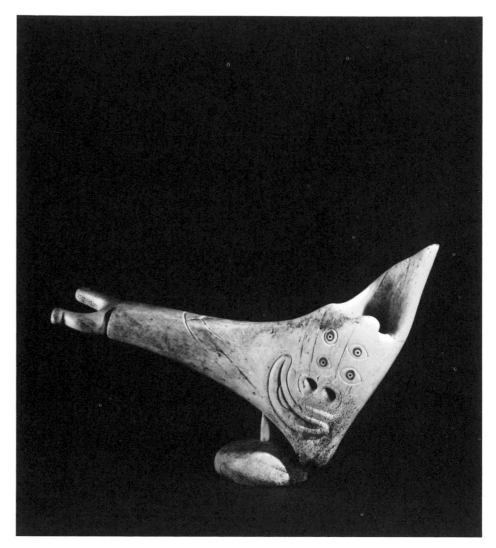

Karoo Ashevak *Spirit* 1973

2
Art for the Glory of God: The Early Explorers and the French Regime

When the first explorers crossed the ocean over four hundred years ago, they had three ways of bringing back information about what they saw: they could write about it, paint or draw pictures of it, or kidnap a few natives. On his expedition to Baffin Island in 1577, Sir Martin Frobisher did all three. He was accompanied by an artist and adventurer named John White, who painted European man's first violent encounter with the Eskimo, in which several people were killed. Frobisher later captured three Eskimos and took them back to Queen Elizabeth as trophies.

Some forty years earlier Jacques Cartier had made his historic expeditions down the Gulf of St. Lawrence, but the only visual records of these voyages are some unusual maps drawn after his return to Europe. One of them, in Nicolas Vallard's *Atlas* (p. 87), shows Jacques Cartier landing near the site of Quebec City with his companions. Samuel de Champlain's exploration of the St. Lawrence produced the first visual documentation of New France – from Champlain's own hand. An amateur artist, Champlain documented his travels with scientific precision. During the next thirty-two years, he devoted all his energies to the colony

of New France and managed to establish a foothold in North America. For the few settlers, missionaries, and *coureurs de bois*, life in the colony was a constant struggle for survival. There was little time for leisure, and even less time for art.

It was not until 1663, when New France became a Royal Province, that there was any development of art among the white settlers of Canada. France had made a firm commitment to the new colony by providing settlers, military support, and a royal government, all of which brought about a great upsurge in the arts. The main force behind this development was the vision of Bishop François de Montmorency Laval, the spiritual leader of the colony from 1663 until 1685. Laval was motivated by an intense missionary zeal. He recognized that the colony had to have its own institutions and its own culture if it was to become anything more than a fur-trade depot. Churches, seminaries, and missionary headquarters were built and decorated with works of art as beautiful as those found in France.

Laval brought artists to the New World and encouraged the development of a craft tradition in Canada. By the time of his death in 1708, the population of New France had risen from three thousand to over sixteen thousand, and French culture was firmly implanted on Canadian soil. A pattern was established that was to be repeated many times in the next three hundred years, as each settler brought with him his particular education and cultural background and adapted it to the New World.

The Church played a vital role in the day-to-day life of the early inhabitants. As the temple of God and the centre of the community, each church was embellished with specially planned decoration. Every piece of sculpture, each painting or work of silver had its own definite place in the scheme. These creations were not considered works of art, but rather expressions of faith. Their sole purpose was to glorify God. Paintings of religious subjects provided a visual interpretation of the Bible for the faithful; portraits of priests and nuns provided a way of remembering those who were dearly loved and had spent their lives in the service of God. Every church had a sculpture of its patron saint to provide inspiration and example for all to follow.

In the seventeenth century, the Counter-Reformation in Europe, with its intense religious revival, created a powerful force that was felt in Catholic countries all over the world. It was the era of Bernini, Poussin, and Rubens, who were admired by royalty and aristocracy. Their works represent the height of the Baroque, a grandiose and impressive style characterized by its direct appeal to the emotions. The Catholic church recognized the importance of art as a propaganda tool and encouraged an art that inspired profound religious feelings. Sculpture, painting, and architecture were combined to create an overwhelming total environment. With the spread of Catholicism, the Baroque style soon radiated outwards to other countries, including America.

By the time it reached New France, the visions of grandeur were radically transformed. The New World had no great masters capable of initiating a new art form, and most artists were regarded as craftsmen. Except in a few rare cases, their sole patron was the Church. They worked according to well-defined traditions, and their job was to imitate established French examples. These they learned through engraved pictures, works brought over from France, or their own previous experience as craftsmen in France. They imitated the prevalent styles found in French provincial centres, rather than the more refined style of Paris or Versailles. There was little room for creative self-expression – an idea that would not have occurred to them. Despite these restrictions, many works by the early Quebec artists have astonishing power and imaginative force, inspired by a simple faith in God.

The most important art form in New France was not painting, but sculpture. Every new church required a profusely decorated interior, including altar pieces, sculptures, and statuettes. Sculpture formed the major part of the decoration, often covering the entire altar wall of a church. Except for a few small silver statuettes, these were carved from wood, then gilded or painted. The rich gilding looked as beautiful as solid gold, and the painted sculptures, with their elaborately-coloured clothing and flesh tones, appeared life-like.

Although some sculptures were sent from France, their bulk made them impractical to ship in great numbers. Because Laval wanted to make the colony self-reliant, artists were brought over from France to train native-born Canadians. Soon the new colony was producing its own art, independent of France. Although French-Canadian art still depended on French models for much of its composition and subject matter, it rapidly developed its own distinctive characteristics – a combination of human warmth, naïveté, and sophistication.

Included among the first immigrants to New France in 1666 were several sculptors. Their names are known, but there are no surviving works that can be attributed to them. As with all the art of this period, there is remarkably little known about the artists or their works. Many early works were destroyed by fire; others were demolished by the English. Most were never signed, many were painted over by later artists, and some were made in France and sent over to Canada.

One of the first Quebec-born sculptors was Noël Levasseur, who formed part of a long lineage of *québécois* carvers that started with his grandfather, Jean Levasseur. It was very common for a family of artisans to work together, passing on traditions from generation to generation. Noël Levasseur worked alongside his cousin Pierre-Noël Levasseur, as well as Noël's two sons. Often they

John White   *Skirmish with Eskimo*   1577

worked on the same project together, making it almost impossible to determine which artist was responsible for an individual sculpture.

One such project was the decoration of the Ursuline Chapel, Quebec City (p. 96), one of the great masterpieces of Quebec art. Contemporary accounts indicate that Pierre-Noël was in charge of the major sculptural decoration, carried out between 1730 and 1736. The project involved an extremely complex scheme of sculpture and ornamentation, including large sculptures in the round, small statuettes, relief carvings, and a wide variety of decorative motifs. The total effect is a magnificent tribute to the Ursuline sisters, who commissioned the work and preserved it to the present day.

Pierre-Noël Levasseur, an accomplished artist, was responsible for the delightful *Angel of the Last Judgment* (p. 99) that surmounts the pulpit in the Ursuline Chapel, as well as many other important pieces in the chapel. Pierre-Noël also sculpted *The Holy Father* (p. 100), a work that shows he was able to transcend the dull and ponderous French models he imitated. In *The Holy Father* he injects his own personal style and gives the work a profound humanity that sets it apart from most other works of the period.

Besides the Levasseurs, there were other families of wood-carvers such as the Baillairgé family, who were active from the 1780s until the mid-nineteenth century. There were also many independent sculptors producing religious art. Most of them remain anonymous, but the works they have left behind, such as the tender and sensitive sculpture of *St. Lawrence* (p. 99), reveal a new tradition, independent of France. This tradition combines technical sophistication with a simplicity of vision that borders on folk art. That combination is one of the outstanding characteristics of early Canadian art.

The first professional painter to arrive in New France was a curé, the Abbé Pommier, who had been invited over by Bishop Laval. Laval had met him in Paris in 1663, when he was recruiting settlers for the colony, and Pommier arrived a year later. Not one painting can be attributed to him with any certainty. The records

25

indicate that he painted a portrait of Mère Catherine de Saint-Augustin after her death in 1668. There is a portrait of *La Mère Marie Catherine de Saint-Augustin* (Hôtel-Dieu, Quebec), but it has been extensively repainted so that the eyes, which were once closed, are now open. Pommier is known to have painted several other posthumous portraits while in Quebec, probably including that of the famous *Mère Marie de l'Incarnation* (Ursuline Convent, Quebec).

The zenith of painting in New France came after the arrival of Frère Luc during the summer of 1670. Frère Luc had been a well-established artist in France before he joined the Recollet Order in 1644. He had trained under Simon Vouet, and had worked under the greatest French artist of the period, Nicolas Poussin. Frère Luc came to Quebec City with the first group of Recollet missionaries, when Bishop Laval invited them to re-establish the order in New France. During the voyage, he painted a portrait of Jean Talon, the Intendent, which has since been lost. Once in Quebec, he undertook a number of important works, including the architectural design of the Recollet headquarters. During his fifteen-month stay he painted several works, including the impressive *Assumption of the Virgin* in the Quebec Hôpital-Général (p. 91) and a painting of *The Holy Family* in the Sainte-Famille church on the Isle d'Orléans.

After his return to France, Frère Luc continued to send paintings to Canadian churches, which had a profound impact on early Quebec art. By the time of his departure for France in the fall of 1671, Frère Luc had set a whole new standard for art in the New World. The *Assumption of the Virgin* was shown to visitors as one of the wonders of Quebec.

Life in the colony presented constant danger for the early settlers, whether it took the form of attack by the British and the Indians, or disease and natural disaster. When catastrophe struck, man turned to God and the Church. As a result, votive – or *ex-voto* – paintings, such as the *Ex-Voto of the Three Castaways* (p. 95), were commissioned by people who had survived a shipwreck, a severe illness, or a frightening accident, and who wished to express their gratitude for being saved.

Most of these works were painted by untrained artists who remain anonymous. They approached their task with sincerity and devotion, depicting the incident in a bold and direct manner. They had no professional training, so they did not worry about perspective, spatial depth, or any other conventions. They also had no pretensions about creating a great masterpiece; they simply wanted to tell the story in as direct and honest a manner as possible. The resulting works have a profound sincerity and humanity that stand in marked contrast to the official paintings of the time.

A number of other painters were active during the French regime, most of them belonging to religious orders. Some were missionaries, such as Father Pierron and Father Chauchetière, who made illustrations of the Bible as teaching aids for the Indians. Another priest, the Abbé Louis Nicolas, wrote the famous *Codex Canadensis*, the first study of Canadian natural history. He may also have produced the spectacular drawings of animals, plants, and Indians that accompany the text.

One of the first native-born *québécois* painters was Pierre Le Ber. His portrait of *Marguerite Bourgeoys* (p. 92) is one of the most striking works of this early period. His sister, Jeanne Le Ber, was a recluse who made many exquisite embroideries during her nineteen years in seclusion.

By the mid-eighteenth century, the French colony had a population of over eighty thousand. The capital of Quebec had grown from a frontier outpost to a bustling seaport of over eight thousand people. According to one writer, "Quebec could boast more and finer public buildings than could any other colonial capital north of Mexico City."[7] These buildings remain symbols of France's early enthusiasm. But now she had withdrawn most of her direct support from the colony and seemed to have little interest in what Voltaire described as *"quelques arpents de neige"*: a few acres of snow. Quebec was forced to become more independent and self-sufficient, both economically and politically. By this time, the people of New France had developed a unique culture that would carry on long after the defeat by the English.

3
The Garrison and the Frontier: Documenting the New Society

After the defeat of the French on the Plains of Abraham, the British became the dominant force in North America. The American Revolution brought about a period of tremendous upheaval and conflicting loyalties. Over forty thousand British Loyalists made their way to Canada, foreshadowing an eventual English majority over the French. The British ruled from their strongholds in Quebec, Montreal, and Halifax, where there ensued a period of peace, prosperity, and growth.

The military presence made itself felt everywhere and played an important role in the formation of the new society. In Quebec alone there was a garrison of about two thousand men. The military officers in charge were gentlemen from the British upper classes, who mingled freely with the English establishment that now ruled Quebec. Together they formed a small, tightly knit community with a rigid social hierarchy and a strong system of *bourgeois* values. This was the garrison society – closed in on itself and colonial in its attitudes – that characterized much of early Canadian life.

One of the first art forms to appear in the new colony was the topographical art of the British army officers, who received art instruction at the famous Woolwich Military Academy in England. In the days before photography, topographical art had an important military function. Every officer had to be able to make accurate maps, drawings of fortifications, and sketches showing the essential features of landscapes. When the British attacked Quebec in 1759, several officers made sketches of the siege and the ruins after the battle, providing the only visual record of this dramatic moment in Canadian history. The most famous portrayal of the battle was by an American artist who painted the event in England, eleven years after it happened. Benjamin West's *The Death of General Wolfe* (National Gallery of Canada) was one of the most revolutionary paintings of its time, and was a precursor of the Romantic movement in art.

During periods of peace, the officers painted views of scenic ruins, waterfalls, or local beauty spots to take home as souvenirs when their tours of duty ended. One of the favourite subjects was Niagara Falls, and nearly everyone who could hold a brush painted it. Its breathtaking splendour perfectly embodied the romantic ideal of the time – it was exotic, primitive, and awe-inspiring. Although most of these water colours have little more than historical interest, those by Thomas Davies (p. 105), George Heriot (p. 106), and J. P. Cockburn are of high quality. They display not only exceptional handling of a difficult medium, but also sensitivity to the Canadian landscape.

Under British rule, Quebec's energetic social life was soon back to its frenetic pace, in both the French and English communities. There were active English and French theatres, elaborate state balls, ceremonies, and processions, and a variety of clubs and societies – all part of a general desire to recreate European culture in Canada, and to emulate European taste. For most people, Canada was still not "home," but a temporary residence.

In the cities, the garrison elite – and the new middle class who emulated them – provided artists with a much-needed source of income. There was a great demand for portraits – portraits of the clergy, government officials, and wealthy merchants and their families. Portraits became such an important sign of prestige that anyone with a modest income insisted on having one. This rage continued for over seventy years, until photography superseded portrait painting. Many artists made a comfortable income and one, Louis Dulongpré, is said to have painted over thirty-five hundred portraits between 1785 and 1815.

A new level of sophistication appeared in the work of Canadian artists during this period. Several of them, such as François Malepart de Beaucourt (p. 110) and François Baillairgé went to France and returned to Canada as graduates of the French Academy, and other professional artists came to Canada from Europe with impressive credentials. This was the Rococo period in European art, which produced works with a spirit of lightness, virtuosity, and refined elegance. By the time the Rococo style reached Canada, it had been transformed into a more serious and sober idiom, which was just what the newly formed society wanted. When the European Rococo style evolved into Neo-Classicism, it was brought to Canada by artists such as William Berczy (p. 109). As always, it was the external trappings of the European trends that were copied, without an understanding of the philosophy behind them.

Artists in Canada began to assume more professional status during this period. In 1792, François Beaucourt advertised his ability to do everything from portraits to historical paintings and theatrical scenery. Although artists such as Louis Dulongpré and William Berczy were accepted among the high society of the time, an artist still had to be a jack-of-all-trades if he was to survive. Many continued to work for the Church, which commissioned sculpture and other decoration for its newly reconstructed sanctuaries. But the Church was no longer the sole patron of the arts and, apart from a few carved church interiors such as that at St. Joachim by François Baillairgé, religious art did not have the same vitality as before.

In the late eighteenth century, art flourished in the French-speaking communities of Quebec and Montreal. The defeat by the English had forged a new sense of identity for the *québécois* that was distinct from that of the British or the French. As contacts with France diminished, artists had to rely on their own inspiration, instead of using France as a model. The presence of Europe still made itself felt, but in different ways. In 1816, the Abbé Desjardins brought more than two hundred European paintings to Canada to save them from the rampant destruction of art following the French Revolution. These were auctioned in 1817, and many of them were purchased by a young man named Joseph Légaré.

Légaré (pp. 10, 117) was a self-taught artist who opened a studio in Quebec to restore paintings and to produce works for churches. At the age of twenty-two he bought many of the Desjardins canvases (of widely varying quality) and made copies of them for his Quebec clientele. These later inspired him to create his own landscapes and historical paintings of Quebec subjects, making him one of the first artists in the country to concentrate on the Canadian landscape. He painted the wild and rugged scenery near Quebec, as well as a large number of dramatically impressive historical paintings that depicted natural disasters, such as L'incendie du Quartier Saint-Jean (p. 10) and the Le choléra à Québec

(National Gallery of Canada). He also established the first museum in Canada open to the public.

Légaré was succeeded by his pupil Antoine Plamondon (p. 113), who virtually dominated art in Quebec from 1830 to 1850. Plamondon had spent four years studying in France and returned as an *élève de l'Ecole française*. He immediately became the most fashion-able portrait painter in Quebec, and turned out some of the most beautiful portraits ever made in Canada. He also painted a series of religious works and some extraordinarily sensitive portraits of nuns. Plamondon jealously guarded his territory from intruders, and burst into abusive rage whenever another artist tried to set up shop in Quebec. When he retired in 1850 he was succeeded by his

Benjamin West   *The Death of General Wolfe*   1770

own pupil, Théophile Hamel (p. 114), who became the leading portrait painter of Quebec society for the next two decades.

The affluent sitters portrayed by Plamondon and Hamel contrast sharply with the rural Quebec society of the time. Rural Quebec was little affected by the Conquest, and its people soon resumed a way of life that centred on agriculture in summer and socializing in winter. The Church and the *seigneur* remained at the core of the culture. Life was peaceful and simple, and was lived in close harmony with nature. This was the period when the rich folk-culture of Quebec flourished in music, dances, and stories.

The person most responsible for providing our visual record of this culture was neither Canadian-born nor French. Cornelius Krieghoff (pp. 5, 118, 121) had grown up in Europe and emigrated to the United States in 1836. There he met a beautiful young French-Canadian girl named Emilie Gautier. Settling with her at Longueuil near Montreal, he began painting a variety of local scenes – his wife and daughter in a sleigh together with some friends, a group of *habitants* playing cards, or Indians hunting in the woods. Some of these paintings are humorous, some are anecdotal, and others depict simple everyday experiences.

Krieghoff sold these paintings in Montreal to wealthy merchants and army officers. Many of the works went to Europe as souvenirs of the "quaint" life of the *habitant*. With an increased demand for his work, Krieghoff moved to Montreal, where he received numerous commissions; but his good fortune did not last long. In a few years the market dried up, and Krieghoff was forced to sell his paintings from door to door for five or ten dollars each. He was eventually rescued by a friend and patron named John Budden, who invited him to Quebec in 1853. Once again Krieghoff became an immense success, catering to the English-speaking population of Quebec. However, the wealthy French-speaking community refused to buy his work, feeling that it was vulgar caricature and an insult to their cultivated lifestyle.

Krieghoff had clearly broken with the conventions of the French-speaking garrison by painting the life of the *habitant*. The *bourgeois* French were trying to recreate an existence similar to that of Europe and considered the *habitant* to be socially inferior. The English found Krieghoff's work interesting because it was exotic and entertaining. Krieghoff himself was an unconventional person who did not fit into either of these moulds. He did not paint the *québécois* to make fun of them or because they were quaint, but because he had a deep sympathy for their way of life and knew it intimately. Although his paintings are partly derived from European prototypes, they are among the few works of this period to show a way of life that was uniquely Canadian.

Toronto's history is very different from that of Quebec or Montreal. In 1820, it had a population of 1,240 and was described as a "place better calculated for a frog pond, or beaver meadow, than for the residence of human beings."[8] By 1850, it had swelled to thirty thousand people, but it remained a cultural backwater. There was little appreciation for the arts and there were few places

Peter Rindisbacher   *Captain Bulger, Governor of the Assiniboia, and the Chiefs & Warriors of the Chippewa Tribe at Red Lake*   1823

for an artist to show his work. In fine art exhibitions, paintings were exhibited along with wax flowers, false teeth, fur coats, and other *objets d'art*.

The town did manage to support a few artists, including George Theodore Berthon. When Berthon settled in Toronto in 1844, he became the leading portrait painter of the Toronto establishment. His portrait of *The Three Robinson Sisters* (p. 114) provides a fascinating glimpse of Toronto society at the time.

The Toronto Society of Arts was formed in 1847, holding its first exhibition that year in what is presently the St. Lawrence Hall. Included in the exhibition were works by Berthon and Krieghoff, as well as paintings of Indians by an unknown artist named Paul Kane (p. 131), who had grown up in Toronto (then known as York) after arriving with his family from Ireland at the age of nine. In 1836, he had set off on a nine-year odyssey to the United States, and then on to Rome and London. It was in London that he discovered the paintings of American artist George Catlin, who was exhibiting his celebrated series on the American Indians.

Kane was profoundly affected by Catlin's work and resolved to create the same record of the Canadian Indian. Two years later he made his first trip westward, with "no companion but my portfolio and box of paints, my gun and a stock of ammunition."[9] The works he painted after his return were among those he included in the Toronto Society of Arts exhibition. The next year he set out on an even longer journey across the country, to Vancouver Island and northwestern United States. It was a voyage of two and a half years, in which he travelled thousands of miles on foot, on horseback, by dog sled, and by canoe. He suffered incredible hardships, including blizzards, starvation, and attacks by wolves and grizzly bears. Kane returned with over 240 sketches and produced his finished canvases. When they were shown in 1851, Kane was hailed as superior to Catlin. Eventually he completed one hundred paintings depicting the North American Indian.

Paul Kane's life and work superbly illustrate the contemporary fascination with the western frontier. Just over forty years before Kane's triumphant exhibition, Simon Fraser made the first overland voyage to the Pacific; less than thirty years after the exhibition, the last spike joined the continent from coast to coast.

Kane was not the only artist to paint and explore the West. In 1821, Peter Rindisbacher emigrated to Lord Selkirk's Red River Colony as a boy of thirteen. A self-taught artist, he was soon selling his meticulous sketches of the Indians to the soldiers and traders at Fort Garry. A few years later he moved to the United States, but died in 1834 at the age of twenty-six.

William Hind (p. 128), another artist-explorer, made his first trip to the North with his brother on the Hind Labrador Expedition of 1861. In 1862, he joined the celebrated Overlanders of '62 on their trip to the Caribou. His sketches on this trip reveal an unusual artistic sensibility that goes far beyond documentation.

By the time of Confederation, British North America had grown from a colonial outpost to a country of over three million people. The soldiers and fur traders had given way to farmers and lumberjacks. Immigrants such as those pictured in William Raphael's painting, *Behind Bonsecours Market, Montreal* (p. 132), had arrived by the thousands from Great Britain. They built the cities and transformed the wilderness into rural farmland, and laid the foundations for maturing artistic expression. Apart from a few exceptional figures such as Hind, Krieghoff, Kane, and Légaré, British colonial art up to this time had been essentially an art of documentation. On the frontier, artists recorded the arduous life of the explorers and the exotic customs of the Indians. Closer to home, topographers preserved the scenic wonders of a raw, primitive land. In the colonial garrison, painters depicted a society trying to build a culture on the basis of what it remembered from Europe. This society dictated the rigid conventions of future Canadian art, holding it within established forms for years to come.

4
Contradictions and Change: Art in the Victorian Era

In the Victorian era Canada became an industrial nation, with more changes telescoped into these decades than in all its previous history. Rapid change brought startling contradictions – in the cities, new wealth and the misery of the sweatshops; on the frontier, the Riel Rebellion, the Gold Rush, and the western wave of emigration; in the Victorian parlour, a rigid sense of morality and propriety; and in the back streets, the brothels and tenements.

A glance at the work of leading Canadian artists of the period makes it difficult to believe that any of these changes were taking place. The landscapes represent either peaceful countryside or wild mountains and lakes untouched by man. The portraits of the period reveal some aspects of Victorian upper-class life, but none of the harsh realities of an industrial society. Victorian artists painted a romantic, ideal world that stood in direct contrast to the technological progress taking place. They no longer were called upon to document their society, for photography had demonstrated that it could do the job more effectively. Art could now serve as a romantic escape from a reality that was often brutal.

There were, as always, a few exceptions. In Robert Whale's painting of the *Canada Southern Railway at Niagara* (National Gallery of Canada), even the mighty Niagara Falls takes second place to the new railroad, suspension bridge, and buildings, revealing the contemporary faith in progress and the future. F.M. Bell-Smith's painting of *Lights of a City Street* (p. 137) portrays the bustling city of Toronto just before the turn of the century.

Robert Harris (p. 138), who illustrated contemporary events for local newspapers in the days before photo-engraving, covered the sensational Donnelly murders of 1880. Harris also received a major commission from the federal government: to paint the Fathers of Confederation at their meeting in Quebec in 1864. It was nineteen years after the event, and Harris had to rely on photographs taken by William Notman for many of the likenesses. The huge painting took two years to complete, and was hung in the Parliament Buildings in Ottawa – where it was destroyed by fire in 1916. The *Fathers of Confederation* brought Harris much acclaim, and established his reputation in Canada.

Harris was chosen for the commission partly because he was Canadian and partly because he had already achieved a reputation in Europe. During the 1880s and 1890s, Europe established the criteria for acceptable art and culture. Everyone who hoped to be a successful artist made an obligatory trip to Paris to study in the French academies. In 1877, Robert Harris and William Brymner were among the first Canadians to discover the Paris art world. Brymner's *A Wreath of Flowers* (p. 7), painted just before he returned to Canada, illustrates his expert knowledge of the correct academic techniques.

Both artists taught "in the French manner" after they returned – Brymner in Montreal and Harris in Toronto. They had great influence on younger artists, and many of them were soon on their way to Paris. Some, such as Paul Peel (pp. 6, 142) and William Blair Bruce (p. 145), ended up living permanently in Europe, but most stayed for only a few years. French-speaking artists also made the pilgrimage, and by 1893 there were over twenty-five Canadian artists working in Paris, primarily because they had few means of studying art in Canada. As one artist wrote: "There were no instructions in drawing, no directions in art outlook, no discussion of principles deduced from great painters or from experience."[10] Artists went to Paris to soak up the creative atmosphere and to live *la vie bohème* amidst an exciting climate of experimentation and discussion, heightened by the ideal of art as a matter of total commitment. Artists enrolled in academies such as the Académie Julian, where they spent all day drawing models and making plaster casts. Twice a week their work was criticized by well-known French artists.

The style to which Canadian artists were attracted was not the innovative art of Van Gogh, Gauguin, and Seurat – or even the Impressionists – who were working in Paris at the time. It was the traditional academic style of Gérôme, Cabanal, and Meissonier, who were the current rage in the Paris Salon. This time-lag in the response of Canadian artists to *avant-garde* trends is one of the recurring patterns of Canadian art. Instead of responding to the leading creative edge, they were attracted to what was already safe, proven, and well-established.

The style that appealed to Canadian artists in the Victorian era was characterized by technical brilliance, photographic realism, and sentimental themes. It demanded the traditional skills of draughtsmanship, a scientific knowledge of anatomy, and an emotional message in the grand manner. It was an art perfectly adapted to the pragmatic materialism of Canadian culture in the late nineteenth century. Once an artist had learned these skills, his one chance for success in Paris was to exhibit in the yearly Salon and hope that he would be noticed. Very few Canadian artists survived the ruthless competition.

When Robert Harris arrived in Canada in 1879 after two years in Paris, he soon became the leading portrait painter of his generation. Despite the growing popularity of photography, portrait painting was still very much in vogue. Artists were quick to assure customers that their paintings had the detail and precision of a photograph – often by working from photographs. They took advantage of the fact that a painting could idealize and flatter a sitter, whereas a photograph showed every blemish and wrinkle. Portraits were commissioned by both the establishment and the new middle class. The men usually assumed forceful poses that indicated moral strength, whereas women chose poses that emphasized feminity and gentility.

Harris excelled in painting the confident and self-assured leaders of the business community: men who were ambitious, materialistic, *bourgeois*, and solidly Anglo-Saxon. Their attitude is best summed up by Sir William Van Horne's statement: "I eat all I can, I drink all I can, I smoke all I can and I don't give a damn for anything."[11] Van Horne was a great art collector as well as a railroad builder, and he later combined these two interests by giving artists free passes to travel across the country to produce promotional pictures for the Canadian Pacific Railway. Van Horne, and others like him, were the patrons of Canadian art.

In the Victorian era great weight was placed on commercial success and public acceptance. The artist either conformed or starved. The basic philosophy was to give the public what it wanted, and what it wanted was an art that was realistic, tasteful, and "modern." Artists worked hard at establishing their pedigrees, boasting proudly of their French training, the medals they had won, and the art societies they belonged to. Their strong craving for public approval was apparent even in their dress – immaculate three-piece suits, and sometimes top hats, even when they were working.

They established a profusion of professional art societies, where they could promote, sell, and exhibit their paintings, mostly in Montreal and Toronto. One of the first art galleries in Canada started in The Notman and Fraser Photographic Gallery, founded by William Notman in Montreal. He later opened several branches, including one in Toronto, under the direction of John Fraser (p. 151), a superb water colourist and painter who played a major role in Canadian art during these years. The company became Canada's most illustrious firm of photographers, and was appointed Photographer to the Queen. It had its own exhibiting space and its own art collection, and employed and trained a large number of young Canadian artists in the laborious process of tinting photographs. They painted in their spare time and were given help by the older artists of the firm, making it unofficially the leading art school in the country.

The advent of photography posed some fascinating aesthetic problems for both painters and photographers. Faced with the astonishing possibilities of the photograph, the artist had two choices. He could make paintings that resembled photographs, as Henry Sandham did in *Hunters Returning with their Spoil* (National Gallery of Canada), or he could turn his back on photography and pursue art for art's sake. For the more perceptive artist, photography meant that he no longer needed to imitate nature slavishly, and he could experiment freely with painterly problems.

Canadian art achieved new prestige with the founding of the Royal Canadian Academy in 1880, primarily through the efforts of the new Governor General, the Marquis of Lorne, who arrived in Canada in 1878. He and his wife, Princess Louise (the daughter of Queen Victoria), were both amateur artists with a passionate interest in painting. Lorne set out to improve Canada's cultural life by creating institutions similar to those in Great Britain. The

F.M. Bell-Smith   *Portrait of Queen Victoria*   1895

academy's first exhibition opened in 1882 in Ottawa, with a great deal of pomp and fanfare. A number of works were purchased for Queen Victoria, including paintings by Homer Watson, John Fraser, and Lucius O'Brien. Canada was coming of age.

Lucius O'Brien (p. 149), the newly elected president of the academy, had the perfect background; born in rural Ontario of respected English parents, he attended Upper Canada College and then worked as a land surveyor, before becoming a professional artist when he was forty. Tactful and diplomatic, O'Brien enjoyed moving in Canada's high society and was a close acquaintance of the Marquis of Lorne. O'Brien was one of the few people who could soothe the fragile temperaments of the other members of the academy.

O'Brien was a landscape painter exclusively, at a time when this type of painting was very much in vogue. He and his contemporaries were heavily influenced by the American painters of the famous Hudson River school, who had been inspired by the beauty of the American landscape in the 1830s and 1840s. Another influence was the early nineteenth-century French Barbizon school, whose artists based their philosophy on Jean-Jacques Rousseau's romantic notion of finding spiritual sustenance in nature. They were among the first to paint outdoors, in an attempt to see nature with fresh eyes.

Canadian artist Horatio Walker (p. 152) was profoundly affected by the Barbizon artists, particularly by François Millet's scenes of peasant life. Walker spent most of his life painting the poor and humble farmers of Quebec, and became very successful – at first in New York, and later in Canada.

Walker's work, along with that of two other Canadian artists, Homer Watson and Ozias Leduc, was based on a rural environment and possessed an independence of spirit that sets it apart from the cosmopolitan art of the period. Watson and Walker both came from farming communities in Ontario; both went to Toronto at about the same time and ended up at the Notman and Fraser Gallery. For Watson, who was nineteen at the time, Toronto had all he needed: "I did not know enough to have Paris or Rome in

Robert Whale   *The Canada Southern Railway at Niagara*   c. 1870

mind."[12] He left for the United States in 1876 to study art in New York; Walker followed in the same year. When Watson came back to Canada, he returned to his native village of Doon, Ontario, and began to paint pastoral landscapes in works such as *The Stone Road* (p. 155). In 1880, his painting *The Pioneer Mill* (Windsor Castle Collection) was purchased by the Marquis of Lorne for Queen Victoria's Royal Collection, which brought instant celebrity to the young artist. He found a gallery to sell his work in Toronto, but continued to live in Doon and to follow his own personal vision.

Ozias Leduc (p. 156), unlike most French-speaking artists who longed for Paris, was content to work in relative seclusion in the little town of St. Hilaire near Montreal. Large church murals provided his main source of income, meagre as it was. His small canvases were done for his own personal satisfaction and he had no intention of selling them. Leduc found inspiration in the simple joys of his immediate surroundings – his young brother copying an illustration from a book, a still life of a few objects sitting on a table, or the familiar landscape of Mont St. Hilaire. By stepping outside the current vogue, Leduc created a new vision that had an enormous effect on artists in succeeding generations, especially Paul-Emile Borduas.

One artist who did take advantage of travel and cosmopolitan life was James Wilson Morrice (pp. 163, 164), who became Canada's first artist of international stature. In contrast to the simple rural upbringing of Leduc and Watson, Morrice grew up in a wealthy, upper-middle-class environment in Montreal. After attending private school, he studied law at the University of Toronto, but soon discovered that he wanted to be a painter and left for France in 1890. Through his American friends in Paris, he discovered the second-generation Impressionists and the works of the American expatriate, James McNeill Whistler. He returned to Canada every winter for short visits and went out to sketch the Quebec countryside with his friend, Maurice Cullen (p. 159). They were among the first artists to apply the principles of European Impressionism to the Canadian landscape. In their winter scenes they painted snow that was not simply white, but included many colours.

Their paintings were attacked by the Montreal critics and spurned by collectors, who were used to the hazy, atmospheric paintings of the Dutch school. The art establishment reacted in the same way that European critics had responded to the first Impressionist paintings, twenty-five years earlier. They even worried that the paintings might discourage immigration! The lack of sales was not a serious problem for Morrice, who had an independent income. But Maurice Cullen was forced to sell over one hundred canvases at auction in 1900, earning an average of eight dollars per painting.

Morrice reacted to the criticism by making fewer and fewer visits to Canada. As he stated in a letter to his friend Edmund Morris: "I have not the slightest desire to improve the taste of the Canadian public."[13] By 1904, he had achieved a considerable reputation in Europe, and had sold Le quai des Grands Augustins (Musée Nationale d'Art Moderne, Paris) to the French government. In 1909, a French critic wrote that Morrice was "unquestionably the American painter who has achieved, in France and at Paris, the most notable and well-merited place in the world of art."[14] He also achieved a reputation as one of the most interesting personalities of the Paris café society, and was the inspiration for several characters in contemporary novels. The poet Cronshaw in Somerset Maugham's Of Human Bondage was based on Morrice, as was Priam Farll in Arnold Bennett's novel, Buried Alive.

After discontinuing his visits to Canada, Morrice kept in touch primarily through exhibitions at the Canadian Art Club. It was founded in 1907 by Edmund Morris and Curtis Williamson, who were frustrated with the prevailing academic styles. Membership in the club was by invitation only, and many of the more innovative artists were asked to join: Morrice, Cullen, and Marc-Aurèle de Foy Suzor-Côté (p 160) from Montreal, and Watson, Franklin Brownell, and several others from Toronto. The club held exhibitions every year until 1915, and was instrumental in awakening younger artists to new styles. For the new generation, Cullen and Morrice were the heroes. As A. Y. Jackson later wrote:

It was through Cullen and Morrice that we in Montreal first became aware of the fresh and invigorating movements going on in the art circles of France; and it was their influence that weakened the respect of the younger generation of painters for the stuffy traditions that prevailed in that city.[15]

5
The Canadian Spirit in Art: The Group of Seven and Their Contemporaries

Early in the twentieth century, the more innovative Canadian artists wanted to break free of dependence on European traditions. They were searching for their roots, and more often than not they found them in the landscape, which came to represent what was distinctive and unique about Canada. This highly romantic spirit led artists to form clubs that went sketching on weekends or held "Canadian evenings," when members sat on benches and sang Canadian songs.

In Toronto, most of these young artists worked at a commercial art firm named Grip, graphic designers for large stores like Eaton's. At one time or another Grip employed five of the future members of the Group of Seven, as well as Tom Thomson. J. E. H. (Jim) MacDonald (pp. 183, 184) was the head designer at Grip and the senior member of the group. Thomson (pp. 9, 173, 174), then in his thirties, had joined the firm in 1907 as a specialist in lettering. Arthur Lismer (p. 178) and Fred Varley (pp. 179, 180) began working for Grip shortly after emigrating to Canada from Sheffield, England; Frank Johnston belonged to the firm briefly before going to New York in 1910; and Frank Carmichael was a young apprentice from 1911 to 1912.

All these artists shared an infectious enthusiasm for the North. At first they went on weekend sketching trips around Toronto, but they soon felt the need to go further. In 1912, Thomson made a three-hundred-mile canoe trip down the Mississagi River with William Broadhead, another Grip employee. When he returned, he talked eagerly about his adventures to his friends at the firm, and showed them his sketches. They were dark and muddy, but bore a strong feeling for the North. Thomson had found his subject matter, but was still searching for a personal style. The solution was soon found in the decorative design techniques practised at Grip, based on European *Art Nouveau* principles.

All the artists at the firm belonged to the Arts and Letters Club. Essentially a social club for those involved in the arts, it played a vital role in the formation of the new art movement. It was here that the artists from Grip met the wealthy and influential people who were to become their first patrons: Dr. James MacCallum, Vincent Massey, and Sir Edmund Walker. They also met Lawren Harris (pp. 8, 177, 200), who became the unspoken leader of the group. An heir to the Massey-Harris fortunes, Harris was the only artist who did not have to worry about earning a living.

At the club the artists spent long hours discussing the exploration of "the whole country for its expressive and creative possibilities in painting."[16] The remote northern landscape, where nature was still wild, pure, and unspoiled, became a romantic symbol for the unique qualities of Canada. These qualities could not be found in the cities, where the pursuit of materialism was the highest ideal; nor in the neighbouring countryside that appealed to Victorian painters. In the North the artists felt "a deeply moving experience of oneness with the spirit of the whole land."[17]

Early in 1913, Lawren Harris and Jim MacDonald went to Buffalo to see an exhibition of Scandinavian art, which made a tremendous impression on them. The Scandinavian artists had painted the landscape using the flat decorative patterns associated with Art Nouveau. Their works inspired Harris and MacDonald to develop an abstract, two-dimensional approach to the Canadian landscape.

A.Y. Jackson (pp. 169, 170), an artist from Montreal, had made several trips to Europe, where he had studied painting and learned a second-generation form of Impressionism. When he returned to Canada in 1913, he held an exhibition of his recent works at the Art Association of Montreal. It was a total failure and left Jackson utterly discouraged with the art scene in Canada. He was considering a move to the United States when he received a letter from J. E. H. MacDonald, who had seen a painting by Jackson called *The Edge of the Maple Wood* (National Gallery of Canada). An enthusiastic exchange of letters followed, through which Jackson became aware of all that was going on in Toronto.

When Jackson arrived in Toronto in the spring of 1913, he was accepted by the Toronto group as a kindred spirit. Jackson had made a commitment to devote himself exclusively to painting, but had no idea how he was going to support himself. While at Georgian Bay that fall, he met Dr. MacCallum, who offered to guarantee Jackson's expenses for a year. After returning to Toronto in October, Jackson created paintings of several of his Georgian Bay sketches, including *Terre Sauvage* (p. 169). Some of the sketches were later shown at the Arts and Letters Club, a show that produced a review in the Toronto *Star* entitled the "Hot Mush School." The paintings were attacked for looking "more like a gargle or gob of porridge than a work of art."[18] This first attack on the Toronto artists was later to become the rallying cry in a battle to defend the new movement.

By the end of 1913, the Toronto artists had become a cohesive group and felt the need for a common working place where they could devote themselves to full-time painting. Harris and Dr. MacCallum contributed enough money to construct a Studio Building for Canadian Art, where artists could work together and be free of financial worries. Early in 1914, Jackson and Tom Thomson became the first tenants, paying a nominal twenty-two dollars per month. Harris and MacDonald soon took over two more studios.

Algonquin Park became the group's main sketching ground, and the artists were informally referred to as the Algonquin school. In the fall of 1914, Jackson, Lismer, and Varley joined Thomson for several weeks of camping and sketching. With Jackson's encouragement, Thomson made a dramatic breakthrough in his painting to a new and daring use of colour.

When they returned to Toronto, the group's high spirits and enthusiasm rapidly disintegrated. World War I disrupted all plans for the future. Each went his separate way, and only MacDonald was left to defend the new art movement single-handedly against increasing criticism. In 1916, Hector Charlesworth accused MacDonald of throwing his "paint pots in the face of the public"[19] with works such as *The Tangled Garden* (p. 183). MacDonald, a shy, sensitive individual, was pushed into the limelight as the most radical member of the group. He defended his work and that of the other artists in a devastating rebuttal, which concluded: "*Tangled Garden, Elements*, and a host more, are but items in a big idea, the spirit of our native land."[20]

For Tom Thomson, it was the beginning of the last and most legendary phase of his career. He spent his winters in the shack behind the Studio Building, and left for Algonquin Park as soon as the snow began to melt. He was discovering his personal style, which reflected a close identification with the wilderness. Then, in the summer of 1917, Thomson set off alone on a fishing trip, never to return. His body was found eight days later.

Thomson's death and the war had a devastating effect on the other artists. Both MacDonald and Harris suffered nervous collapse. In the fall of 1918, Harris arranged to rent a boxcar from the Algoma Central Railroad, outfitting the car with bunks, a stove, a table, and chairs. It was a virtual studio on wheels that could be left on sidings while the artists went out to sketch the spectacular scenery. The Algoma trip of 1918, which included Harris, MacDonald, Johnston, and MacCallum, rekindled the earlier enthusiasm for the North. Another trip was made the following year, with Jackson taking the place of Dr. MacCallum. Like most other Canadians, the artists were experiencing a strong upsurge of national feeling as a result of the war. In 1919, MacDonald wrote that "the Canadian Spirit in Art is just entering on possession of its heritage. It is opening a new world."[21]

The group was labelled radical and revolutionary when it exhibited its works in Toronto. The artists felt the need to formalize their relationship in order to hold their own exhibitions and defend themselves from their detractors. In 1920, they officially became the Group of Seven, and held an exhibition in May that included Lawren Harris, Jim MacDonald, A.Y. Jackson, Arthur Lismer, Fred Varley, Frank Johnston, and Frank Carmichael. Most of the "young revolutionaries" were no longer young: MacDonald was oldest at forty-seven, and Carmichael the youngest at thirty; the rest were in their late thirties.

Contrary to popular myth, the first exhibition by the Group of Seven received very little adverse criticism from the press; it was not until the later exhibitions of the 1920s that the reactions became hostile. By this time the group was actively promoting their art, sending works across the country, giving lecture tours, and writing articles in the press. Never before had Canadian artists been so aggressively outspoken, or motivated by such missionary zeal. They criticized the academics and insisted that the only true art was one inspired by the northern landscape.

By 1930, the Group of Seven had done paintings of the country from coast to coast. Algoma was called "MacDonald's Country," Jackson became known for his scenes of Quebec, Harris for his paintings of Lake Superior, and Lismer for Georgian Bay. As Harris said, "We lived in a continuous blaze of enthusiasm. We were at times very serious and concerned, at other times hilarious and carefree. Above all we loved this country and loved exploring and painting it."[22]

Each artist established his individual style. Jackson and Carmichael remained essentially outward looking, concerned with documenting the external landscape in a lyrical and poetic way. Harris, MacDonald, and Varley explored a more spiritual dimension. They believed that by contemplating nature it was

Franklin Carmichael   *Northern Silver Mine*   1930

possible to reveal a universal landscape of the human spirit.

The active period of the Group of Seven lasted a surprisingly short time. In 1921, Frank Johnston left for Winnipeg, and he resigned from the group three years later. He was replaced in 1926 by the young A.J. Casson, a close friend of Carmichael. Fred Varley moved to Vancouver in the same year and had little to do with the group from that time onward. In an attempt to broaden the membership, the remaining artists invited Montreal artist Edwin Holgate (p. 194) to join in 1930. LeMoine FitzGerald (p. 193) was offered an honorary membership in 1932, but by this time the group had unofficially disbanded. In 1931, they held their eighth and final exhibition at The Art Gallery of Ontario. Aside from the official group members, there were twenty-four invited contributors.

After the preview of the exhibition, they announced that the Group of Seven "had ceased to exist as such" and that a "bigger association is to take its place . . . widened to include a far reaching representation of all creative Canadian artists."[23] That association became known as the Canadian Group of Painters, which was to continue the Group of Seven tradition through the 1930s. A.Y. Jackson and Arthur Lismer remained the great patriarchs for the younger members of the new group. Although they encouraged figure painting and an openness to "modernism," the emphasis was still on landscape. Many excellent painters, such as Carl Schaefer, Charles Comfort (p. 195), and Yvonne McKague, continued to explore the expressive possibilities of landscape painting.

The Group of Seven formed such a powerful and dominant force during the 1920s and 1930s that other artists of stature were virtually ignored. Three artists of major importance were working contemporaneously with the group, but were almost unheard-of until the late 1930s. They were Emily Carr, David Milne, and LeMoine FitzGerald. All three worked in semi-isolation, pursuing their own personal vision; all three had to struggle for years with extreme financial hardship and lack of recognition, and all three remained deeply attached to the region in which they had grown up: Emily Carr to the rain forests of the west coast; FitzGerald to

the Prairies; and Milne to the Ontario countryside.

Emily Carr (p. 187) spent her childhood in Victoria, BC, a city that had little to offer an aspiring artist. She travelled alone to England and France to study art, and discovered the bright colours of the Fauves. Long before Thomson made his first trip to Algonquin Park, she travelled north to the remote villages of the Northwest Coast Indian, and painted the dense forests and disappearing totem poles. Her paintings met with either indifference or hostility, and she was forced to give up painting in order to support herself. For fifteen years she did everything from running a boarding house to making pottery and raising 350 bobtail puppies. In 1927, Eric Brown, Director of The National Gallery of Canada, introduced her to the Group of Seven, and as a result she began painting again at the age of fifty-seven. Once more she visited the Indian villages and immersed herself in the wilderness of British Columbia. She even outfitted an old caravan for herself and all her animals, including her pet monkey, so that she could live closer to nature. Her later paintings are an exultant celebration of nature and its mysteries. Like the Indians she admired so much, she believed that everything in nature was alive and filled with energy.

David Milne (pp. 188-190) represents a far different attitude. He was a "painter's painter," more concerned with individual aesthetic expression and the solving of painterly problems. He had none of the national consciousness of the group, and felt that art should exist for its own sake, independent of any social purpose. It was the process of art that interested him – the content was secondary. For Milne, "The thing that 'makes' a picture is the thing that 'makes' dynamite – compression. It isn't a fire in the grass; it is an explosion."[24] In works such as Across the Lake (p. 189), he simplified his technique down to the barest essentials so that the impact on the viewer was immediate. He managed to preserve the intensity of his original impression, creating great dramatic tension. His works are modest statements of extraordinary power and strength, revealing a unique personal vision.

Although LeMoine FitzGerald was connected briefly with the Group of Seven, he was allied in temperament to David Milne. Like

Goodridge Roberts *Nude* 1943

Milne, he was a quiet and solitary figure who worked in isolation from the major art centres. He slowly and methodically developed his personal style, based on a concern for light and space. Although he did produce some abstract works in his later years, he believed that art was much more than an exercise in solving formal problems:

> Art is not design, structure, volume, tensions and all the modern vocabulary only. Surely there are some human values. . . .[25]

For FitzGerald, the human values were to be found in nature, which had to be studied intensely and understood from the inside. He drew inspiration from his immediate surroundings—whether it was the trees and houses outside his front window, or a plant and a few apples sitting beside him on a table. It was a peaceful and self-contained world, inviting quiet contemplation, and was far removed from contemporary international art trends.

Canadian artists were slow to react to the radical transformations in art that had taken place in Europe early in the twentieth century. The Impressionists had developed a new mode of perception based on the scientific study of optics and colour; Post-Impressionist Paul Cézanne became one of the most influential artists of the century. Later, the Cubist style of Pablo Picasso and Georges Braque formed the basis of most abstract art. Early in 1910, Wassily Kandinsky created what was claimed to be the first abstract painting, and sought to express the "inner necessity" of the human spirit.

Lawren Harris had the same interest in exploring the spiritual realm. Kandinsky's book, *Concerning the Spiritual in Art*, made a great impact on him when he first read it around 1926. He showed it to his friend Bertram Brooker (p. 199), who responded by painting a series of abstract works based on music. These were exhibited at the Arts and Letters Club in 1927. It was the first exhibition of abstract art in Canada, and the response was similar to the "Hot Mush School" reaction fourteen years earlier: "Human Soul Is Not Pink as Some Psychiatrists Say, But Only the Artist Himself Can Paint It – Says His Only Subject Was His Own Feeling."[26]

In the same year, Harris helped to arrange a large exhibition of European abstract art at The Art Gallery of Toronto. But Canadian artists showed little interest, and there were no more exhibitions of abstract art in Toronto for twenty years. Harris was the only artist to explore new directions, expressing spiritual concepts through the symbolic use of light, form, and colour. He believed that art could embody a vast range of experiences without having to imitate anything in nature. To him, the closest analogy to non-representational art was music. He was criticized for his abstractions, and members of the Group of Seven refused to take them seriously. The former revolutionaries were now the traditionalists.

The Depression years made survival more difficult than ever for Canadian artists. Although it was possible to exhibit with different art societies, there were only a handful of collectors in Canada who were purchasing art. An artist was lucky to earn a few dollars per year from sales. Unlike the United States, which had an active program of government support, Canada provided no help whatsoever for its artists. The only alternative was to take on teaching jobs or commercial work – if they could be found. Some artists had breakdowns, others gave up painting, and more just held on. Many artists became active politically. There were a few who produced propaganda art, such as Miller Brittain and Fritz Brandtner, who depicted working-class life.

In the 1930s, Montreal was the one centre in Canada that encouraged a "modernist" approach to art, because of the influence of a single artist: John Lyman (p. 196). Lyman started his art studies as a young man of twenty-one in Paris. Befriended by Canadian expatriate James Wilson Morrice, he soon discovered the work of Matisse, which was to have a great influence on him. In 1913, he exhibited some of his latest works in Montreal and was viciously attacked by the critics. The artistic climate of Montreal was not yet ready for modern art, and he went to live in Europe for another eighteen years. When he returned in 1931, he was shocked to see the hold that the Group of Seven had on Canadian art. He objected to their nationalistic outlook, saying that "the real adventure takes place in the sensibility and imagination of the individual. The real trail must be blazed towards a perception of universal relations that are present in every parcel of creation, not towards the Arctic Circle."[27]

Lyman brought back with him an awareness of recent European styles and awakened younger Canadian artists to developments in Europe. He started a studio called The Atelier and arranged several exhibitions. Lyman also wrote an art column in the *Montrealer* and became a focal inspiration for young painters, such as Goodridge Roberts and Jack Humphrey. In 1939, he helped form an organization called the Contemporary Art Society. Members such as Paul-Emile Borduas, Goodridge Roberts, and Marian Scott all had vastly different approaches; but they all adhered to the "modernist" philosophy of the Paris school, best summarized by Maurice Denis's famous statement that "a painting – before it is a battlehorse, a nude woman, or some anecdote – is essentially a flat surface covered with colours assembled in a certain order."[28] This philosophy inspired the concept of "pure" painting, with an emphasis on the formal qualities of line, colour, and form – rather than subject matter. With the founding of the Contemporary Art Society, Canadian artists were exposed to these new developments in twentieth-century art.

6
The Search Within: Contemporary Art

One of the greatest revolutions in the history of art took place in the 1940s – the birth of Abstract Expressionism. It occurred simultaneously with the shift of the centre of the art world from Paris to New York. During the war, European artists came to New York, bringing with them the creative ferment that spurred North American artists to radical innovation. Instead of lagging behind the rest of the world, Canadian artists linked into the New York centre and joined the vanguard. The event that precipitated these changes more than anything else was World War II. Out of the torment of the war came reaffirmation of individual artistic freedom, re-establishment of humanitarian values, and the emergence of a radical new art form.

In Canada, the convulsions of World War II were accompanied by new international communications that blasted open a provincial consciousness, and it was the French-speaking community in Montreal that became the focal point for these changes. John Lyman had succeeded in introducing European "modernism" to the English-speaking community, and had founded the influential Contemporary Art Society in 1939. However, the only two *québécois* artists involved in the society were Louise Gadbois and Paul-Emile Borduas (pp. 12, 205), who was still a young artist known primarily for his religious murals. He had painted a few portraits and landscapes, but they gave little indication of his immense talent. The established *québécois* artists of the day were still painting picturesque scenes of rural Quebec. They had little awareness of current European trends, and no desire to find out more about them.

> What French Canadian art needed in order to be resurrected after these centuries of lethargic slumber was a vigorous blow from the outside, and Pellan provided just that blow.[29]

In 1940, artist Alfred Pellan (p. 206) returned to Montreal after fourteen years in Europe, bringing with him over four hundred of his works, and in the fall of 1940 he exhibited a selection of them in Quebec and Montreal. The exhibition had a staggering impact. Pellan was hailed as "the synthesis and the moving image of the modern era."[30] The works had a flair and maturity of vision never before seen in Quebec. Pellan had assimilated the salient characteristics of European Cubism and Surrealism and transformed them into a highly personal idiom.

Younger artists began to form a radical group of supporters around Pellan. Through them Pellan met John Lyman, Borduas, and the influential artist and critic, Father Marie-Alain Couturier, who had fled from Europe at the same time as Pellan. Father Couturier, like Pellan, was deeply committed to the idea of liberating art from its academic restrictions.

Paul-Emile Borduas became the catalyst for a second group of revolutionary young artists, including Jean-Paul Riopelle (p. 209), Fernand Leduc, Pierre Gauvreau, Marcel Barbeau, and Jean-Paul Mousseau. Borduas created his first "automatic paintings" in 1941, and exhibited them in his first one-man show of Surrealist paintings in April of the following year. The critics described the exhibition as a turning point in the history of Canadian painting.

Borduas had been profoundly affected by the writings of the Surrealist poet André Breton, and wanted to adapt the technique of automatic writing to painting. His interest in Surrealism and his sensitivity to dream images opened up a new point of departure: he recognized that man's creative energies flowed from the unconscious. His ideas were rapidly assimilated by younger artists, generating a tremendous surge of creative activity. They were united by high ideals, a sense of discovery, and the exhilaration of being part of a revolution. They held various group shows, as well as their first Surrealist exhibition in New York in 1946. When the same show opened in Montreal, it was the first by a group of Canadian abstract artists ever held in this country. It was at their second show the next year that they were first called *automatistes*, based on a painting then called *Automatisme 1.47*, which was in fact Borduas's *Sous le vent de l'île* (p. 205).

As Borduas and his supporters experimented, they broke through to a new mode of perception. They rapidly became more radical than those who were considered revolutionary just a few years earlier. They reacted against Lyman and the Contemporary Art Society and considered Pellan to be retrogressive for not going beyond the restrictions of Surrealism. In preparation for their 1948 exhibition, Borduas and his friends prepared a small mimeographed pamphlet stating their views on art. The key article by Borduas himself, entitled *Le Refus global*, became one of the greatest revolutionary documents in Canadian history. It appeared at a time when Quebec society was engulfed in a suffocating environment that crushed not only personal freedom, but also the cultural expression of the people. Borduas lashed out against both in an impassioned cry for liberation from tyranny and authority.

The immediate repercussions of *Le Refus global* were traumatic for Borduas. He was fired from his job at Ecole du Meuble; he was denounced as insane by members of the Church; he was deserted by influential friends, who could not accept his flagrant criticism of Church and government. Borduas moved to the United States in April, 1953. For the next two years, New York was to be his home.

Jackson Pollock, more than any other artist, characterizes the new approach to painting that Borduas discovered in New York. Pollock's "drip" paintings of the early 1940s were achieved by putting the canvas on the floor and splattering paint on it from different angles. It was a spontaneous, automatic process, emphasizing the process of painting itself, rather than the creation of a specific image. A radical new pictorial space was created, where there was no distinction between the figure and the ground and no attempt to model form. It was a direct and immediate expression of feeling through the sweeping gestures of swirling paint onto canvas.

Borduas soon discovered the work of Pollock and others, such as Franz Kline, and as a result had to revise his "entire vocabulary" of painting. His stay in the United States was an exhilarating experience, especially after the tragic events of the past few years. He produced works at a prolific rate, holding successful exhibitions in New York and Montreal. Partly because of this success, he decided to move to Paris in the summer of 1955.

Borduas found Paris a major disappointment. He became severely depressed and homesick, turning more and more into himself. His work became serene and stark, painted in black and white. Despite increasing critical acclaim, his health continued to suffer, and on February 22, 1960, he died of a heart attack in his Paris studio.

As late as the 1940s, the Toronto scene was still dominated by the Group of Seven and their successors, the Canadian Group of Painters. There were only one or two art galleries in the city and all artists exhibited in the annual shows held by different art societies. A.Y. Jackson was considered an *avant-garde* figure in Canada, and the Canadian landscape was still the major source of inspiration for most artists. Young artists from Toronto such as Charles Comfort, Carl Schaefer, Will Ogilvie, and Jack Nichols were creating moving, yet understated, war paintings that had, by necessity, little to do with modernism or abstraction. People who wanted to experiment and gain recognition went to New York.

The turning point for Toronto art came with the arrival of Oscar Cahén and Jock Macdonald (p. 210) after World War II. Cahén had received his art training in Europe, and had become a successful artist in Prague before being sent to a Canadian internment camp during the war. When he settled near Toronto he quickly established his reputation as a brilliant commercial artist. He also became a patriarch for younger artists such as Harold Town and was able to introduce them to the latest concepts in European art and philosophy.

As an inspired teacher and a deeply committed artist, Jock Macdonald played a role similar to that filled by Jim MacDonald for the Group of Seven. Jock Macdonald had been a teacher for many years before coming to the Ontario College of Art in 1947. He soon attracted a group of loyal and talented students. By this time, Macdonald was committed to abstract art, which he had been experimenting with since 1934. His work was a revelation to his students in Toronto, most of whom had never seen any abstract paintings. One of these students – William Ronald (p. 213) – became his star pupil.

In the fall of 1953, Ronald organized an exhibition called Abstracts at Home at the Robert Simpson Company, displaying abstract paintings with home furnishings to show that such art could exist in a home environment. Ronald invited six other artists to exhibit: Jack Bush (p. 219), Oscar Cahén, Alexandra Luke, Kazuo Nakamura, Ray Mead, and Tom Hodgson. The artists, who scarcely knew each other, decided to meet again at Alexandra Luke's studio to make plans for another exhibition. Four additional artists came to that meeting: Jock Macdonald, Harold Town (p. 216), Hortense Gordon, and Walter Yarwood. A diverse and volatile group, they managed to agree to disagree harmoniously, and to establish a name for themselves: Painters Eleven.

When the first exhibition of Painters Eleven opened at the Roberts Gallery on February 12, 1954, there were huge crowds, and that special kind of excitement that accompanies a landmark event. But there were no important sales and there was little intelligent criticism. Another exhibition was held a year later, but the response of most of the critics and the public was bewilderment, apathy, and few sales. It was an almost identical situation to that of the Group of Seven thirty-five years earlier, except that the Group of Seven were now the establishment and Painters Eleven the revolutionaries.

Once again there was a need for outside approval to give Painters Eleven respectability at home. This came through an exhibition held in New York as part of the annual American Abstract Artists' Exhibition. It was arranged by William Ronald, who had moved to New York in 1955. Much to everyone's surprise, American critics praised the show, and so did the critics at home.

From this point onwards, the situation improved for the Toronto painters. New art galleries opened, including the Greenwich Gallery run by Avrom Isaacs, the Park Gallery, and the Gallery of Contemporary Art. Collectors were beginning to purchase their works, and the more successful artists were able to give up their jobs in commercial art in order to paint full-time. There was a new spirit of adventure and experimentation among the younger artists, such as Michael Snow (pp. 220, 254), Graham

Coughtry (p. 214), and Joyce Wieland (p. 253), who were beginning to emerge as the new *avant garde.*

At William Ronald's first major exhibition at the Kootz Gallery in New York in 1957, Ronald approached the influential American art critic, Clement Greenberg, about coming to Toronto to criticize works by other members of Painters Eleven. This was arranged, although not without fierce argument with two other artists, Harold Town and Walter Yarwood, who refused to have their works "approved" by an American critic.

Greenberg came to Toronto in June of 1957, and spent half a day in each of the artist's studios. What Greenberg favoured was a new style of painting that he later called "Post-Painterly Abstraction," or Colour-Field painting, which rejected what he considered to be the "rhetoric" of Abstract Expressionism. The approach placed enormous emphasis on the primacy of pure colour. The aim was to make the painting as flat and two-dimensional as possible.

By the time of Greenberg's visit, Painters Eleven was beginning to receive recognition in Canada. When the prestigious Park Gallery opened in 1957, Painters Eleven made up the first show. In 1958, they were invited to repeat the same exhibition in Montreal, where they were received with great acclaim. That same year, the Park Gallery reciprocated by inviting ten Quebec artists, including Borduas and Riopelle, to exhibit in Toronto.

Almost as quickly as Painters Eleven became accepted, they began to disintegrate as a group. In 1956, Oscar Cahén was killed in a car accident; in 1957, William Ronald resigned; and in 1958, they held their last exhibition at the Park Gallery. The next year the remaining members met and decided to disband: "We accomplished what we set out to do, and then each went our separate ways—grateful to each other for the fun it was."[31]

In the 1960s, art in Toronto became part of a much larger phenomenon known as the "Toronto Look." Artists were glorified as heroes by the media. Harold Town, with his flamboyant and outspoken personality, came to personify the new image of what an artist should be. All the artists shared a fun-loving

Claude Breeze   *Sunday Afternoon: From an Old American Photograph*   1965

spirit, and enjoyed nothing more than shocking the staid Toronto public. Dennis Burton exhibited his striking garter-belt series (Garter-beltmania) in the mid-1960s. Robert Markle delighted in painting freshly erotic sketches of nudes in high heels and little else. These were among the works included in Dorothy Cameron's famous EROS 65 show, which was raided by the police. That same year a giant spontaneous happening was staged by Burton, Gordon Rayner (p. 215), and Richard Gorman at The Art Gallery of Ontario, with over two thousand people attending. Music became a central part of the total artistic experience. It was the era of the jazz greats – John Coltrane, Miles Davis, Thelonius Monk. Artists played jazz while they painted, haunted the jazz spots, and formed their own groups.

In 1962, Michael Snow and Joyce Wieland left Toronto for New York, where they lived for the next ten years. They became central figures in the New York art scene, creating works that were in the vanguard of international art. Snow explored the countless permutations of the Walking Woman theme, working through Pop art, Environmental art, and Minimal art before the terms were invented. His revolutionary experimental film, *Wavelength*, won international awards and catapulted him to the position of the leading *avant-garde* film-maker. Joyce Wieland produced *La Raison avant la Passion*, a film that is now considered one of the most important made in the sixties. Both artists, who have worked in sculpture, painting, printmaking, video, film, and photography, illustrate an important new trend that emerged in the sixties. Art was "coming off the canvas," and artists were experimenting in a variety of media.

In the more traditional arena of painting in Montreal, the *automatistes* had found acceptance among a small group of collectors by the mid-1950s. Young painters began to search for a new form of expression, and four of them, known as *les plasticiens*, exhibited together in 1955.

Although the *plasticiens* never made a great impact on Montreal art, two artists who were sympathetic to their ideas were soon to transform them into a radical new style. Guido Molinari (p. 228) and Claude Tousignant (p. 231) were producing severe and uncompromising hard-edge, geometric paintings by the mid-1950s. Their work was misunderstood for several years, until they exhibited in a large *Art abstrait* exhibition in 1959. This show established a new direction for Montreal painting, with Molinari and Tousignant at the forefront as head of the *nouveaux plasticiens*.

In the 1950s and 1960s, the Montreal art community went through an explosion similar to that of Toronto, with new galleries, new patrons, and a profusion of art in every form imaginable. This creative outpouring culminated in Expo 67, which was an art form in itself, as well as a symbol for the optimism and vitality of the age.

For more than one hundred years, Montreal and Toronto were the undisputed art centres in Canada. Beginning in the 1950s, artists in the rest of the country were able to keep in touch with developments in New York and elsewhere as easily as anyone in Toronto or Montreal. A new consciousness developed; artists recognized that their particular region was unique, and yet part of a larger whole.

In the Prairies, the sole art centre until the mid-1950s was Calgary. With the exception of a few talented artists, such as Maxwell Bates and Marion Nicholl, the artistic climate was insular and parochial. Regina was even more isolated, but in 1950 a young artist named Kenneth Lochhead (p. 224) arrived to become Director of the Regina School of Art. Lochhead was only twenty-four at the time, and fresh out of art school. He began making innovative changes to the program, and was joined two years later by another young artist, Arthur McKay. In 1955, they decided to use facilities at Emma Lake for a two-week workshop, and invited Jack Shadbolt (p. 235) to lead it. The workshop's overwhelming success led to additional sessions.

In 1959, Barnett Newman, an unknown artist from New York, agreed to make the trip from New York to Emma Lake to conduct the summer session. For those participating in the workshop, it was a momentous experience. Newman introduced them to the idea of using bold, simplified areas of colour, providing them with a challenging alternative to Abstract Expressionism. Newman was on the verge of becoming recognized as one of the great painters of his generation, and the Regina artists were exposed to his innovative work before most painters in New York were. It had seminal influence on five artists, who broke with their past styles and within a year formed a group called The Regina Five: Ron Bloore (p. 227), Kenneth Lochhead, Art McKay, Ted Godwin, and Doug Morton. They held their first exhibition in 1960, and a year later a show entitled The Regina Five toured Canada, bringing them to the attention of the rest of the country. In following years, New Yorkers Clement Greenberg, Kenneth Noland, and Jules Olitsky conducted workshops at Emma Lake, establishing strong dependency on New York influences.

Many Canadian artists paid little attention to current New York trends and created regional art that reflected their own environment and a unique sense of place. They found all the creative inspiration they needed in their own immediate surroundings, in the belief that it was only through the particular that they could arrive at the universal.

In the Maritimes, Alex Colville (p. 237) returned to Sackville, New Brunswick, after serving for two years as a war artist, and began teaching art at Mount Allison University. He continued to paint within the Realist tradition, choosing familiar, everyday scenes for his subject matter, but imparting a heightened sense of reality. The altered perception inherent in his work, and the emphasis on precise photographic realism, creates ambiguous and haunting images of great power. Despite criticism for being behind the times, Colville persisted with his High-Realist style during the passing trends of Abstract Expressionism, Pop, and Op, and was only gradually recognized for his significant contribution to Canadian art. As a teacher, he also had an important influence on many younger artists, such as Christopher Pratt (p. 236), Tom Forrestall, and D.P. Brown, who later developed their own personal approaches to High Realism.

The work of Jack Shadbolt also cannot be dissociated from his local environment. Shadbolt grew up in Victoria, BC, and from an early age was influenced not only by Emily Carr, but also by the dramatic wilderness and lush vegetation of the West Coast. Shadbolt was fascinated with evocations of growing nature, and the rich traditions of the Northwest Coast Indians. An incredibly prolific artist, he has worked through various approaches to Abstract Expressionism and Realism, without ever losing his deep affinity for nature. As a teacher, writer, poet, philosopher, and artist, he was the focal personality for an astonishing surge of creative activity in Vancouver during the 1950s.

In the Prairies, a similar role was played by Ernest Lindner, who influenced over three generations of students during his thirty years as a teacher and educator. After retiring from teaching in 1962 at the age of sixty-five, his work went through a remarkable creative flowering. He had been a passionate observer of nature for many years, observing its miraculous transformations through death, decay, and rebirth. In the 1960s, his infinitely detailed water colours of tree stumps became richer in colour, and gradually came to assume a deeper meaning as a "landscape of life experience."[32] He developed a brilliant drawing technique, and in works such as *Walking through the Woods* (artist's collection) began to explore the immensely difficult challenge of integrating the nude figure into the environment.

Colville, Shadbolt, and Lindner are just three of many artists across Canada who continue to pursue their own personal vision, without feeling any necessity to emulate the international style of New York. In London, Ontario, a small group of artists produced a creative explosion that seemed completely out of keeping with the city's staid, conservative environment. The London school had a well-defined philosophy that soon came to epitomize regional art in Canada. This philosophy was largely the inspiration of two artists, Jack Chambers (pp. 11, 242) and Greg Curnoe (p. 245), who were born and brought up there. Their aim was to produce an art that went to the roots of their own experience and their own cultural heritage, starting with themselves, their families, their friends, their homes, their studios, and only after that: "street, block, neighbourhood, city, township, county, province, dominion, world, solar system, cosmos...."[33]

Curnoe left London in 1956 to spend four years at the Ontario College of Art, where he soon became disenchanted with conventional fine art. He discovered the Dada Movement, with its deliberate anti-art and anti-sense philosophy. Once back in London, he and some friends, including writer James Reaney,

started to explore the popular culture around them. It was an exciting world of great sports figures, comic-book heroes, pop bottles, and popular music. For Curnoe, art is to be found everywhere, and the most beautiful objects are often the most commonplace – there is no separation between life and art. All Curnoe's works reveal a unique perception of his everyday world.

Jack Chambers approached regionalism from a different direction. When he returned to London in 1961, after almost nine years of studying art in Spain, he was an accomplished artist with rigorous academic training behind him. He produced a series of evocative and dream-like paintings based on his life and his

Ernest Lindner   *Walking through the Woods*   1972

ancestors. He also made a number of experimental films, including the enigmatic *Heart of London*, which uses real images from everyday life to make a moving statement about life and death. His most celebrated works, *Sunday Morning No. 2* (p. 242) and *401 Towards London* (Northern and Central Gas Corp. Ltd.), are painted in a style he called "Perceptual Realism." These visionary paintings represent familiar scenes of his close family and the landscape around London. Their exacting photographic realism extends far beyond regionalism or the surface quality of a photograph. For Chambers, they represented a miraculous moment of perception, when ordinary objects become extraordinary objects – a moment of revelation, when the invisible becomes visible.

Although Chambers and Curnoe were without doubt the unspoken leaders of the London School, there were other artists of importance who helped to create the artistic climate for this major creative breakthrough. The nucleus was made up of those artists who were in the radical Heart of London exhibition, which toured Canada in 1968. Besides Chambers and Curnoe, it included John Boyle (p. 251), Murray Favro, Bev Kelly, Ron Martin, David Rabinowitch, Royden Rabinowitch, Walt Redinger, Tony Urquhart (p. 252), and Ed Zelenak. It was a group characterized by its diversity, originality, and dynamic energy. Even though some of the artists have moved elsewhere, and Jack Chambers died in 1978, London still remains a focal point for some of the most original creative developments in Canadian art.

The emphasis on regionalism inevitably led to a new surge of nationalism in Canadian art, far surpassing the nationalism of the Group of Seven in its intensity. This awakening coincided with a number of external factors – increased government support of the arts through the Canada Council, a new sense of pride in the country as a result of Expo 67, and an increased awareness of American domination of Canadian culture. Artists became involved in radical politics and did not hesitate to express their views through art. Some of their works contain violently anti-American statements, particularly those of Greg Curnoe and John Boyle. Boyle celebrated mythic Canadian folk heroes, such as

Tom Thomson, Stephen Leacock, and Louis Riel, in his impressive historical paintings. Joyce Wieland created an incredible variety of "patriotic" works, from quilts to films, paintings, sculptures, and an Arctic Passion Cake for Canada.

For these artists, the very survival of Canada depended on a strong and independent expression of Canadian culture, which included social protest. In Vancouver, Claude Breeze shocked a staid Canadian audience with his large painting *Sunday Afternoon: From an Old American Photograph* (Department of External Affairs, Ottawa), in which he showed two lynched blacks hanging from a tree. Not all of Breeze's work involves social comment; his heroic Canadian Atlas Series includes joyful and expressive landscapes that celebrate the beauty of nature.

Montreal artist Mark Prent's life-size tableaux such as *Death in the Chair* (Canada Council Art Bank) are powerful indictments of contemporary man. Although his works still intimidate Canadian buyers, both the prestigious Stedlijk Museum in Amsterdam and the Akademier der Kunst in Berlin have given him one-man shows. Many of the paintings by the late Toronto artist William Kurelek (p. 238) also make a strong statement about man's inhumanity to man.

In the 1960s, a new consciousness evolved, which transcended the old forms of nationalism and internationalism. This was the global outlook made popular by one of the great visionaries of the twentieth century – Marshall McLuhan. An expert in communications and technology, McLuhan has long stressed the importance of the poet and the artist as someone who "sharpens our perceptions." He has spoken of the artist as a "distant early warning system," a person with a special gift to see environments as they really are. According to McLuhan, "The artist *reprograms* the senses to render us able to survive in the technological environment."[34]

A number of artists are already reflecting this global awareness in their art. In 1966, the N.E. Thing Co. Ltd. (p. 254) was formed in Vancouver, with Iain and Ingrid Baxter as co-presidents. The purpose of the company is to disseminate "Sensitivity Information (SI), based on the idea that everything in the world is information."[35] The company developed a number of projects and set up various departments to carry them out. One department gave certificates to those things that the company felt did not deserve a place in eternity, such as works by some pretentious *avant-garde* artists. It was a way of poking fun at the establishment and the art purists who take themselves with deadly seriousness. Another department extended the stripes of a Ken Noland painting fifteen feet in either direction. The inevitable question arises, "but is it art?", and the company's inevitable answer is that "N.E. Thing is Art." Their work plays with perceptions and stretches our conception of what art is or can be. Many of the company's works, such as *Inflatable Landscapes* (National Gallery of Canada), also happen to be beautiful objects in themselves. According to a brightly coloured button handed out by the N.E. Thing Co. Ltd., "*Art is all over.*"

In the 1960s, television, photography, and film threatened to render art obsolete. Colour reproductions of art works reached such a high quality that they became an acceptable substitute for the work itself. As a result, art lost its uniqueness and exclusivity — it was available to everyone. The art establishment responded by stressing even more the value of an original art work, and prices soared. The *avant-garde* artists responded by "arranging the entire human environment as a work of art."[36] They made conceptual art, earth art, and body art; they used film, photography, and video; they created environments, happenings, and performances. Art went through one radical transformation after another. It not only came off the canvas and went out into the environment, but it also went beyond the object altogether.

The artist was still faced with the enormous challenge of preserving his own identity in the new technological age. One artist who uses technology without losing humanistic values is Michael Snow. For Snow, seeing is a form of knowing — he is a modern day Leonardo da Vinci who explores the universe around him with intense curiosity and scientific detachment. As a painter, sculptor, film-maker, photographer, musician, and "time-sound-light-poet," Snow has crossed new frontiers in all media. His work breaks down preconceived notions of reality and creates an entirely new way of seeing.

Snow is just one artist exploring new ways of perceiving technology and environment. Robin Mackenzie is another innovator who once brought hay bales, rocks, and logs into the art gallery environment in a bold statement about landscape and natural forces. He uses photography extensively in his work, investigating what he calls "a sense of site" through variations in time, space, and colour.

Murray Favro has made a number of environmental works, including one made of fibreglass, rubber, steel, canvas, and engines. It is called *Synthetic Lake* (National Gallery of Canada), and represents a "projected reconstruction" of a portion of Lake Huron. While a wave machine simulates the movement of waves, a film loop of the waves on Lake Huron is projected onto the machine. The work creates a dynamic interplay between illusion and reality, and provides a new perception of a familiar experience.

Edmund Alleyn, in *La suite québécoise* (artist's collection), painted six large sunsets on canvas and placed about thirty life-size figures in front of them. These highly realistic figures are painted on plexiglass and represent the average crowd found at an amusement park on a Sunday afternoon. They remain suspended in time before their exotic postcard sunsets. The work contains elements of the past and the present in a profound statement that evokes a sense of mystery and ritual.

These and many other artists are reconnecting us with our environment. Their art appeals directly to our emotions. It is an art that celebrates the human experience and reaffirms the importance of nature. It transcends conventional reality and attempts to open the way to the human spirit. In many ways, the contemporary artist has come full circle to the role of the artists of the far-distant past. Like the artist-shaman of prehistoric times, the contemporary artist has become the prophet and the visionary of our times, creating a balance between the concrete world and that of the spirit.

NOTES

1. Quoted by Bill Reid in Olive Patricia Dickason, *Indian Arts in Canada* (Ottawa: Department of Indian Affairs and Northern Development, 1972), p. 110.

2. Bill Reid, *Out of the Silence* (Fort Worth: Amon Carter Museum of Western Art, 1971), p. 8.

3. Franz Boas, *The Social Organization and Secret Societies of the Kwakiutl Indians* (Washington: Report of the U.S. National Museum, 1895), p. 488.

4. Quoted in William E. Taylor, Jr., and George Swinton, "Prehistoric Dorset Art," *The Beaver* (Autumn 1967): 41.

5. Pitseolak, *Pictures out of My Life*, ed. Dorothy Eber (Toronto: Oxford University Press, 1977), n.p.

6. Quoted in George Swinton, *Sculpture of the Eskimo* (Toronto: McClelland and Stewart, 1972), p. 129.

7. Quoted in Dennis Reid, *A Concise History of Canadian Painting* (Toronto: Oxford University Press, 1973), p. 20.

8. Jacob Spelt, *Toronto* (Toronto: Collier-Macmillan Canada, 1973), p. 11.

9. Quoted in J. Russell Harper, *Painting in Canada: A History*, 2nd ed. (Toronto: University of Toronto Press, 1977), p. 121.

10. J.W.L. Forster, *Under the Studio Light* (Toronto: Oxford University Press, 1928), p. 11.

11. W.L. Morton and L.F. Shannon, *This Land, These People* (Toronto: Gage Publishing, 1977), p. 181.

12. National Gallery of Canada, *Homer Watson 1855-1936* (Ottawa: 1963), n.p.; from the introduction by J. Russell Harper.

13. J.W. Morrice to Edmund Morris, Feb. 12, 1911. Artist's file, National Gallery of Canada.

14. Quoted in D.W. Buchanan, *James Wilson Morrice, A Biography* (Toronto: Ryerson Press, 1936), p. 47.

15. A.Y. Jackson, *A Painter's Country* (Toronto: Clarke, Irwin, 1958), p. 19.

16. Quoted in Peter Mellen, *The Group of Seven* (Toronto: McClelland and Stewart, 1970), p. 24.

17. Lawren Harris, "The Group of Seven in Canadian History," *The Canadian Historical Association: "Report of the Annual Meeting Held at Victoria and Vancouver, June 16-19, 1948,"* p. 36.

18. H.F. Gadsby, "The Hot Mush School," *Toronto Star*, 12 December 1913.

19. H. Charlesworth, "Pictures that Can Be Heard," *Saturday Night* 29, no. 23 (18 March 1916): 5.

20. J.E.H. MacDonald, "Bouquets from a Tangled Garden," *The Globe and Mail*, 17 March 1916.

21. J.E.H. MacDonald, "The Canadian Spirit in Art," *The Statesman* 1, no. 35 (22 March 1919): 6-7.

22. Harris, *op. cit.*, p. 32.

23. Mellen, *op. cit.*, p. 184.

24. Agnes Etherington Art Centre, *David Milne 1882-1953* (Kingston, Ont., 1967), n.p.; from the introduction by David Silcox.

25. Robert Ayre, "LeMoine FitzGerald 1890-1956," *Canadian Art* 14, no. 1 (1956): 16.

26. Dennis Reid, *Bertram Brooker, 1888-1955* (Ottawa: National Gallery of Canada, 1973), p. 9.

27. John Lyman, "Canadian Art, Letter to the Editor," *Canadian Forum* (May 1932): 313.

28. Quoted in Linda Nochlin, *Impressionism and Post Impressionism, 1874-1904* (New Jersey: Prentice Hall, 1966), p. 187.

29. National Gallery of Canada, *Alfred Pellan* (Ottawa: 1960), n.p.; from the introduction by Donald Buchanan.

30. Germain Lefebvre, *Pellan* (Toronto: McClelland and Stewart, 1973), p. 54.

31. Kathryn Reid Woods, *A History of Painters Eleven* (Oshawa: McLaughlin Gallery, n.d.), n.p.

32. Ronald Bloore, "A Note on Ernest Lindner," *artscanada* (June 1970): 32.

33. National Gallery of Canada, *Greg Curnoe* (Ottawa: 1969), p. 67.

34. Derrick de Kerckhove Varent, "McLuhan and Art," *Vie des Arts* (Autumn 1973): 91.

35. Ann Rosenberg, "An Illustrated Introduction to the N.E. Thing Co. Ltd.," *Capilano Review* (Spring 1976): n.p.

36. Marshall McLuhan and Quentin Fiore, *The Medium Is the Message* (New York: Bantam Books, 1967), p. 68.

The Native Peoples

"In the very earliest time, when both people and animals lived on earth, a person could become an animal if he wanted to and an animal could become a human being. Sometimes they were people and sometimes animals and there was no difference. All spoke the same language. That was the time when words were like magic. The human mind had mysterious powers."

"*Magic Words*" (after Nalungiuq), 1972

Dorset Shaman's Mask

A few years ago a young Eskimo walking along a beach near Button Point, on Bylot Island, noticed a lump of turf that had fallen from an eroding bank at the edge of the beach. Protruding from the soil was a wooden mask (opposite) that had been preserved in the permafrost for almost a thousand years. It had been left behind by the Dorset people (800 BC-1300 AD), nomadic hunters who followed the walrus, caribou, and seal according to the seasons. The people of this sea culture believed in an animistic world filled with spirits. To survive, each person had to have a helping spirit, and the person who acted as a mediator with the spirit world was the shaman, or medicine man. He was said to be a healer, a conjuror, a maker of words, songs, and images, and a visionary.

This mask was almost certainly made for or by a shaman. It may have been worn by him in some ceremony or ritual, or it may have been a death mask placed over the face of a corpse. It served as a bridge between this world and that of the spirit, and embodied the energy of a powerful *inua*, or soul.

The mask is made of driftwood, a material that was considered rare and special. (Although the Dorset Eskimos lived in a warmer era than the present-day Eskimo, the nearest trees were a thousand miles away.) Crafted with great skill, the mask consists of several different pieces of wood joined together. Parts of it are stained with red ochre, and there are tiny pegs that once held a moustache, hair, and eyebrows. Although frozen for centuries in the earth, even in its present form the mask has astonishing power.

from LAMENT FOR THE DORSETS

Animal bones and some mossy tent rings
scrapers and spearheads carved ivory swans
all that remains of the Dorset giants
who drove the Vikings back to their long ships
talked to spirits of earth and water
−a picture of terrifying old men
so large they broke the backs of bears
so small they lurk behind bone rafters
in the brain of modern hunters
among good thoughts and warm things
and come out at night
to spit on the stars

-Al Purdy, 1971

PLATE 9
Dorset
Shaman's Mask   C. 500 AD-1000 AD
wood stained with red ochre   19.3 x 13.8 x 4.3 cm
National Museum of Man

PLATE 9

PLATE 10

PLATE 11

Dorset Shaman's Tube/Comb with Face

Only 6.4 centimetres high, this small carving (opposite, left) was probably carved from a walrus tusk during the Dorset period. It may have once been used by the shaman to hold his tiny amulets, or it may have been his sucking tube, for healing the sick. The striking face, with its open mouth and dilated nostrils, is similar to faces on other cylindrical tubes used for blowing out power or sucking away illness. Such tubes were "soul catchers," for they contained the shaman's breath, which represented the spirit. The open mouth and wide nostrils on this tube unite the concept of breathing—the essence of life—with the magical power of the shaman.

Although the carving looks like a comb, scholars believe that at one time it was a shaman's tube, and was reworked by a later Thule carver, who perhaps had little interest in its magical qualities. In its present form, the carving represents an unusual combination; it is at once a face, a hand, a comb, and an object of sacred power.

"My breath—this is what I call this song, for it is just as necessary for me to sing as it is to breathe. I will sing this song, a song that is strong."

—Orpingalik, a shaman and poet of the Netsilik Eskimo, to Knud Rasmussen, 1923

PLATE 10
Dorset
Shaman's Tube/Comb with Face   C. 500 AD-1200 AD
walrus ivory   6.4 x 2.5 x 0.7 cm
National Museum of Man

Dorset Dragline Handle

The small *Dragline Handle* (opposite, right) is made from a walrus tooth, and seems to have been used either as a toggle to drag seals across the ice, or as a fastening for a belt. Like the *Shaman's Tube* (right), it was probably an amulet made in Dorset times and later modified by a Thule carver, who drilled the hole in the centre. On one side, the handle takes on the shape of a whale; on another, the head of a fox appears. On either side of the hole are two seals; and at the top is an extraordinary human face.

The *Dragline Handle* illustrates the special care that the Eskimo lavished on common utilitarian objects, in an attempt to create sympathetic magic. Most of these objects, such as harpoon heads, fish spears, and the *Dragline Handle*, were used in hunting, which was a sacred activity and a matter of survival. The Dorsets sought to invest their tools with a power that would help the hunter in his task. The carver attempted to transform the object into a carrier of magic, so that he would have a greater chance of making a kill. These carvings of the Dorset culture, found in scattered sites from Alaska across Canada to Greenland, expressed the profound belief in magic that was inherent in their loosely woven, animistic religion.

PLATE 11
Dorset
Dragline Handle   900 AD-1300 AD
walrus tooth   5.8 x 1.7 x 1.6 cm (hole: 7 mm diameter)
National Museum of Man

The Sechelt Image

The powerful *Sechelt Image* (opposite, left) is a prehistoric stone sculpture found in southern British Columbia. It may depict the strength-testing contest of some of the Northwest Coast tribes: at marriage ceremonies, men would lift heavy oval boulders – which were often greased – to demonstrate their strength. The contest symbolized sexual power as well as physical strength.

The *Sechelt Image* (named after the place in BC where it was found), translates this theme into a complex interplay of ambiguous imagery. The powerful masculine head that leans back is gripping not a stone, but a phallus, and from a certain angle the whole stone takes on a phallic shape. However, the figure's arms clasp what could be a child. At its base is a clearly delineated vulva – so that a male figure of strength simultaneously becomes an image of mother and child. This preoccupation with the fundamental drives of sex and survival is found in many prehistoric sculptures from the West Coast.

PLATE 12
Northwest Coast Indian
The Sechelt Image   100 BC-500 AD
stone   50.8 cm (height)
Centennial Museum, Vancouver

The Death Bringer Club

The stone club on the opposite page (right) was found in 1922 near Hazelton, BC, near the site where thirty-five other clubs were discovered in 1898. These clubs are images of power and were probably not used as weapons. They may be replicas of functional clubs or they may simply be symbols of potency and strength. Since many clubs are unmistakably phallic in shape, they may also represent male sexual power.

The Death Bringer, with its lethal blade and its handle surmounted by a mysterious head, is the most impressive of all the clubs. The head, with its eyes closed, is almost sinister in appearance – at once an image of life and of death. Like the *Sechelt Image*, its meaning is ambiguous; it could represent either the preservation or the destruction of life. The head might be a new-born infant with its eyes still closed, or an old man with his eyes closed in death.

"Stone is about life and death. Stone is about time. If a club could be devised to kill death, it would be made of stone. If a design could be devised to thwart time, it would exist in stone."

– Wilson Duff, *Images Stone B.C.*, 1975

PLATE 13
Northwest Coast Indian
The Death Bringer Club   1200 AD-1600 AD
stone   45.7 cm (length)
Museum of the American Indian, New York

PLATE 12

PLATE 13

59

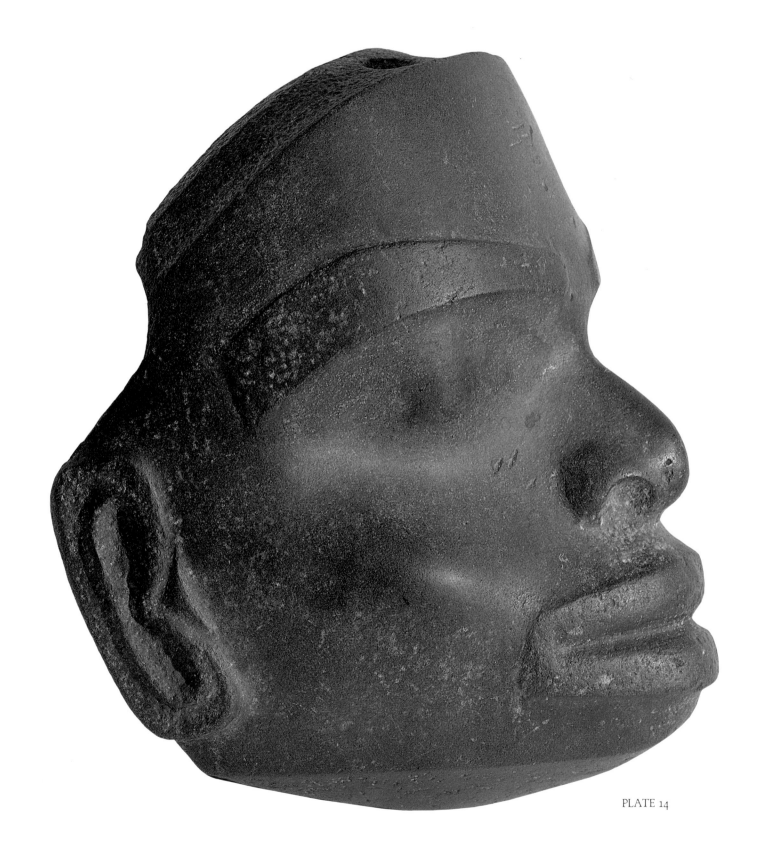

PLATE 14

The Twin Mask

In 1974, when Wilson Duff was preparing his exhibition "Images Stone B.C." for the Art Gallery of Greater Victoria, he flew to Paris to bring back a prehistoric stone mask in the collection of the Musée de l'Homme. When he placed it next to its "twin" at the National Museum of Canada, he was astonished to see that the Paris mask fit snugly within the other mask and that they were a perfectly matched pair. The masks were identical, except that the National Museum of Canada mask had no opening for eyes, whereas the Paris mask was "sighted."

The Paris mask had several holes drilled in it for a harness, probably so that it could be held firmly on a dancer's face. The Ottawa mask was probably held in the hands, so that it could be placed quickly in front of the other mask, dramatically altering the expression. Scholars speculate that these masks were worn by a performer in the sacred winter dances of the Northwest Coast Indians.

The eyes of these masks are not like mortal eyes. As Wilson Duff said, "Their kind of vision is of a purer kind, eternally open to the inner light." Stone is an extremely difficult and intractable medium, and the carver's sensitivity to its characteristics is truly astounding. It is the one material suited for making a statement of eternal truth; it defies time and the transitory nature of human existence. The "unsighted" *Twin Mask* (opposite) becomes an image of lasting power, preserving forever the spirit of man in stone.

"They are about seeing and masking. They are about self-recognition. I cannot help but think that if they could speak, their message would be what Raven's grandfather said to Raven in one of the Haida creation myths: I am you. That is you."

—Wilson Duff, *Images Stone* B.C., 1975

PLATE 14
Northwest Coast Indian
The Twin Mask   1200 AD-1600 AD
basalt   22.8 cm (diameter)
National Museum of Man

Tsimshian Chilkat Blanket

Among the most elaborate works of the Northwest Coast Indian were Chilkat blankets, which were expressions of social prestige and wealth. These deep-fringed capes were worn by the chief or other important individuals on ceremonial occasions, to show to full advantage the wearer's totemic emblems. Chilkat blankets were originally invented by the Tsimshian tribe, but were later woven exclusively by the northern Tlingit Indians and traded down the coast. These people were among the few who had access to goat's wool, which was used in making the blankets. The bold designs were painted by men on wooden pattern boards and then woven by women over a warp of cedar bark and goat's wool.

This blanket (opposite) is unique because of the touch of red woven into the lower pattern, and its design is so unusual that it may be an early Tsimshian blanket. Its black squares represent animal forms and the yellow squares represent human heads. Along the lower part of the design are two inverted eyes flanked by the two rectangular red mouth designs. The blanket was intended to be seen worn over the shoulders, or in motion while dancing, with the heavy fringe swaying back and forth. It was also used as a shroud for a chief. Occasionally, when a body was cremated, the blanket was hung permanently on the front of the grave house, as a mark of esteem.

PLATE 15
Tsimshian
Chilkat Blanket   early nineteenth century
mountain goat wool, cedar bark
78.5 cm (height without fringe)
159.0 cm (width without fringe)
56.5 cm (length of bottom fringe)
22.8 cm (length of side fringe)
National Museum of Man

Tsimshian Ceremonial Frontlet

Ceremonial frontlets were worn only by chiefs and, like crowns, were symbolic of the chief's authority. This frontlet (p. 64) was attached to a frame that held it in place in front of the chief's forehead. On top of the frontlet were vertical sea-lion whiskers; hanging down were long flowing trailers of ermine, usually attached to a royal scarlet trade cloth to enhance its appearance. The designs on frontlets represent the crests of the chiefs who commissioned them; the central motif of this one is a large head with gleaming eyes and teeth of inlaid abalone shell. Below the face is a stylized rendering of arms and legs, and circling the central motif are eight frogs, with eyes of black stone. Between them is a plaque of shell inlay, adding lustre and texture.

"A Northwest Coast chief in full regalia must have been about the most gorgeously panoplied human ever to strut the face of this earth. These costumes weren't as colourful or elaborate as, say, a Chinese emperor's brocade robes, or a Renaissance churchman's gold and velvet, but the power of these designs more than makes up for that. The combination of a garment … with the right headdress and the rest of the outfit would be overwhelming. Even hanging lifeless by itself, it's a gorgeous thing. Savile Row, eat your heart out!"

— Bill Reid, *Indian Art of the Northwest Coast*, 1976

PLATE 16
Tsimshian
Ceremonial Frontlet   c. 1900
wood, haliotis, and black stone inlay   17.2 x 14.6 cm
National Museum of Man

PLATE 15

PLATE 16

PLATE 17

PLATE 18

Kwakiutl Bookwus Mask: Wild Man of the Woods

This Kwakiutl ceremonial mask (p. 65) represents the legendary figure Bookwus, more familiarly known as the "Wild Man of the Woods." According to the legend, Bookwus lives deep in the woods, where he eats snails and crawling things. When people become lost in the forest, he entices them to eat with him, and they turn into ghosts. Bookwus is chief of the dead, and his grimacing expression comes from shielding his face to make certain he is not being watched.

The mask was worn in a traditional dance ceremony in which the dancer imitates the actions of Bookwus, occasionally letting out high pitched whoops or blowing on a small whistle. He shrouds his body in hemlock boughs and moves about the dance floor, cautiously at first, then making dramatic leaps into the air. It has been said that this terrifying creature still exists, and can be seen early in the morning, prowling the western beaches in search of cockles, his favourite food.

PLATE 17
Kwakiutl
Bookwus Mask: Wild Man of the Woods　late nineteenth century
wood, horsehair, paint, nails　32.5 cm (height)
Provincial Museum of British Columbia, Victoria

Tsimshian Sea Monster Headdress

Sea Monster Headdress (opposite) represents a mythological, whale-like creature and has six humanoid figures riding on its back. It was carved in wood and brightly painted, with copper eyes and mother of pearl teeth. Attached to the back of the headdress is a piece of skin, which the last figure clings to. The headdress was worn in ceremonial dances, but does not relate to any known legend. It may possibly have been worn at funeral ceremonies and may represent human souls being transported to the spirit world; it may also relate to legends in which people were taken beneath the sea on the back of a monster to a world of wealth; or it may have been used in a dance before executing a person condemned to death.

For the Northwest Coast Indians, the deep waters they lived beside were filled with frightening monsters who could stir up storms or dangerous rip-tides, and who guarded their great wealth under the sea.

"These were objects of bright pride, to be admired in the newness of their crisply carved lines, the powerful flow of sure elegant curves and recesses – yes, and in the brightness of fresh paint. They told the people of the completeness of their culture, the continuing lineages of the great families, their closeness to the magic world of universal myth and legend."

– Bill Reid, *Arts of the Raven*, 1967

PLATE 18
Tsimshian
Sea Monster Headdress　c. 1870
wood, paint, hide　55 cm (length)
Royal Ontario Museum

Stoney Ceremonial Headdress

A Plains Indian in full ceremonial regalia was an impressive and majestic sight: beaded moccasins, leggings, an elaborately decorated war shirt or tunic, a magnificent headdress, and in his hand a spear or lance decorated with feathers. At the time this headdress (opposite, left and centre) was made the costume was worn as a showpiece on festive occasions. But in earlier years, the headdresses of the Stoney Indian were "given" to the warrior in a dream by the Great Being, who instructed him on how to make it. The headdress had sacred power that protected him in battle, and was worn only at religious ceremonies and when riding into war.

This headdress (shown from the back and the side) has a bonnet and trailer made of buckskin lined with red cloth. Attached to it are large eagle feathers tipped with rabbit fur and white horsehair. On the back is a magnificent beaded piece with floral patterns, and a red medallion with a black eagle set into it. The headdress was probably made by the warrior who owned it; the ornamentation would have been done by a woman.

PLATE 19
Stoney
Ceremonial Headdress   c. 1900
unsmoked buckskin, red cloth, eagle feathers,
rabbit fur, horsehair, down, and beads
172.8 cm (length)
Glenbow-Alberta Institute, Calgary

Iroquois Mask: Crooked Nose

According to Iroquois legend, when Manitou had finished creating the world he met with an unknown being – a giant – who claimed that he was creator of the world. The giant suggested that they have a contest to see who was strongest. He summoned the cliffs of the highest mountains to move forward, and they did. Then Manitou commanded the mountains to come forward until they stood right behind the giant. The mountains obeyed, and when the giant turned around, his face struck the mountain and his nose was broken. Grimacing with pain, and with his tongue drooping, he said to Manitou, "It is true that You are the creator of Mother Earth." Manitou said he would allow the giant to remain in the rocky hills of the west, near the Great World Rim. There, False Face, as the giant was called, could use his power to protect the people from disease and to blow warm air over the fields and the trees.

The Iroquois of the Medicine Mask (or False Face) Society created masks representing the giant, like the one on the opposite page (right). The masks were carved directly into the trunks of living trees and were made only by those who had seen the image of Manitou in a dream. Once the mask was carved and freed from the tree, it was painted either red or black, because the face of the great giant was so high up that it was red in the morning sun and black in the evening shadow.

PLATE 20
Iroquois
Mask: Crooked Nose   nineteenth century
painted poplar, inlaid brass, and horsehair
31.0 cm (height)
Royal Ontario Museum

PLATE 19

PLATE 20

69

PLATE 21

ATTRIBUTED TO MYEENGUN
Mishipeshu Rock Painting

Mishipeshu, or the Great Lynx, is an underwater monster and the most dangerous of the Ojibwa water beings. With his powerful dragon-like tail he can create terrible storms or shift currents if someone fails to show proper respect for his power. According to legend, a nineteenth-century shaman named Myeengun (Wolf) was inspired by a vision to venture out across the treacherous waters of Lake Superior. It was a dangerous expedition involving three days' travel over open water, where at any time the great Mishipeshu could have destroyed Myeengun and his party of five canoes. When Myeengun reached the other side, he painted an image of Mishipeshu (opposite) on the granite cliffs at Agawa as a tribute to Mishipeshu for safe passage.

The rock painting shows the water spirit as half-lynx, half-serpent, with the body in profile and the head straight on; and underneath are two snakes, symbolizing "swiftness and power over life." The dramatic image is intended for the eyes of Manitou alone. Even today, the Ojibwa are reluctant to talk about Mishipeshu, who they feel may still live beneath the icy waters of Lake Superior.

PLATE 21
Attributed to Myeengun
Mishipeshu Rock Painting   c. 1800
red ochre on stone   approx. 91.0 cm
Agawa Site, Lake Superior

"An Indian family was travelling one summer near the area called Agawa Rock. On one of the beaches the Ojibway Indian said to his wife, 'Let us make a fire, to eat.' They left for the bush, the woman to get wood, the man for bark, leaving their only child, wrapped in a tikinagan, or carrier, near the canoe, although the old-time Ojibway feared Lake Superior.

"On returning they found their baby gone. When they looked at the sand, they saw Misshipeshu's footprints. The tracks were seen leading into the water, with the baby. The couple did not know what to do. Finally the man spoke, 'I will call on my protectors, the birds of thunder, to come to our help. Although we shall not see our child again, I will do what I can through the help of my protectors. Let us now go under the canoe,' and then he started to play his drum.

"In about half an hour the thunderbirds, or thunderstorm, arrived in that area. The lightning began to pour on a mountain close by and it got dark. For two hours the storm lasted. Misshipeshu tried to hide but lightning fell all over the place and he was killed. Then the rain and lightning ceased, the skies cleared and the sun shone again. On the waters of Lake Superior, by the shore, an empty cradle was seen floating and beside it two small dead cubs. So ends this legend."

— Norval Morriseau, *Legends of My People, the Great Ojibway*, 1965

OSHAWEETUK-A
Mother and Child

For many years Oshaweetuk-A was a successful hunter, living along the south coast of Baffin Island near Cape Dorset. During the winter months he was the camp boss at Akeeaktoloolavik (the place we last had enough to eat). The rest of the year he followed walrus in autumn, seals in winter, caribou in spring, and fish in the summer, as Eskimos had done for centuries. In the early 1950s, encouraged by James Houston, he created a few astounding stone carvings. His production was always small, and almost exclusively represented the theme of a mother and child.

When contemporary sculptor Henry Moore saw this particular piece (opposite), through Gimpel Fils in London, he felt it was one of the most impressive Eskimo carvings he had seen. The carving bears an uncanny resemblance to Moore's own work in its powerful and dramatically simple forms. Oshaweetuk has carved directly into the stone with amazing confidence. He was not concerned with rules of sculpture or techniques of carving; for him, the stone already contained the spirit of mother and child before he began carving, and his task was to release the form that was already there – to find the life within the stone. The carving, which fits in the palm of the hand, has the same impact as a huge Moore sculpture, and qualifies for a place among the other great works throughout history that are based on this traditional theme.

"It is still in the house;
The snowstorm wails outside.
My little boy is sleeping on my back;
His stomach is bulging round.
Is it strange if I start to cry with joy?"

—Eskimo Song

PLATE 22
Oshaweetuk-A   (1913-   )
Mother and Child   1951
soapstone   20.3 x 9.0 cm
Metropolitan Museum of Art, New York

PLATE 22

73

PLATE 23

PLATE 24

MANNO
Bear on Ice

The bear plays a significant role in Eskimo life and mythology as the most powerful and most sacred of all the animals. Eskimo artists have created images of spirit-bears, hunters being attacked by bears, enraged bears standing on their hind legs, and bears transforming into humans. This carving (opposite, left) by Manno is unique in its portrayal of the bear looking at his own reflection in the ice – an extraordinary concept. The image was probably suggested by the shape of the stone itself, for the Eskimo carver studied each piece of stone with care before carving, trying to find "the life within the stone." As he carved, the form of the bear began to emerge; probably the "reflection" evolved later, as he worked on the stone.

Bear on Ice reveals Manno's acute powers of observation. As a hunter, he literally knew the bear inside-out from countless hours of observing it, and from carving it up for food after the kill. This knowledge is readily apparent in the graceful flow of the bear's torso and limbs and its cautious stance on slippery ice.

Manno is not concerned with photographic realism, but with conveying the essence of "bear-ness."

PLATE 23
Manno (1923-   )
Bear on Ice   1964
soapstone   9.0 x 17.0 x 8.5 cm
Private collection, Toronto

TIKTAK
Mother and Child

Tiktak's work centres on the fundamental themes of mother and child, the family, man and woman. Some pieces represent a single head carved in stone; others portray family groups with faces emerging out of rock. The Mother and Child (opposite, right) is one of his most moving works, and makes a timeless statement about basic human relationships. It has the restraint characteristic of his people, whose emotions are usually kept firmly in control.

Tiktak did not become a full-time sculptor until late in his life. Born near Eskimo Point in 1916, he moved to Rankin Inlet in 1958, where he worked in a nickel mine. Three years later, after his leg was crushed in an accident, he began carving. He had been making small souvenir sculptures since his youth, but his work began to assume a new authority. Tiktak commands much love and respect from his friends, who admire his sensitivity, honesty, and humility. When praised for his work, he laughs, saying in the polite Eskimo manner, "I am a bad carver."

"I do not think out what I will do. My thought comes out while I work. My work expresses my thought. My work is what I think. My work is my thought."

– Tiktak, 1970

PLATE 24
Tiktak (1916-   )
Mother and Child   1966
soapstone   48.0 x 12.0 x 21.0 cm
Private collection, Ottawa

JESSIE OONARK
Untitled Wall Hanging

Jessie Oonark's huge wall hanging (opposite) in the National Arts Centre, Ottawa, illustrates many of the changes that have taken place in Inuit art in recent years—changes that incorporate modern innovations with centuries-old traditions. The most striking digression from earlier Eskimo art is the hanging's enormous scale. While most traditional works could be held in the palm of the hand, this wall hanging stretches over six metres by four metres. Yet it was hand-stitched in a tiny room, where the artist could not see the final design until the work was completed and hung.

Wall hangings were introduced to Baker Lake in 1970 by Jack and Sheila Butler, who were then acting as advisers to the Eskimo co-operative and trying to find new means of employment for the people there. The first works produced were small appliquéd pictures made from scraps of material, but it was not long before artists were bringing large and impressive wall hangings to the co-operative. Although the concept is new, the appliqué technique goes back to the traditional skin clothing of the early Eskimo: the white belly-fur of the caribou was cut in geometric designs and sewn on darker garments. Much of Oonark's early life was spent mending and sewing, the traditional and time-consuming occupation of Eskimo women.

The imagery of this wall hanging combines elements of past and present. There are traditional hunting scenes, sleds, animals, and objects such as the triangle-shaped *ulu* (woman's knife). Since Jessie Oonark is a devout Christian, the figure in the centre of the hanging probably represents an angel, or the Virgin, with the other figures bowed down in worship around her. Drawing on the mythology of her people as well as the icons of Christianity, the work presents an epic story of Eskimo life.

Born in 1906 in Back River country, about one hundred and fifty miles north of Baker Lake, Jessie Oonark grew up in a traditional Eskimo community. She married young, had eight children, and lost her husband. She was near starvation, along with many of her people, when an airlift brought her and her family to Baker Lake in the 1950s. In 1959 she was living in a snowhouse in Baker Lake when Andrew Macpherson, a Federal civil servant, gave her drawing materials. She produced some unusual drawings, two of which were later made into prints at Cape Dorset—the first prints by an Eskimo artist from outside that settlement. Oonark went on to produce many more drawings, prints, and wall hangings, which were purchased by public art galleries and institutions; she was elected to the Royal Canadian Academy; she received the Order of Canada medal; and two of her children, William Noah and Janet Kigusiuq (Plate 27), became well-known artists.

PLATE 25
Jessie Oonark   (1906-   )
Untitled Wall Hanging   1972-73
wool, felt, and embroidery floss   396.2 x 640.1 cm
Collection of National Arts Centre

PLATE 25

PLATE 26

PLATE 27

KENOJUAK
Sun Owl

Eskimo graphic art originated in the incised images created during the Thule period. Just over twenty years ago, James Houston introduced the concept of print-making to the artists of Cape Dorset. A series of innovative experiments produced new stone-cut and stencil techniques—along with many unusual problems, including frozen inks and lack of paper and printing presses. One of the most celebrated graphic artists to emerge from these early efforts was a Cape Dorset woman named Kenojuak. Kenojuak has produced hundreds of prints, stencils, and drawings, one of the most familiar of which is her emblematic *Sun Owl* (opposite, top). The owl is the traditional symbol of wisdom; the sun-like rays of its feathers reach out "to drive away the darkness." As Kenojuak herself explained, "I am an owl, and I am a happy owl. I like to make people happy and everything happy. I am the light of happiness and I am a dancing owl."

This print was made from Kenojuak's drawing, which was first traced on a large flat stone. Then the stone-cutter chiselled away all but the owl and its feathers, so that only these surfaces would receive ink. After the ink was rolled on, paper was placed face down on the inked stone and carefully rubbed. The small red igloo signifies the Cape Dorset co-op; above it, in Inuit syllabics, is "Iyola," the print-maker's "chop"; and above that, the signature of Kenojuak.

PLATE 26
Kenojuak (1927-   )
Sun Owl   1963
Stone cut   62.0 x 74.0 cm (sheet)
               46.0 x 60.3 cm (image)
National Museum of Man

JANET KIGUSIUQ
A Giant, Half Human, Half Animal, Attacks

Janet Kigusiuq, a Baker Lake artist, is the daughter of Jessie Oonark (Plate 25). Born in 1926, she experienced the traditional way of life before she and her family moved to the settlement in the 1950s. Her drawings were inspired by an unexpected amalgam of influences; they refer not only to the legendary monsters from what is known as the Qiviug cycle, but also to her fascination with comic book monsters. Qiviug was a hero who undertook many Ulysses-like exploits and encountered various half-human, half-animal beings. In her drawing, *A Giant, Half Human, Half Animal, Attacks* (opposite, bottom), Janet Kigusiuq created her own exotic creatures. Using pencils, she completely colours in the supernatural creatures—the giant, the wolf, and the head of the bird/human—and lightly outlines the humans and the small dog. Her perception of space is radically different from the traditional western perspective: she uses overlapping figures to indicate depth; all the action radiates from the centre of the drawing; and the balance is asymmetrical because of the emphasis on the supernatural creatures. Each figure has its own independent space, and several events occur simultaneously. In this unusual image, Janet Kigusiuq demonstrates that seeing is a form of knowing; she is not concerned with depiction of concrete reality, but instead seeks to make visible the invisible.

PLATE 27
Janet Kigusiuq   (1926-   )
A Giant, Half Human, Half Animal, Attacks   c. 1971
graphite pencil and coloured pencil   55.9 x 76.2 cm
Winnipeg Art Gallery

NORVAL MORRISEAU
Warrior with Thunderbirds

Norval Morriseau spent his childhood on an isolated reserve along the shore of Lake Nipigon. When he finished school at age fifteen, he had a Grade Four education. Along with his strict Catholic upbringing, he absorbed the rich heritage of his Ojibwa past through the stories told by his grandfather – wonderful stories about the sea monster Mishipeshu, the breath-taking exploits of Nanabozho, and about Mikkinnuk the Turtle and the Shaking Tent. As a young man, Morriseau created pictorial versions of these legends, at first by drawing in the sand. But he soon stopped, fearing the ancient taboos against making images or writing about the past.

The next years were difficult ones. He worked as a guide, trapper, and miner, and eventually contracted tuberculosis and ended up in a sanatorium. There he had a dream that radically changed his life and gave him the strength to paint again.

Warrior with Thunderbirds (opposite) was painted in 1973 and represents a theme that occurs again and again in Morriseau's works – the transformation of man into the powerful spirit, Thunderbird, which emerges from the Indian's right shoulder. The Thunderbird has four beaks, which may possibly refer to the four wives that Morriseau has seen in visions of past lives. It is painted in vibrant colours, with the same profile silhouettes found in the early art of the Ojibwa. The work is a unique amalgamation of Morriseau's personal vision and the mythology of his people.

"It was a dream, you understand. It was the Great Manitou. You see, I was confused. Indians believe that our legends and myths should not be written down. I wanted to paint them. I didn't know what to do. Then I had a dream. Behind me is a grizzly bear. In front of me, two water gods chewing on bones. Something stronger than myself is protecting me from them. Like a shadow. The shadow starts moving. The bear shows his claws. The water gods are coming towards me. I know fear. I run after the shadow. 'Great Spirit! Help me! I am much afraid!' The shadow speaks to me, not in words, but I can hear its mind. 'Do not be afraid!' it says, 'I'm the Great Manitou. I'm testing you. Now here is a charm for you.' And he throws down two pieces of silk, like flags, yes. Light blue and dark blue. Day sky and night sky. 'These will protect you. Go ahead and do these things. Never fear. I will help you.' I woke up. Since then I am not afraid."

– Norval Morriseau, 1964

PLATE 28
Norval Morriseau   (1930-   )
Warrior with Thunderbirds   1973
oil on canvas   123 x 123 cm
Collection of Helen E. Band

PLATE 28

PLATE 29

BILL REID
Box: Haida Myth of Bear Mother

After the golden age of Northwest Coast Indian art in the nineteenth century, the traditional high standards of workmanship almost disappeared. There was no longer the same internal social motivation for producing art, and its cultural significance was lost. Recently, however, there has been a tremendous revitalization of West Coast art, largely because of the efforts of a few individuals, especially Bill Reid.

Born in 1920 in Victoria, BC, to an American father and a Haida mother, Bill Reid was brought up in an Anglo-Saxon environment and was not aware of his native heritage until he was a teenager. Eventually he met his grandfather, a Haida artist who had studied under the great carver, Charles Edenshaw. (At this point Reid was working as a Canadian Broadcasting Corporation announcer and had no artistic training.) He started taking courses in jewellery-making and, after several years, established his own workshop, where he began to explore the old Haida designs, including Edenshaw's. He came to understand the underlying dynamics of Haida art, producing highly original work.

Although the *Haida Myth of Bear Mother* (opposite) is a container only 7.5 centimetres high, designed to be held in the hand, it has a monumental effect that transcends its size. The gold box portrays the famous Haida legend of the beautiful young girl who mates with a bear and gives birth to semi-divine, bear-human children. The girl, suckling her bear-children, surmounts the bear-shaped container. It is a work of exquisite craftsmanship, executed with the traditional Haida traits of elegance and refinement.

"If every structure, be it box or totem pole, spoon handle or rattle, must have for every thrust a counter thrust, then each object becomes a frozen universe, filled with latent energy. The basic lines of a box design start with a major image, rush to the limits of the field, turn back on themselves, are pushed and squeezed towards the centre, and rippling over and around the internal patterns, start the motion again. Where form touches form, the line is compressed, and the tension almost reaches the breaking point before it is released in another broad flowing curve.... All is containment and control, and yet always there seems to be an effort to escape. The rules were there, and they were a part of a pattern that went far beyond the conventions of art, were more than a part of the life of the people, were the very essence of their lives."

– Bill Reid, 1967

PLATE 29
Bill Reid   (1920-   )
Box: Haida Myth of Bear Mother   1972
gold   7.3 x 7.0 x 5.2 cm
National Museum of Man

1500-1760

"Do you know that over here hearts have to have a completely
different sensibility from what one enjoys in France? Here there is
absolutely nothing that can satisfy the senses; one's affections must
be completely divine and spiritual, for God apparently wants the
heart to be stripped bare of everything else...."

Réverende Mère Marie de l'Incarnation, 1641

NICOLAS VALLARD'S ATLAS
Jacques Cartier Landing with Colonists

Early explorers brought back elaborate descriptions of their voyages to the New World – and occasionally a few natives who were looked upon with great curiosity. Based on these descriptions and other information gathered from a variety of sources, contemporary cartographers produced highly decorated maps. Although they often contained accurate descriptions, they also included fanciful elaborations based on the cartographer's – or explorers' – own imaginings.

This map (opposite) has the name of Nicolas Vallard inscribed on it, but it is not certain whether he was the map-maker or the owner of the atlas. The map itself depicts the coastline of North America, with numerous place names in French and Spanish. Newfoundland is on the left, and the St. Lawrence River runs horizontally across the map. The lower section shows Jacques Cartier landing at the Indian village of Stadacona, near present-day Quebec City, in 1541. Cartier had been sent out by Francis I, King of France, in the hope of finding the waterway to the west – or at least gold and precious stones. Cartier (at the centre, with the long black robe) is accompanied by a group of soldiers, ladies, and other colonists, including the Sieur de Roberval, the leader of the expedition. Roberval (dressed in the black cloak and red tunic) was sent to establish the first colony in the New World, but the experiment ended in failure. Behind him, some men have already built a stockade, and in the woods are bears, deer, and other animals. The Indians are shown, inaccurately, wearing fur garments. The natives that Cartier met were in fact the Iroquois, who helped him survive his first winter in Canada.

"The sayd men did moreover certify unto us, that there was the way and beginning of the great river of Hochelaga and ready way to Canada, which river the further it went the narrower it came, even into Canada, and that there was fresh water, which went so farre upwards, that they had never heard of any man who had gone to the head of it and that there is no other passage but with small boates."

– Jacques Cartier, 1589

PLATE 30
Nicolas Vallard's *Atlas*
Jacques Cartier Landing with Colonists   1546
gouache on vellum   47.5 x 36.6 cm
Huntington Library, San Marino, California

PLATE 31

France Bringing Faith to the Indians of New France

This large allegorical painting (opposite) epitomizes the attitude of the Roman Catholic church towards colonization of the New World. An Indian, clothed in a cape embroidered with *fleurs-de-lis*, kneels before a painting representing Christ and the Holy Family. Behind the painting is a female figure who personifies France – and who resembles the Queen Mother, Anne of Austria. She points heavenward to the spiritual gathering of the Holy Trinity, which appears in the clouds. Behind her is a ship decorated with flags and a coat of arms, and to the left are two small missionary churches. In the background, a river with rugged mountains on each side – probably the St. Lawrence – stretches out into the distance.

The work was intended for use by the missionaries working in New France, and was placed in the inner chapel of the Ursuline Convent (Plate 35). The concept of a painting within a painting not only illustrates the use of art as an educational tool, but also indicates that it is the Trinity in heaven that must be worshipped, not the painting itself. The Indian, who for centuries had lived in a land where all inter-relationships among men, animals, and nature were sacred, now was taught to pledge allegiance to France and the Catholic church.

The attribution of the painting is uncertain – it has been hanging in the Ursuline Chapel since well before the early nineteenth century, when it was described as a work by Frère Luc (Plate 32), However, as with many works from the period, it is almost impossible to ascertain who painted it,

"In France the great number and good examples of the Christians, the solemnity of the festivals, the majesty of the magnificently adorned churches preach piety to you. And in our houses, the fervor of our brethren, their modesty, and the many virtues which shine forth in all their actions, are so many powerful voices that cry to you unceasingly, *respice et fac similiter.*

"Certainly we have here none of these external trappings that awaken and sustain devotion. We see nothing but what may be called the essentials of our religion, the Holy Sacrament of the Altar, to the marvels of which our faith must open our eyes without being helped by any sensible mark of its grandeur, any more than were in olden times the Magi in the stable."

– Jean de Brébeuf   c. 1648

PLATE 31
Anonymous
*France Bringing Faith to
the Indians of New France*   c. 1671
oil on canvas   218.4 x 218.4 cm
Monastère des Ursulines, Québec

FRÈRE LUC
Assumption of the Virgin

When the *Assumption of the Virgin* (opposite) was completed by Frère Luc in 1671, it was considered to be one of the wonders of New France and one of the great treasures of the Recollet Order. It was of such a high level of sophistication compared to previous works done in Canada that it set an impressive new standard for other artists.

The work, designed especially for the altar wall in the chapel of the Recollet headquarters (now the Hôpital Général in Quebec), represents the Virgin rising heavenward from her grave. She is surrounded by angels, one of whom carries a halo, another clasps her sceptre, a third holds her cloak, and a fourth points towards heaven. On the left are flowers symbolizing purity, and on the right cliffs rise up from the water. In front of the painting is a large gilded altar piece made by Noël Levasseur in 1722. For the early settlers and missionaries, far from the comforts of home, this setting must have looked like a vision from heaven.

The painting follows the accepted Baroque style of the time, although it has a stiffness and awkwardness not found in the work of the more accomplished European artists. Frère Luc had trained as an artist in Paris and in Rome and had worked for the two great artists of the period, Nicolas Poussin and Simon Vouet. After he entered the Recollet in 1645, he continued to paint and was invited to come to the colony in 1670 with the first group of Recollet missionaries. His fifteen-month stay there left a great impression on him, and he continued to send works back long after his return to France.

His painting of *The Holy Family* in the Sainte-Famille church on the Isle d'Orléans played an important role in the defence of Quebec in 1690, when the British Navy under Admiral Phips placed Quebec under siege. Bishop Laval ordered that Frère Luc's painting be placed on the parish-church tower, in the hope that it would invoke divine protection for the city. During the week-long siege, cannon-fire damaged much of Quebec, but the painting remained unharmed, and the British attack failed.

"Frère Luc, the Frenchman, rather well known throughout France as one of the most skilful painters of his time, and who never dedicated his brush to anything but works of piety, the sight of which inspires the spirit of devotion, this good religious man laboured for fifteen months on many works, which he has left as so many marks of his zeal; the painting over the high altar of our Church and that of the chapel; he enriched the parish church with a large painting of the Holy Family, that of the reverend Jesuit Fathers with a painting of the Assumption of the Blessed Virgin; and he completed that of the high altar, representing the Adoration of the Kings, the churches of Ange Gardien, Chateau-Richer, the coté de Baupré [sic], the one of the Holy Family on the Ile d'Orléans and the Hospital of Quebec were likewise indebted to him for his works."

–Chretien Le Clercq, 1691

PLATE 32
Frère Luc   (1614-1685)
Assumption of the Virgin   1671
oil on canvas   205.7 x 157.5 cm
Hôpital-Général, Québec

PLATE 32

PLATE 33

PIERRE LE BER
Marguerite Bourgeoys

Pierre Le Ber's portrait of *Marguerite Bourgeoys* (opposite) represents one of God's most loyal and humble servants in Canada. A devout Christian, Pierre Le Ber was one of the first artists born in New France. His parents belonged to the two wealthiest families in Montreal, but Pierre used this wealth to make large contributions to charities and to build an alms house for the poor. This painting was executed after Marguerite Bourgeoys' death in 1700 and later was completely covered over twice by two different artists. The original underneath was not discovered until it was X-rayed in 1965. The work still has immense emotive power, with its stark, forceful design and bold simplicity. Its sombre colours, angular features, and simplified background are ideally suited to Marguerite Bourgeoys' strong character and deep piety.

Marguerite Bourgeoys died on January 12, 1700, in her eightieth year. Her death was mourned by all, for she was one of New France's most admired spiritual leaders, and the founder of the Congrégation de Notre Dame in Montreal. Inspired by a vision, she came to the colony in 1653, where she set up a school for teaching poor children. She also established a mission for teaching young Indian girls, and in her later years managed to have the sisters of the congregation recognized by the new bishop. After her death, Pierre Le Ber was asked to paint her portrait while she lay on her death bed. According to legend, her humility was such that she seemed even then to reject the vanity of a portrait.

"The Sisters, for their consolation, hoping to have the portrait of their dear departed Mother, had Mr. Pierre Le Ber, brother of the celebrated recluse Jeanne Le Ber, who did a little painting, asked to have the goodness to draw her. He was fervent: but he was not perhaps among the most clever. Howsoever it may be, he prepared himself for his work, by the holy communion which he received that day, in the Eglise de Soeurs. It appears that God wished them to glorify his servant (Marguerite) by a new miracle, because as the painter went to take up his brush to work he found himself seized with such a headache, that it was impossible for him to do his work; but having put under his wig several of the hairs of the departed they say that he was cured immediately, and ready to work. The portrait which he then did is the same which we see today in the Chapelle des Soeurs."

—Etienne Montgolfier *La Vie de la Vénérable Soeur Marguerite Bourgeoys Dite du Saint-Sacrement* (Ville-Marie 1818), pp. 168-169.

PLATE 33
Pierre Le Ber   (1669-1707)
Marguerite Bourgeoys   1700
oil on canvas   62.2 x 49.5 cm
Congrégation de Notre Dame, Montréal

Ex-Voto of the Three Castaways

At two o'clock in the morning in the summer of 1754, two young men and three women were crossing the St. Lawrence River between Lévis and Beaupré when their boat overturned. The men managed to climb on the hull of the boat and to pull one woman to safety, but the remaining two drowned. The survivors later commissioned a painting (opposite) to give thanks to St. Anne for their safe arrival. Executed by an untrained artist and hung in the church vestibule at Sainte-Anne de Beaupré, the work became a reminder of the saint's benevolence and divine intervention.

The artist has depicted the dramatic moment when one of the men pulls his friend to safety, while the two drowning women reach heavenward. In the sky a vision of St. Anne appears, surrounded by clouds, and to the left is the church at Beaupré. The painting is executed in an unselfconscious manner, with little concern for perspective, subtle colours, or polished technique.

There were many similar votive paintings in New France, showing people being saved from shipwrecks, fallen trees, or severe illness. Their exciting stories tell of the terrible power of nature and the need for faith in order to survive. As examples of folk art, they all have in common a sincerity of expression inspired by a profound belief in God.

"Ex voto
J. B. T. Aucler, Louis Bouvier, Marthe Feuïllet'eau, all 3 saved. M^{ra} chamar, aged 21

Marg ^{te} champagne aged 20 years one day both of them drowned. The 17th June 1754. at 2 o'clock in the morning all 5 in this unhappy state are recommending themselves to the blessed Ste. Ane."

- inscription on the Ex-Voto of the Three Castaways

PLATE 34
Anonymous
Ex-Voto of the Three Castaways   1754
oil on panel   32.4 x 52.1 cm
Chapelle Commémorative, The Museum, Sainte-Anne de Beaupré, Québec

PLATE 34

95

PLATE 35

PIERRE-NOËL LEVASSEUR
Altar Wall, Ursuline Chapel

One of the great masterpieces of early Canadian art is the decoration in the Ursuline Chapel in Quebec (opposite). Marie de l'Incarnation and the Ursuline sisters arrived in 1639, when the population of Quebec totalled two hundred and fifty people. The first Ursuline convent was finished in 1648 – and burned two years later. A second one was built, and it, too, was destroyed by fire – in 1686. Once again construction started, and when the decoration was finally completed for the one-hundredth anniversary celebrations in 1739, it was one of the most beautiful buildings in all Quebec. After surviving bombardment by the British during the Seven Years' War, the building has been preserved almost intact by the Ursuline sisters until the present day.

The person who was responsible for the interior decoration of the main chapel was Pierre-Noël Levasseur, one of a long dynasty of Quebec sculptors. He was helped by members of his family in carrying out the work on the main chapel (1730 - 1736), but drew up the plans himself, in consultation with the Ursuline sisters. Although he never visited France, he based his design on the traditional French altar wall, which he would have known about through engravings and copy books. The altar wall is in the form of a triumphal arch, symbolizing the entrance to heaven. It has a complex iconographical plan involving a multitude of sculptures, reliefs, decorated columns, and statuettes, all carved in wood. At the top of the altar wall, over the altar, is a sculpture of St. Joseph with Jesus in his arms, framed by kneeling angels on either side; in the niches of the lower section are statues of St. Ursuline and St. Augustine.

"Next morning I went to the chapel of the Ursulines, in the expectation of seeing the nuns at their devotions; but in that I was disappointed. An old priest was saying mass at a magnificent altar, the tabernacle uncommonly splendid, Corinthian columns, gilded statues, a bishop on one side, and a queen on the other, (probably Ann of Austria, the mother of Lewis XIV as this institution was founded in 1639,) St. Joseph with the child in his arms overhead; seraphs are reclining in the angles of the pediment, and cherubs spread their wings above and below the niches; bas-reliefs of apostles and evangelists, with their appropriate emblems, occupying the pannels of the pedestals. All this in the finest style of the age of Lewis XIV. both sculpture and architecture.

"This rich chapel may be eighty feet long, forty wide, and forty high. It is now dark with age, though it has always been neatly kept, by the piety of the nuns, and has therefore suffered nothing else from time."

- Joseph Sanson, *Travels in Lower Canada*, 1820

PLATE 35
Pierre-Noël Levasseur   (1690-1770)
Altar Wall   1730-1736
wood, painted and gilded   approx. 10.7 x 9.1 m
Monastère des Ursulines, Québec

St. Lawrence

This sculpture (opposite, left), from a church in St. Laurent parish on the Ile d'Orléans near Quebec, represents St. Lawrence, the patron saint of many churches in New France. Known for his gentleness and his courage, his image appears often in early French-Canadian sculpture and painting. Martyred by the Roman state in the third century for distributing the wealth of the church to the poor, St. Lawrence was slowly burned to death on a gridiron. He is usually shown in the dress of a deacon, bearing a palm, the symbol of his martyrdom.

In this life-like sculpture, the saint looks thoughtfully downwards, with his right arm upraised and his left hand in a meditative gesture. It is a sensitive and unassuming pose of dignified restraint. Carved in wood, the basic shape is extremely simple, but lends the impression of a human form beneath the clothing.

For the early settlers, this sculpture would have been a symbol of courage and faith in the face of adversity. It was probably carved by a skilled carpenter as an extension of his role as woodworker. It has a simplicity that verges on folk art, but at the same time achieves a high level of sophistication. Like many other works from this period, it was long hidden in a museum basement before it was discovered.

PLATE 36

Anonymous
St. Lawrence   early eighteenth century
wood, gilded and polychromed   170.2 cm
National Gallery of Canada,
on loan from the National Museum of Man

PIERRE-NOËL LEVASSEUR
Angel of the Last Judgment

The graceful *Angel of the Last Judgment* (opposite, right) is a small statuette in wood that surmounts the *abat-voix* above the pulpit in the Ursuline Chapel. As the priest spoke in the pulpit below, the angel gave added weight to his words. Effortlessly balanced on a globe, this crowning element of the pulpit appears to float in the air, with her right foot stretched out behind her. She is blowing the trumpet of the Last Judgment; the laurel leaves on her head symbolize triumph over death.

The superb aesthetic quality of the angel clearly indicates that it is the work of Pierre-Noël Levasseur, who was in charge of the decoration for the chapel. The pulpit was begun in 1726 as the first stage in the chapel's decoration. Although there are similar pulpit decorations in the provincial churches of France, this is the first such example in New France; others were soon to follow.

The flowing garments of the angel and her magnificent wings have been covered in a layer of thin gold-leaf by the Ursuline sisters themselves, who were experts in the art of gilding and decorated other churches for additional income.

PLATE 37
Pierre-Noël Levasseur   (1690-1770)
Angel of the Last Judgment   1726
wood, painted and gilded   84.5 cm
Monastère des Ursulines, Québec

PLATE 37

PLATE 38

PIERRE-NOËL LEVASSEUR
The Holy Father

Documents from the 1760s show that this sculpture (opposite) was originally in the church of Saint Vallier at Bellechasse, outside Quebec. The church's decoration was carried out by Pierre-Noël Levasseur, undoubtedly the most important woodcarver of his day, with the help of his son, Stanislas. In its original setting it was placed high on the altar wall, probably above the altar. It was carefully designed to be viewed from below, as part of the total decoration.

Even when seen out of its original context, *The Holy Father* is one of the most moving and eloquent images in Canadian art. Carved in high relief rather than in the round, the figure sits in heaven with the globe resting on his lap and his crown by his right hand. Painted in polychrome, with blue for the clouds and the sky, and gold for the robe and crown, he looks down towards his faithful subjects. He is not an idealized, distant figure; there is an expression of profound compassion on his face. His hand is not stiff and wooden; it is a life-like hand with the veins clearly visible.

In a rare personal document from the period, Pierre-Noël Lavasseur reveals his own deeply compassionate nature in a letter written after his son left him to apprentice with a Montreal sculptor:

"I have the honour of replying to this (letter), which you gave me pleasure in writing (and) by which you inform me that my son is with you. I thank you for the kind welcome that you have given him for our sake. My wish is that he be firm in his will to learn woodworking with you....I trust that you will give him some moments to read, write and draw, and that you will watch over his behaviour as though he belonged to you, in order that he goes often to the Churches and (takes part in) the sacraments, and does not associate with drunkards and libertines. If he needs paper to write and draw, I will send it to him as soon as I know that he will be staying with you and that you will give me good evidence of his diligence....I hope that God will grant him the grace to be wiser in the future, and that he will profit from your (advice) and that of your wife to whom I take the liberty of entrusting him. I beg of you to hide from him the affections which I still have for him, and let him know only the resentment (I harbour) for his bad behaviour towards me. I await news from you upon the first occasion and remain respectfully yours.

"Your very humble servant, Levasseur, Sculptor."

PLATE 38
Pierre-Noël Levasseur (1690-1770)
The Holy Father c. 1768
high relief, wood, gilded and polychrome 1,321.0 cm (height)
Musée du Québec, Québec

1760-1867

"I had been accustomed to see hundreds of Indians about my native village, then Little York, muddy and dirty, just struggling into existence . . . . But now the face of the red man is no longer seen."

Paul Kane, 1850

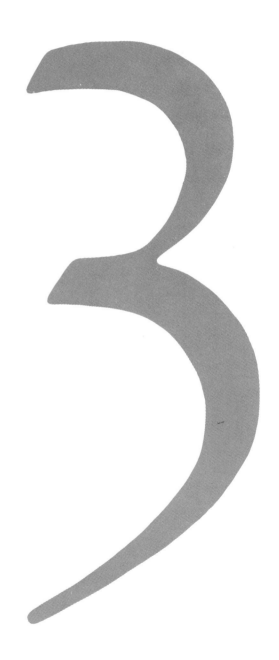

THOMAS DAVIES
A View of the Lower Part of the Falls of St. Anne

Topography was a popular art form in the eighteenth century and was practised by many of the British military officers, who learned it as a regular part of their military training. In wartime it was used as a means of documenting fortifications and battles, and in peacetime it was considered to be a "gentlemanly pursuit," along with fishing, hunting, and having elegant picnics with the ladies.

One of the most outstanding topographical artists to work in Canada was Thomas Davies, who spent over twenty years here during four different visits, between 1757 and 1790. Davies had received art lessons under G. Massiot at the Woolwich Military Academy in England, and first came to Canada in 1757. Beginning as Lieutenant of Fireworks – the lowest commissioned rank in the Royal Artillery – he worked his way up to Colonel-Commandant. During these years he did both military water colours and works for pleasure, including many views of waterfalls. He also became a well-known naturalist and ornithologist. Eventually he settled in Quebec during four years of peace, from 1786 to 1790. During this period he produced some of his most spectacular works, including *The Falls of St. Anne* (opposite). By this time he had achieved a full command of the water-colour medium, becoming a superb draughtsman and a brilliant colourist, with his own rhythmic, stylized patterns and flowing forms. His later works also reveal a deep understanding of nature and of the distinctive characteristics of the Canadian landscape.

"A rough path conducts the visitor...into a most solitary vale of rocks and trees, almost a natural grotto, through the centre of which the stream rushes until it escapes by a narrow channel between the rocks, and continues roaring and tumbling with augmenting velocity. From below there is a striking view of the cataract, which combined with the natural wildness and extraordinary features of the scene defies description; the painter alone could convey to the mind the representation with effect."

– Joseph Bouchette, 1815

PLATE 39
Thomas Davies   (c. 1737-1812)
A View of the Lower Part of the Falls of St. Anne   1790
water colour   51.4 x 34.3 cm
National Gallery of Canada

PLATE 39

PLATE 40

GEORGE HERIOT
Lake St. Charles near Quebec

George Heriot attended the Royal Military Academy at Woolwich and studied under G. Massiot's successor, the famous Paul Sandby. After Heriot came to Canada in 1792, he became completely divorced from army life when he was appointed deputy postmaster-general for British North America, a post he retained until his return to England in 1816. This position required extensive travel throughout Canada, and provided ample opportunity to do what he enjoyed most – sketching views of the landscape and writing his *Travels Through the Canadas*, published in 1807.

Heriot was a member of the garrison society, which considered nature to be either "picturesque" or "sublime" – exotic and awe-inspiring. Books such as Uvedale Price's *Essay on the Picturesque* and Edmund Burke's *The Sublime and the Beautiful* clearly set out the correct limits of taste.

In *Lake St. Charles near Quebec* (opposite), Heriot creates an eminently picturesque scene, with towering trees in the foreground and fishermen quietly enjoying the day in their skiffs. In the distance, the rugged mountains fade into the mist. It is a romantic reverie, echoing the landscapes of the French artist Claude Lorraine, who originated the picturesque style. Heriot would have known of Lorraine through his instructor Paul Sandby, who was a great admirer of the French artist. However, Heriot goes beyond these early influences to reflect a mood and atmosphere peculiar to the Canadian landscape.

"On arriving at the vicinity of the lake, the spectator is delighted by the beauty and picturesque wildness of its banks. It is, around small collections of water like this, that nature is displayed to the highest advantage. The extent of the lake is about five miles, and it is almost divided into two, by a neck of land, which forms a narrow passage, nearly at the centre. Trees grow immediately on the borders of the water, which is indented by several points advancing into it, and forming little bays. The lofty hills which suddenly rise toward the north, in shapes, singular and diversified, are overlooked by mountains which exalt beyond them, their more distant summits.

"The effect produced by clouds, is here solemn and sublime, particularly during thunder storms, when they float in rugged masses, around the tops of the hills, whose caverns, and defiles, re-echo to the trembling forests, the hoarse and awful roar."

–George Heriot, 1807

PLATE 40
George Heriot   (1766-1844)
Lake St. Charles near Quebec   c. 1800
water colour   27.2 x 44.5 cm
National Gallery of Canada

WILLIAM BERCZY
The Woolsey Family

In July, 1808, William Berczy arrived in Quebec City to spend a few months painting his group portrait of the Woolsey Family. But the work took so long that he was not able to return to his wife and family in Montreal for a full year. Born in Saxony, Berczy had worked as a writer, painter, and architect in Italy and England before he came to Canada in 1794, having set out two years earlier as the leader of a group of German settlers.

His painting of *The Woolsey Family* (opposite) depicts John Woolsey and his family in their drawingroom. Woolsey was an English merchant who lived comfortably in the prosperous society of Quebec merchants. He wanted a portrait that would create an image of wealth and refinement and would serve as a symbol of his success. The family members are all dressed in the latest styles, and the room is decorated in fashionable Neo-Classical style – Regency chairs, geometric motifs on the floor, and an Adams-style mantelpiece. Outside the large window is a view of the ramparts of Quebec. Woolsey himself stands self-assuredly in the background, looking down at his wife, who holds their youngest child on her lap. The three other children, with their wistful expressions and exquisite clothes, are pictures of propriety. Behind the table sits Woolsey's mother, and the young man with the flute is his brother-in-law. The work is an example of "conversation piece" portraits, which show two or more people conversing with each other in a casual setting. Berczy would have seen many precedents by Neo-Classical artists while in Europe and England. He was extremely proud of *The Woolsey Family*, for which he charged ten pounds for each human figure – the dog was added for free.

"I spent this afternoon after dinner with the Woolsey family, whom I assembled together at their house so that I could examine the group closely. After correcting the composition of my rough sketch, I spent the evening with William at their house...Today I began to trace my family painting on to the canvas ...and the rest of the week I shall devote entirely to the Woolsey family and to my chess player. But especially, I long to see my eight figures on canvas, it is a painting which pleases me. To proceed quickly, I have nearly finished drawing the correct outlines for each figure on paper, all of them in proportion, which I shall shade in as preliminary sketches after tracing them onto the canvas. Many of the parts, especially the sketches of the clothing, I shall try to finish at the first opportunity; having the sketches sorted out before me, they will come to me with that much more spirit and clarity."

– William Berczy, 1808

PLATE 41
William Berczy   (1744-1813)
The Woolsey Family   1809
oil on canvas   60.3 x 87.0 cm
National Gallery of Canada

PLATE 41

PLATE 42

110

FRANÇOIS BEAUCOURT
Marguerite Mailhot

During the late eighteenth century, the wealthy French-speaking community in Quebec and Montreal was still trying to emulate the lifestyle of France. They felt a strong need to adopt the social conventions of the upper classes, and to combat the wilderness with "civilization." There was a proliferation of theatres, clubs, libraries, and music. Art prospered as it never had before, but it was now supported by the privileged few rather than the church. There was a great demand for portraits, and artists such as François Beaucourt became immensely successful.

Born near Montreal, Beaucourt was one of the first Canadian artists to study art in Europe. He remained there almost twenty-three years, returning to Canada in 1786, where he settled in Montreal and established himself as an artist of many talents. His painting of *Marguerite Mailhot* (opposite) shows that Beaucourt had absorbed the Rococo tradition in France, with its pastel colours and refined elegance. The affluent woman is seen opening a gold box as she prepares tea in her elegant samovar. All the objects in the painting reflect her wealth, respectability, and social position. A companion portrait shows her husband, *Eustache-Ignace Trottier* (National Gallery of Canada), in a green velvet jacket and lacy cravat, gambling at cards. Although Beaucourt does his best to portray them as sophisticated gentry, their *petit-bourgeois* nature is still apparent.

"BEAUCOURT, Canadian Painter.
"Member of the Academy of Painting, Sculpture, and Civil and Naval Architecture of Bordeaux, aggregated to that of Paris.

"Begs leave to inform the amateurs of those arts, that he paints Portraits in oil; also executes historical, and landscape painting. He undertakes to paint theatrical scenery. Having made geometrical and aerial perspective his particular study, he has met with considerable encouragement in several Cities of Europe, viz. Paris, Petersburg, Nantz, Bordeaux, & c, in which he followed his art as a profession. He understands the art of ornamenting, in the newest stile and taste, apartments, by painting to imitate either architecture, baso-relievos, flowers, or the arabesque stile. He will undertake to teach a few students in any branch of drawing agreeable to their wish and taste.
"Apply at Mr. Belair, near St. Laurent's Gate, N° 9."

– The Montreal *Gazette*, 1792

PLATE 42
François Beaucourt (1740-1794)
Marguerite Mailhot 1793
oil on canvas 79.5 x 63.8 cm
Musée du Québec, Québec

ANTOINE PLAMONDON
Soeur Saint-Alphonse

Antoine Plamondon painted the portrait of *Soeur Saint-Alphonse* (opposite) in 1841, two years after she had taken her vows. Born into a wealthy Quebec merchant family, her name was Marie Louise Emilie Pelletier before she became a nun at twenty-two. As a young girl she had attended religious schools and enjoyed dances and parties, where she dressed sumptuously and had a reputation for being elegant and gracious. A portrait of her in these years by Plamondon (Private Collection, Quebec), stands in striking contrast to this one. Here she wears the habit of an Augustinian nun, with a band of white cloth over the forehead. She has a determined and intelligent expression in her eyes and the hint of a smile on her face.

Plamondon has carefully structured the work to capture her character with amazing psychological insight. The pyramidal composition provides solidity and structure; the textures and colours of the clothing set off her tender and beautiful face; and the subtle tonalities and simplified background add dignity and warmth.

Plamondon's talent was acquired through years of training, first as pupil of Joseph Légaré (Plates 6, 46) and later in Paris with Paulin Guérin, a disciple of the great Classical painter, Jacques-Louis David. On his return to Quebec City in 1830, Plamondon opened a studio as a "pupil of the French School" and set out to monopolize all the painting commissions in the city. A difficult and quarrelsome bachelor, he wrote vindictive reviews whenever another artist tried to invade his territory. Despite his fierce reputation, he painted a number of superb paintings that reveal a profound artistic sensitivity.

"Mr. Plamondon's work is for the benefit of the public and not of individuals. Because of this, regardless of the fee that he receives, he is not miserly with his time, nor are the products of his brush any less splendid. The great collection in the church of Montreal offers recent proof of this. The pictures mentioned above are portraits of three nuns... The painter had to overcome great difficulties, especially in regard to the face, which is almost entirely covered by a wide, tight band, which pulls together and constricts the forehead and cheeks, depriving them of that graceful openness and freedom which the painter so delights to depict and the viewer to admire....

"I shall now consider the costume, which attracts me with a charm I cannot master. What beauty there is in this costume! How naturally and impulsively he has clothed his subjects! What freedom there is in the folds of the mantle! What grace and finesse of outline. What suppleness! What flowing sleeves!

"Mr. Plamondon's use of colour – which is the most impressive aspect of his talent – is the best on this side of the ocean. Our comments here do not merely represent our own opinion, but are corroborated by a host of foreign connoisseurs and by all knowledgeable people."

–Le Canadien, 1841

PLATE 43
Antoine Plamondon   (1804-1895)
Soeur Saint-Alphonse   1841
oil on canvas   91.4 x 72.4 cm
National Gallery of Canada

PLATE 43

PLATE 44

PLATE 45

THÉOPHILE HAMEL
Madame Renaud and Her Daughters Wilhelmine and Emma

Théophile Hamel was born at Sainte-Foy, a suburb of Quebec. At age seventeen, he began to serve an apprenticeship under Antoine Plamondon (Plate 43), which continued until 1840, when he opened his own studio in Quebec. His early works, with their cold, clear tones, blue underpainting, and dramatic lighting, show the Neo-Classical orientation of his teacher.

Hamel's figures were always fresher and more fluid than Plamondon's, which are more precise and linear. His sensibility shows itself in a simple honesty of handling and in his ability to suggest emotion and affection in his group portraits. In *Madame Renaud and Her Daughters Wilhelmine and Emma* (opposite, left) Wilhelmine, the elder daughter, affectionately clasps her mother as she leans over her shoulder; Madame Renaud in turn lays her hand on baby Emma's bare leg, gently teasing her for her shoe. The panoply of fashion and rich living is there (Hamel was the painter of the Quebec establishment), but the effect is of wealth moderated by familial affection. Portrait painting was Hamel's main business. To round up trade, he visited Montreal, Kingston, Toronto and Hamilton, and his other portrait subjects read like a Who's Who of pre-Confederation politics and the Catholic clergy.

PLATE 44
Théophile Hamel   (1817-1870)
Madame Renaud and Her Daughters Wilhelmine and Emma   1853
oil on canvas   115.6 x 87.0 cm
Musée du Québec, Québec

GEORGE THEODORE BERTHON
The Three Robinson Sisters

Born in Vienna, George Theodore Berthon received instruction in the basics of painting and drawing from his father, René Theodore Berthon, court painter to Napoleon.

The artist settled in Toronto about 1841, the year Upper and Lower Canada were united. His first major commission (c. 1845) was from Sir John Beverley Robinson, a prominent member of the Family Compact, who had written the Hon. William Morris in England to advise Berthon to try his future in Canada. Berthon later painted portraits of almost all of the members of the Law Society of Upper Canada, and these works hang today in Toronto's Osgoode Hall.

The Three Robinson Sisters (opposite, right) portrays Sir John Beverley Robinson's daughters Augusta, Louisa, and Emily, on the day of the marriage of the latter two. The work was a gift to the girls' mother from her three sons-in-law. There is an atmosphere of gracious dignity, stately ease, and comfortable self-assurance in the painting: the three girls are "presented" to the viewer in a decorous way, as though at a ball, with meticulous attention to detail. Their ringlets and Victorian dresses, with pointed waistlines, were the fashionable ideal. Although their faces are amiable, they have little depth of expression beyond beauty of flesh and texture, along with a well-bred reserve.

PLATE 45
George Theodore Berthon   (1806-1892)
The Three Robinson Sisters   1846
oil on canvas   112.1 x 83.8 cm
On loan to Art Gallery of Ontario from
Mr. and Mrs. J.B. Robinson

JOSEPH LÉGARÉ
Les chutes de Saint-Ferréol

When Quebec was cut off from France during the Napoleonic wars, the *québécois* realized a new spirit of independence and self-reliance. The Quebec-born artist Joseph Légaré is a perfect example of this new-found initiative. From an early age he had three great loves: art, politics, and the mountainous landscape near Quebec City. A self-taught artist, by age twenty-two Légaré had learned how to restore and copy old paintings and had purchased many of the two hundred European paintings brought to Canada by the Abbé Desjardins. These paintings, including originals and copies by European artists, belonged to French aristocrats before the French Revolution. Légaré set up a shop and proceeded to make copies of them for other clients. He enlarged on his own collection and later opened a public museum – the first in Canada. He also created a number of impressive historical paintings representing natural disasters in Quebec history.

L'incendie du Quartier Saint-Jean (Plate 6), one such work, shows the terrible fire that swept through the Saint Jean Quarter of Quebec City in 1845, destroying over a thousand homes. In this painting, the raging inferno is at its height, with sparks and flames reaching high into the air.

A versatile artist, Légaré was the first Canadian to paint landscape for its own sake. *Les chutes de Saint-Ferréol* (opposite), on the St. Anne River near Quebec, depicts a ruggedly beautiful landscape, very different from the civilized views of the topographical artists. The vegetation in the foreground indicates Légaré's debt to the Italian paintings in his collection, but there is a forcefulness and directness of approach that is entirely his own.

"He has emerged from the dusty and prozing society of vigil worn saints and other goodly canonized notables, to give his pencil a revel amid the fair and fresh of nature's loveliness; and he is now, as I love to see him, surrounded by heaps of mountains, and sunny valleys, and dear gray hills of his own country....it has often excited my wonder that our native painters have not devoted some part of their time and study to the scenery of Canada – and to their shame be it spoken they have not; and truly they have neglected a field from which rare laurels will yet be won....Old worn copies upon copies of European landscapes, or anything else, seem preferable to the rich and novel material which our picturesque land affords."

– The Quebec *Gazette*, 1833

PLATE 46
Joseph Légaré   (1795-1855)
Les chutes de Saint-Ferréol   c. 1840
oil on canvas   75.1 x 88.4 cm
Musée du Québec, Québec

PLATE 46

PLATE 47

CORNELIUS KRIEGHOFF
Indians Portaging Furs

Cornelius Krieghoff was born in Amsterdam, Holland, and spent his youth in different parts of Europe, where he was an itinerant painter and musician. He travelled to New York in 1836 and enlisted in the army, fighting against the Seminole Indians of Florida. Later he fell in love with the beautiful Emilie Gautier, a young *québécoise* from Boucherville, near Montreal, and married her. By 1846 he had settled in Longueuil and had started to paint everyday scenes of life in Quebec.

Krieghoff was particularly interested in Indians and painted numerous scenes of their way of life. *Indians Portaging Furs* (opposite) is a superb example of his early Canadian work – he revels in the rich fall colours and the unspoiled wilderness. A woodsman, hunter, and naturalist, Krieghoff identified with the Indians and their close relationship to the natural environment.

Krieghoff moved to Montreal in 1849 and, after a brief period of success, moved to Quebec City in 1853, at the invitation of his friend, John Budden. The following years were extremely prolific ones, culminating in his masterpiece, *Merrymaking*, in 1860 (Plate 1). The all-night revel at Jolifou's Inn is just ending, and the guests are leaving for home. Krieghoff's cast of over sixty characters – including himself, standing on the steps of the inn – act out a fascinating variety of scenes. Packed with rich, anecdotal detail, this painting is not only a timeless portrait of the fun-loving and convivial *québécois*, but also a reflection of Krieghoff's own adventurous life.

"The exhibition of Mr. Krieghoff's collection of paintings ... attracted all the art connoisseurs of the city and vicinity and an immense number of visitors.... The pictures on exhibition comprise nearly all the popular artist's favourite subjects, and form a rare collection of Canadian landscapes and incidents of rural life. Among these the celebrated *Merrymaking* is conspicuous by its variety of figures and fidelity of detail, colouring and attitudes. It is generally considered the finest canvas of the collection. We may here remark that fidelity to nature is the great merit of these paintings. We have seen Canadian subjects treated by foreign artists, but they always lacked the native brilliancy of sky and forest which is the leading characteristic of Mr. Krieghoff's work. All his autumnal pieces and winter scenes are remarkable for a fidelity which rivals the photograph and cannot be surpassed. Some of the forests reflected in calm lakes and lonely streams, are worthy to rank with the best works of modern landscape painters. The only difficulty which the man of taste experiences is an 'embarras de richesses.'"

– The Quebec *Chronicle*, 1862

PLATE 47
Cornelius Krieghoff   (1815-1872)
Indians Portaging Furs   c. 1858
oil on canvas   31.8 x 44.4 cm
Hudson's Bay Company

CORNELIUS KRIEGHOFF
The Habitant Farm

In his time, Cornelius Krieghoff was the epitome of the passionate and sensitive artist. A romantic adventurer, he experienced failure and deprivation, as well as success and adulation. As an artist, he lived on the edge of society, at home with the wealthy upper class of English-speaking Quebec and with the poor *québécois* who peopled Jolifou's inn. He was a musician, story-teller, actor, and dancer, who was always the last to leave a good party. He was also a woodsman and hunter – reputed to have eyesight as keen as an Indian's. A keen botanist, he often went on long trips with his close friend, Gabriel Teoriolen, a Huron Indian, collecting plants and insects; some of these specimens were later used to make brilliant, non-fading colours.

During his productive years in Quebec City, Krieghoff turned out an astonishing number of works, including many copies of the most popular ones. *The Habitant Farm* (opposite) was one of his favourite themes, presenting a vivid picture of life in rural Quebec. The husband has just returned from the market and has brought the grandmother home for a visit. The painting abounds in minute details of country life at that time. Although the work may now appear quaint, for Krieghoff it was part of a sincere attempt at photographic accuracy. He appealed to popular tastes with his personal and perceptive characterization of the *habitant* family, telling a story forthrightly, with no attempt to cater to refined aesthetic tastes.

PLATE 48
Cornelius Krieghoff   (1815-1872)
The Habitant Farm   1856
oil on canvas   61.0 x 91.4 cm
National Gallery of Canada

ROBERT TODD
The Ice Cone, Montmorency Falls

Before Krieghoff's arrival, the one English-speaking artist of repute in Quebec was Robert Todd. He had arrived in 1834, advertising himself as a "house, sign, carriage and ornamental painter," claiming that he had done work for the gentry and nobility of England. He was probably not a very successful businessman, for he could not find enough work and left Quebec in 1853 – just as Krieghoff arrived. He went to Toronto in search of better opportunities, but fared even more poorly there, commenting that "Toronto is too new and too poor to support an ornamental artist."

During his Quebec stay, Todd specialized in bright, decorative paintings such as *The Ice Cone, Montmorency Falls* (p. 122), his most famous painting. This may have been a "horse portrait," commissioned by an officer or merchant who wanted to see his favourite tandem shown against the picturesque background of the falls, or perhaps a "souvenir painting" of the falls itself. Montmorency Falls was a favourite attraction in winter, when a huge ice cone was formed by the spray from the falls. In this picture, tiny figures can be seen sliding down the ice cone, while others look on. The work has a charm that is both honest and unassuming.

PLATE 49
Robert C. Todd   (1809-1866)
The Ice Cone, Montmorency Falls   c. 1845
oil on canvas   34.3 x 45.7 cm
National Gallery of Canada

PLATE 48

PLATE 49

PLATE 50

PLATE 51

Micmac Indians

Micmac Indians (p. 123) typifies a popular art form that has existed in all parts of Canada from the arrival of the white man to the present day. Generally called folk art, primitive art, or naïve painting, it is created by untrained artists and reflects a concern for personal self-expression, rather than the latest international art styles. It is a people's art, intended for the enjoyment of common folk everywhere. Folk art includes painting, sculpture, and quilts, as well as a delightful – and sometimes eccentric – range of media. Direct and unpretentious, it has a universal appeal, reflecting not only the personality of its maker, but the spirit of its age.

Many of the early examples of folk art are unsigned and were obviously painted for personal pleasure rather than commercial sale. The artists usually came from small rural communities, where everyone would have known them. *Micmac Indians*, the work of an unknown artist, depicts the life of the Indians of eastern Canada. It contains many precise details of their lifestyle, including their dress, canoes, cooking utensils, and hunting methods. The work has a well-organized composition and an intuitive sense of design – even the awkward perspective adds to the painting's charm. Several other works exist that are clearly by the same hand, but the name of the artist will probably remain unknown forever.

PLATE 50
Anonymous
Micmac Indians   c. 1850
oil on canvas   45.7 x 61.0 cm
National Gallery of Canada

EBENEZER BIRRELL
Good Friends

In *Good Friends* (opposite), Ebenezer Birrell carefully and lovingly presented all his favourite animals in a painting of his own farm – his prize cattle, his sturdy work horses, his sheep, and even a flock of geese safely off in the distance. He knew each of the animals intimately and by name. As president of the Pickering Agricultural Society, he obviously had immense pride in his livestock, as well as affection for the Ontario countryside in its autumn splendour. In this painting, which was not discovered until recently, Birrell has provided a glimpse of the farming community of nineteenth-century Ontario.

Birrell was born in Scotland and emigrated to Canada in 1834, where he settled on a five-hundred-acre farm near Pickering, Ontario. Besides looking after his farm, he was a surveyor, a justice of the peace, a lieutenant colonel commanding the 14th battalion of the Ontario County Militia, an elder of the Presbyterian Church at Claremont, a superintendent of education, and an art judge at the Upper Canada Provincial Exhibitions. Painting was clearly only one of his many pursuits, and something he did for pleasure. He chose as his subjects the things that were dear to him, depicting them with dignity and pride.

PLATE 51
Ebenezer Birrell   (1801-1888)
Good Friends   c. 1834
oil on canvas   58.4 x 71.1 cm
Art Gallery of Hamilton

JOHN O'BRIEN
British Naval Squadron off Nova Scotia

Although the east coast of Canada had been a part of British North America since the fall of Louisbourg in 1758, there were no artists of significance living in the Maritimes until after 1800.

One painter of note who emerged briefly during this period was John O'Brien. According to tradition, he was born off the coast of Nova Scotia on a ship on which his parents were emigrating from Ireland. He later became one of the most celebrated marine painters on the east coast. Ship-building was one of the major industries of Nova Scotia, and paintings of the newly built ships were commissioned by ship owners, captains, and naval officers. O'Brien made his first paintings as a youth in Halifax, and the local merchants were so impressed that they raised enough money when he was eighteen to send him to London and Paris to study art. He was influenced by Flemish marine scenes, toning down his colours to restrained greys and emphasizing atmospheric effects.

On his return to Halifax, he produced many marine paintings, such as *British Naval Squadron off Nova Scotia* (opposite). It conveys the drama of a storm at sea, as waves and wind batter the twenty-six-gun frigates. In this highly romantic work, the stormy sky and wave-tossed sea are dramatically portrayed in subtle grey tonalities. The sun breaks through the clouds to light up the ships and set off the stormy sky and sea. Although it is based on European marine prints, the work has a controlled composition and subtle colouring remarkable for a young artist of twenty-four.

"It will always be said of us, with unabated reverence: *They built ships of the line.* Take it all in all, a ship of the line is the most honourable thing that man, as a gregarious animal, has ever produced. By himself, unhelped, he can do better things than ships of the line; he can make poems and pictures, and other such concentrations of what is best in him. But as a group, he has put into ships of the line as much of his human patience, common sense, forethought, experimental philosophy, self-control, habits of order and obedience, thoroughly wrought handwork, defiance of brute elements, careless courage, careful patriotism and calm expectation of the judgement of God, as can well be put in a space of 300 feet long by 80 broad.''

– John Ruskin, 1856

PLATE 52
John O'Brien   (c. 1832-1891)
British Naval Squadron off Nova Scotia   1856
oil on canvas   63.5 x 88.9 cm
National Gallery of Canada

PLATE 52

PLATE 53

WILLIAM HIND
Self-Portrait

Along with the explorers, surveyors, engineers, and gold-seekers who explored the Canadian West were a number of artists eager to document the new frontier. William Hind was one of these artists. Born in England, he had come to Toronto in 1851 after his older brother, Henry Youle Hind, had established himself in Canada as a celebrated explorer, geologist, and author. In 1861 Henry organized the Hind Labrador Expedition and invited his brother along as official artist.

Two years later the artist joined the Overlanders of 62 on their famous trek across the country to Fort Garry, Edmonton, and the Caribou. On that voyage he filled sketchbooks with pencil drawings and water colours documenting the hardships of the trip. These works are filled with minutely detailed observations of nature, and reflect through their photographic accuracy the scientific spirit of the Darwinian age.

From the Caribou, Hind went on to Victoria, BC, where he spent about seven years, before returning East. His extraordinary *Self-Portrait* (opposite), dating from this period, demonstrates his precise technique, which was derived from the Pre-Raphaelite painters in England. It is one of the most psychologically penetrating self-portraits in Canadian art, in its nakedly honest depiction of the artist's introspective personality. It reveals Hind as the direct antithesis of the rugged and aggressive artist-explorer. The journals of people who travelled with him indicate the difficult times he had with the heterogeneous collection of Englishmen, Frenchmen, Germans, Italians, Hungarians, Poles, Mexicans, and Chinese on the trips.

After leaving Victoria in 1865, Hind travelled back to the Caribou, and then to Fort Garry, before making the long journey east to the Maritimes, where he settled permanently. For the next few years he worked for the Intercolonial Railway as a draughtsman, and continued to paint minutely-detailed scenes, portraying each blade of grass and leaf. His unique perception of nature in these later works approaches the metaphysical in its heightened view of reality.

When Hind died in Sussex, New Brunswick, in 1899, this obituary appeared in the *King's County Record*:

"Mr. Hind was a gentleman whose presence will be missed in Sussex, which he has made his home for the past nine years. Well informed, a good talker, when inclined to be communicative, fond of sports and with a tendency to artistic matters, he found many friends by his grand and occasionally eccentric habits. He had been ailing for the past few weeks but not until recently did his friends anticipate his death. His brother, Professor Hind of Windsor, was in attendance on him. Mr. Hind died on Monday morning about five o'clock having been a considerable sufferer, but all was done that could be done to relieve his wants by kind friends and attendants. The body will be taken to Windsor for interment."

PLATE 53
William Hind   (1833-1899)
Self-Portrait   c. 1863
water colour   30.5 x 22.9 cm
McCord Museum, Montreal

PAUL KANE
Assiniboin Hunting Buffalo

Of all the artist-explorers in Canada, Paul Kane was the most famous. Inspired by the Indian paintings of the American artist George Catlin, he made his first trip westward in the summer of 1845, travelling around the Great Lakes region and sketching the Ojibwa and other tribes. On this trip he painted a portrait of the Ojibwa chief and warrior *Mani-tow-wah-bay* or *He-Devil* (Glenbow Foundation, Calgary), who let Kane paint him only after the artist promised to show the work to Queen Victoria. The next summer, Kane set out for the West with Sir George Simpson, governor of the Hudson's Bay Company. Accompanying Simpson and the spring fur brigade to Fort Garry, he was twice left behind and had to borrow boats and give chase. After Fort Garry, he participated in some of the last great buffalo hunts, which he sketched and wrote about in his journals. Kane continued on to the Rockies, Fort Vancouver, Oregon City, and Victoria. It was mid-October of 1848 before he finally arrived back in Toronto with over five hundred sketches.

He later made a series of three hundred paintings based on this voyage, including *Assiniboin Hunting Buffalo* (opposite). Kane had great difficulty representing animals in movement, and had never made a sketch of charging buffalo. He consulted a book of early nineteenth-century Italian engravings, which had a plate showing Italian youths chasing a wild bull on horseback. Kane borrowed the composition, substituting the Indians and the buffalo for the Italians and the bull, and adding a Prairie landscape with a dramatic, stormy sky in the background. The final result is a theatrical painting presenting a romantic and idealized view of the Indian.

"The scene now became one of intense excitement; the huge bulls thundering over the plain in headlong confusion, whilst the fearless hunters rode recklessly in their midst, keeping up an incessant fire at but a few yards' distance from their victims....

"Coming up with a large bull, I had the satisfaction of bringing him down at the first fire. Excited by my success, I threw down my cap and galloping on, soon put a bullet through another enormous animal. He did not, however, fall, but stopped and faced me, pawing the earth, bellowing and glaring savagely at me. The blood was streaming profusely from his mouth, and I thought he would soon drop. The position in which he stood was so fine that I could not resist the desire of making a sketch. I accordingly dismounted, and had just commenced, when he suddenly made a dash at me. I had hardly time to spring on my horse and get away from him, leaving my gun and everything else behind."

— Paul Kane, 1859

PLATE 54
Paul Kane (1810-1871)
Assiniboin Hunting Buffalo c. 1851-1856
oil on canvas 47.0 x 75.6 cm
National Gallery of Canada

PLATE 54

PLATE 55

WILLIAM RAPHAEL
Behind Bonsecours Market, Montreal

By the time William Raphael painted *Behind Bonsecours Market, Montreal* (opposite), in the year before Confederation, the population of Canada had expanded to over three million – six times what it had been fifty years earlier. During the summer months, over one hundred and eighty ocean-going ships arrived in Montreal. In Raphael's painting, the windships can be seen sailing up the St. Lawrence, along with one of the new steamers that were soon to replace them. On the street behind the old Bonsecours Church, some immigrants have just landed, their possessions piled high; old-timers watch the show, and two young boys sit on the road, uncertain of what the future will bring – a scene repeated thousands of times during these years.

Born in Prussia, William Raphael attended the Berlin Academy for a year at age twenty-one, and emigrated to New York in 1856. A year later he had moved to Canada and was working as an artist in Quebec and Montreal. Raphael's sophisticated scenes of everyday life in Canada derive stylistically from the German Romantic paintings that he saw during his brief stay in Berlin. His works reveal an astonishing proficiency in handling light and form, particularly for an artist who had such brief exposure to European styles.

"I was greatly disappointed in my first acquaintance with the interior of Montreal; a place of which travellers had said so much. I could compare it only to the fruits of the Dead Sea, which are said to be fair and tempting to look upon, but yield only ashes and bitterness when tasted by the thirsty traveller. … But nothing of this kind gladdened our eyes as we toiled along the hot streets. Every house of public resort was crowded from the top to the bottom with emigrants of all ages, English, Irish, and Scotch. The sounds of riotous merriment that burst from them seemed but ill assorted with the haggard, care-worn faces of many of the thoughtless revellers. … The river-side portion of the town is entirely mercantile. Its narrow, dirty streets and dark houses, with heavy iron shutters, have a disagreeable appearance, which cannot but make an unfavourable impression on the mind of a British traveller."

– Catherine Parr Traill, *The Backwoods of Canada*, 1832

PLATE 55
William Raphael   (1833-1914)
Behind Bonsecours Market, Montreal   1866
oil on canvas   67.4 x 109.2 cm
National Gallery of Canada

1867-1910

"Toronto is the best art centre in Canada at present, and there are more artists here than anywhere else, and no lack of portrait painters or rather colourers of photographs. Still, judging from what I have seen, your work would be among the best, if not better than anything else we have...."

Lucius O'Brien to Robert Harris, 1879

F. M. BELL-SMITH
Lights of a City Street

In the latter part of the nineteenth century, all Canadian artists who could manage to do so—like artists the world over—studied in Paris at the various art schools, such as the Ecole Nationale des Beaux-Arts, the Académie Colarossi (where Bell-Smith studied), or the more popular Académie Julian. At these schools the main aim was good craftsmanship. Artists followed the tenets of the great French academician, Jean-Auguste Ingres, who said that "drawing is the probity of art." Drawing, either from plaster casts of Classic Greco-Roman sculptures or from life, was of great importance. Three-dimensional qualities were emphasized in the assignments, which often consisted of figure compositions with bold, heroic themes.

In *Lights of a City Street* (opposite), showing a corner of King and Yonge streets in Toronto, F. M. Bell-Smith demonstrates that he learned all his lessons well: the group action is a true interaction, as people surge towards the viewer—not without courtesy, for one figure tips his hat. Others stare or stand idly by, and a newsboy runs from the spectator's space towards a tall figure with a top hat, who closely resembles the artist. The scene is pervaded with a misty atmosphere, as though taking place after rain, so that the lights of the street dimly flicker. The painting's grey colouration and subtle, somber handling also reflect French training. However, the snapshot-like view of arrested movement probably comes from Bell-Smith's employment as a young man with the well-known photographer, William Notman of Montreal.

In the same year, he painted another major genre work, *The Queen's Tribute to Canada* (its present location is unknown), in which Queen Victoria lays a wreath on the coffin of Sir John Thompson, the Premier of Canada, who had died suddenly at Windsor Castle. An ardent admirer of Queen Victoria, Bell-Smith painted her from life at Windsor Castle on July 5, 1895. In a booklet that he wrote on his adventure, *How I Painted Queen Victoria*, he remarks that Princess Louise, herself an artist (she had assisted in founding the Royal Canadian Academy with her husband, the Marquis of Lorne, in 1880), "volunteered remarks, criticism, and advice, and once, taking the brush from my hands, illustrated her words with a firm well directed touch."

A Canadian nationalist—despite his French training and his admiration for the Queen—Bell-Smith wrote His Excellency the Earl Grey, Governor General of Canada, in 1905 that "our Country is ripe for the development of a distinctly Canadian art, which if intelligently recognized should result in masterworks comparable with those of older lands."

PLATE 56
Frederick Marlett Bell-Smith   (1846-1923)
Lights of a City Street   1894
oil on canvas   137.2 x 200.0 cm
Robert Simpson Co. Ltd., Toronto

PLATE 56

PLATE 57

138

ROBERT HARRIS
A Meeting of the School Trustees

Just after Christmas, 1885, Robert Harris wrote to his mother in Charlottetown, Prince Edward Island, where he had grown up, that he had painted a "meeting of the school trustees of a country district and the teacher, a most towering-looking young woman talking them over to her view of the question before them." By February the painting was on view in the Royal Canadian Academy exhibition. Harris told his mother that "all the artists in Ottawa said the school trustees was the best picture I have painted yet."

The painting (opposite) was set in Pine Creek School, a one-room school in PEI that Harris had visited with his new wife upon a return visit from Paris. Harris painted this image of Canadian pioneer life in the three-dimensional-figure style that he had studied at Bonnat's *atelier* in Paris in 1877. There, realism was the order of the day, and Harris found his mentors in Léon Bonnat and François Millet, whose three-dimensional-figure style is also echoed here.

In this painting, Harris has placed Kate Henderson, the teacher, in the foreground; the viewer's eye must go over her figure into the background. She only towers slightly over the trustees—who gaze at her with the quizzical fixed stare men reserve for assertive females even today. She is in motion, pleading her cause; they do not move—she symbolizes progress. It is a work full of sympathy for both women and education (Harris used his beloved young wife, Bessie, as a model for Kate), and is the first work with a feminist theme in Canadian art. With this painting the artist began to receive portrait commissions, for he had made a name for himself beyond that carved in the picture's wooden desk.

William Brymner, Harris's close friend, used the same somber colouration found in the *School Trustees* in his own painting, A *Wreath of Flowers* (Plate 3). Harris's work has a nobler theme, high moral seriousness, and greater dramatic instinct. One critic of the period, J.E. Hodgson, called it a "sober, earnest, conscientious work" and found the character of the backwoods trustees "big with brief authority ... admirably given."

Harris was to remain a nationalist all of his life, particularly devoted to the island where he had grown up.

"The sunny slopes of Italy ... must not be looked for here, but our Island has, in autumn, colours which even Titian could not rival; the spring here has many a lightsome spray of maple or of birch to toss against the fir and we may get some little glimpse of the blue loveliness of far off hills."

—Robert Harris, 1871

PLATE 57
Robert Harris   (1849-1919)
A *Meeting of the School Trustees*   1886
oil on canvas   99.7 x 123.2 cm
National Gallery of Canada

G. A. REID
Mortgaging the Homestead

The transmission of a teaching tradition is a common occurrence in Canadian art. G. A. Reid studied under Robert Harris (Plate 57) at Toronto's Central Ontario School of Art, and even copied his instructor's well-known painting of *The News-boy* (the original is in the Art Gallery of Ontario; the copy in the Confederation Centre of the Arts, Charlottetown). Reid became a teacher himself, and later was principal of the college of his youth.

The artist's early training in drawing the figure in the three-dimensional, monumental tradition of the Beaux-Arts was the leading influence on his work. In the early years of this century, he belatedly began to use the *plein air* (pictures painted in the open air) techniques of the Impressionists. Reid himself described his training as "drawing with the brush about in the same way that the sculptor feels form with his fingers shaping the clay."

Born on a farm near Wingham, Ontario, the artist always favoured the rural Ontario scene as his subject. At the time it was painted, *Mortgaging the Homestead* (opposite) was said to depict faithfully the "trials and vicissitudes of Canadian agricultural life," and to be a "strong work, well drawn, finely coloured and having its characters delightfully grouped." An important canvas for Reid, it conveys the full impact of his training at the *ateliers* in Paris in its heavy, stolid figures and in its attempt at portraying a complex group interaction united by a story-telling element. The subject comes from the artist's own experience. When his family was forced to mortgage their farm, Reid announced to them his intention to become an artist.

A complementary picture with parallel elements of handling and composition, done three years later, is *The Foreclosure of the Mortgage* (destroyed by fire in 1919; a replica exists in the Parliament Buildings, Toronto). Also a document of pioneer life in Upper Canada, it was exhibited at the Royal Academy, London, and in nearly all important art centres in Canada and the United States.

Other story-telling works of the same period, like *Forbidden Fruit* (Art Gallery of Hamilton), a subject utilizing another memory from the artist's youth, added to Reid's popularity. By 1890 he was recognized as Canada's foremost genre painter. His interests had changed to mural work by 1895, and later to landscapes.

"I have ... arrived at the belief that all representation in art must rest on some solid foundation, and I would state this to be included in the two aspects of representation: anatomy and perspective. The term anatomy must be made broad enough to cover all forms and their structure, and perspective to include all visual relations of form and their colour and tone. I can conceive these factors being used in endless variation to serve the artist for all flights of the imagination."

−G. A. Reid, 1928

PLATE 58
G. A. Reid   (1860-1947)
Mortgaging the Homestead   c. 1890
oil on canvas   128.3 x 212.1 cm
National Gallery of Canada

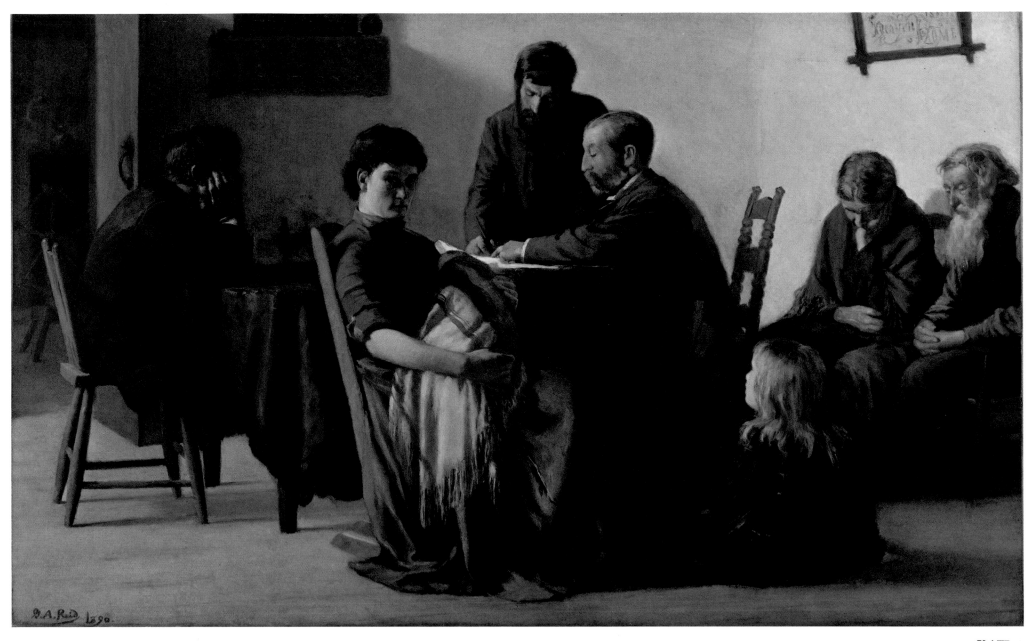

PLATE 58

PLATE 59

PAUL PEEL
A Venetian Bather

Like most Canadian artists of his generation, Paul Peel studied in Paris, where he became a close friend of George Reid (Plate 58). Peel's studio pieces lack the excitement of his smaller works, and are imbued with the monumental-figure tradition prevalent in the Paris *ateliers*. However, his attention to vibrancy of handling and warm colouration shows that he did not forget the lessons he had learned in the sketch medium. His canvases often convey remarkably intimate subject matter, provoking natural sympathy and interest. The works are effective because they reveal Peel's empathy with young children—in *After the Bath* (Plate 2), he uses as subjects his own boy and girl, Robert and Marguerite.

The artist's delight in radiant flesh tones reflects the work of his teacher, Jean-Léon Gérôme. But his interest in a variety of textures, as in *A Venetian Bather* (opposite), shows a sensuous appreciation that is rare, if not unique, in Canadian art. Indeed, this work is one of the most erotic in Canadian art up to this time. As Peel himself said, "Flesh is never flesh until you feel you can pinch it with your fingers." When *A Venetian Bather* was auctioned in 1890, it brought the ridiculously low price of $325—the highest price paid in the sale—and the artist was heartbroken at the auction's results.

After the Bath exists in at least six known versions and was an immensely popular and critical success from the time of its appearance. For it, Peel was awarded a Bronze Medal in the Paris Salon of 1890—a significant milestone in the artist's career and in Canadian art in general, for it was the second time a Canadian artist won important international recognition (the first was Daniel Fowler [Plate 61]). Reputedly sought by Sarah Bernhardt for her collection, *After the Bath* was bought by the Hungarian government and later passed into the collection of Colonel Sam McLaughlin of Oshawa, who left it to the people of Ontario.

Peel lived in Paris as an expatriate artist and was just beginning to acquire an international reputation when he died of tuberculosis at the age of thirty-one.

PLATE 59
Paul Peel   (1860-1892)
A *Venetian Bather*   1889
oil on canvas   156.2 x 113.0 cm
National Gallery of Canada

WILLIAM BLAIR BRUCE
The Phantom Hunter

"For I saw by the sickly moonlight,
  As I followed, bending low,
That the walking of the stranger
  Left no footmarks on the snow."

C. D. Shanly's poem, *The Walker of the Snow*, was the source for this painting (opposite) by William Blair Bruce. He believed that the subject was an old Canadian legend: the "walker" was simply "old Jack Frost" personified and his victims were "killed by his frosty breath." He wrote that the hunters "in their love of the supernatural have put their story in such a form that this walking ghost has been the result." Certainly Bruce, who found the ghost hard to paint, intended the work to do honour to Canada by representing "our national works in France." Bruce sought out Canadian sources as a basis for the painting, such as a snowbank picture done in the lane of his home in Hamilton, Ontario. His father sent him a pair of snowshoes and the appropriate costume so that he might complete the canvas in Giverny, France, where he was working.

Bruce's work was received with acclaim in Paris, a triumph for this student of the Académie Julian. He had recently recovered from a nervous breakdown because in 1885 his work, which he was shipping home to Canada for sale, had been totally lost in the wreck of the steamer Brooklin at Anticosti Island in the Gulf of St. Lawrence. He hoped that he would have other Salon successes after this canvas, but although he painted unceasingly in later years in France, Italy, and Sweden, pre-eminence did not come to him.

"I have been working rather hard these last two months or so on my Salon picture. I believe I have never given you much details as to the subject—otherwise than its being a Canadian one. It is from an old Canadian legend which has had a poem written of it, entitled the 'Walker of the Snow.' Burrows I believe is the writer as it occurs in his works. —As I had to paint a 'ghost' in it, it was rather difficult. However, I have succeeded well enough, as I hear to-day that I have been successful in passing the jury, and have every hope of a good successful reception by the public as well.—As this is the first time I have attempted to show anything of our national works in France—I must say I am just a little contented—and hope that this news may find you the same—just as soon as the photographs are ready I will send you one—My Salon title is very swell 'The Phantom of the Snow (Canadian Legend)—' —I am to exhibit it afterwards at the great international exhibition of Munich where I have already applied for my wall space. If I have success with this picture, I will have plenty of chances to follow up with others in something of the same style and may have a good chance of seeing you again —when I am making my studies in Canada."

—William Blair Bruce, 1888

PLATE 60
William Blair Bruce   (1859-1906)
The Phantom Hunter   1888
oil on canvas   151.1 x 191.1 cm
Art Gallery of Hamilton

PLATE 60

145

PLATE 61

DANIEL FOWLER
Fallen Birch

As a young man, the English-born Daniel Fowler studied with J. D. Harding, the water colourist and draftsman who was one of the earliest advocates of pictures painted directly in the open air, and who was known for his drawing textbooks, such as *Elementary Art, or the Lead Pencil Advocated and Explained* (1834). During and perhaps after his initial training, Fowler travelled widely in Europe. As a drawing master in London, he felt frustrated; health problems caused his emigration to Canada, where he settled on a farm on Amherst Island, near Kingston, then the capital of Upper and Lower Canada. After fourteen years of farming in Canada, where he did practically no painting, he revisited England in 1857 and 1859, taking with him a water-colour sketch of his farm, "The Cedars," to show friends. It revived his old interest in art, as did the exhibitions in England and a visit to his old master. From that time (he was forty-seven) until his death, he painted his island home. At age sixty-six, Fowler achieved his greatest honour, winning the first medal that a Canadian had ever won in an international art competition. This was for his water colour, *Hollyhocks*, at Philadelphia's International Centennial Exposition in 1876, the first American World's Fair.

In works such as *Fallen Birch* (opposite), Fowler refused to use the traditional European subject matter and chose instead a scene from the new land, painting from nature with a fresh vision. A gentle spirit imbued his work with a clarity sometimes lacking in his Canadian contemporaries. Fowler's Canadian water colours have a more lucid tone, a sparkle and brilliance, and a clearer atmosphere than one finds in his English works.

"In England a perpetual haze broods over the land—a beautiful haze if you will, but still a haze.... There are plenty of cloudless days, but the sky is not blue; but a delicate pale hazy lilac...rather than the brilliant azure of Canada...Contrasted with the dancing light and life of the Canadian atmosphere the lights on the English landscapes are all toned down, the shadows deep and obscure. The dense masses of foliage looked heavy and dark, almost black, indeed, in comparison with the feathery dazzling spring greenery I had left behind me."

—Daniel Fowler, 1894

PLATE 61
Daniel Fowler   (1810-1894)
Fallen Birch   1886
pen, brown ink, and water colour   49.3 x 70.5 cm
National Gallery of Canada

LUCIUS R. O'BRIEN
Sunrise on the Saguenay

With the founding of the Royal Canadian Academy (RCA) in 1880, Canadian artists felt a surge of ambition and a desire to prove worthy of the new institution. Lucius O'Brien, a civil engineer with genuine social graces, was nominated the first president of the RCA. President for the academy's first ten years, he must have wanted his diploma painting for that institution (all artists upon election contributed one work as a condition of entry) to be of special significance. Certainly *Sunrise on the Saguenay* (opposite), the work submitted, is distinct from the body of his work in its grandeur and size.

Depicting Cap Trinité on the River Saguenay, the painting is a model of all the tenets O'Brien held most dear: the site is sublime, picturesque, and noble. Even the time of day chosen by the artist is spectacular—sunrise, the time of the most radiant colours.

"The Saguenay is one of the most remarkable streams on this continent. It is gloomy, forbidding, and lonely in its character; the shores often rise in high crags; and Cape Eternity, whose sheer cliff rises hundreds of feet from the river's edge, is one of the most majestic and famous rocks in America."

–Wilfred Campbell, 1907

PLATE 62
Lucius R. O'Brien   (1832-1899)
Sunrise on the Saguenay   1880
oil on canvas   87.6 x 125.7 cm
National Gallery of Canada

ALLAN EDSON
Mount Orford and the Owl's Head from Lake Memphremagog

Allan Edson was born in the Eastern Townships near the impressive Mount Orford, which dominates the area. When he was fifteen he moved to Montreal with his family, and a year or two later began taking art lessons. At age eighteen he went to England for two years to study art, returning in 1867. Shortly after his return he painted *Mount Orford and the Owl's Head from Lake Memphremagog* (p. 150), which reveals his profoundly lyrical style. Edson combines a feeling for photographic realism with a romantic, quiet mood. Like many other artists of the period, he was affected by the scientific precision of the camera, and developed a technique that incorporated great clarity and detail, suffusing each object with light.

"The mountain, looming in the distance, is almost enveloped by a mist, its summit only being visible. The pond forms the foreground, and on the left bank are beautifully mirrored the forest glories which adorn its margin. Here is also visible a splendid study of rock with stunted herbage. The sunlight is very effective, and altogether the picture is 'nature in her own unexaggerated richness.' "

–*Art News*, 1871

PLATE 63
Allan Edson   (1846-1888)
Mount Orford and the Owl's Head from Lake Memphremagog   1870
oil on canvas   91.4 x 152.4 cm
National Gallery of Canada

PLATE 62

149

PLATE 63

PLATE 64

PLATE 65

JOHN A. FRASER
Laurentian Splendour

John Fraser emigrated to Canada as a young man, and in 1860 began to work for William Notman, the well-known photographer in Montreal, colouring photographs by painting over light prints on drawing paper. A full partner of the firm by 1868, he moved to Toronto to open the business there. Fraser helped found both the Society of Canadian Artists in Montreal (1867) and the Ontario Society of Artists in Toronto (1872), before assisting with the founding of the Royal Canadian Academy (1880).

A supremely confident man, he frequently stood in front of his own completed picture and remarked, "A man who can paint like that ought to wear a gold hat." Fraser showed something of the same audacity and verve in his choice of subjects.

In his early years he painted the mountainous landscape of the Eastern Townships. *Laurentian Splendour* (p. 151), a painting of Mount Orford, was submitted as his diploma work for entry to the RCA, and is a *tour-de-force* in its dramatic lighting and attention to detail. Like Edson (Plate 63), Fraser achieved a balance between Realist and Romantic elements.

Later, Fraser explored the far West, startling "the eagle and the grizzly by the unwonted apparition of an easel and sketching umbrella," as J. E. Hodgson, Professor of Painting and Librarian to the Royal Academy, London, said in 1887.

PLATE 64
John A. Fraser   (1838-1898)
Laurentian Splendour   1880
oil on canvas   48.9 x 95.3 cm
National Gallery of Canada

HORATIO WALKER
Oxen Drinking

Of all Canadian artists at the turn of the century, Horatio Walker was the one received with the most acclaim in North America. He even became a member of the Society of American Artists, along with the well-known Americans, Albert Ryder, Theodore Robinson, Winslow Homer, and many others. He won numerous awards abroad and at home, and his works were purchased by institutions such as the Metropolitan Museum, the National Gallery of Art, the Albright Gallery, and the National Gallery of Canada. This acclaim solidified the artist's truculent, trenchant independence in an area he considered his personal domain – and his alone – the Ile d'Orléans, Quebec. *Oxen Drinking* (opposite), purchased by the National Gallery of Canada for $10,000, was one of the first Canadian purchases made by that institution.

A member of the Canadian Art Club along with Maurice Cullen (Plate 68) and James Morrice (Plates 70, 71), Walker studied the more advanced art movements of his day, but found François Millet more important for his figure work, and the French Barbizon school for its landscapes. In *Oxen Drinking*, the handling of light and pigment, as well as the luminous colour, show that Walker was aware of the qualities of the *avant-garde* Impressionist movement; but this tranquil, subdued moment of Quebec rural life is Walker's original contribution.

PLATE 65
Horatio Walker   (1858-1938)
Oxen Drinking   1899
oil on canvas   120.6 x 90.2 cm
National Gallery of Canada

HOMER WATSON
The Stone Road

In 1880, the Marquis of Lorne spoke to an assembled crowd at the founding of the Royal Canadian Academy about the importance of the development of a Canadian school of painting. As though in response to this challenge, Homer Watson painted *The Stone Road* (opposite). Just twenty-six years old and recently returned from New York, where he had visited the well-known Hudson River school painter, George Inness, Watson wanted his painting to reveal the gently unfolding vistas of his home in Doon, a hamlet in the Grand River valley of Ontario, where he had been born. He specifically chose to depict a stretch of winding road along the old Dundas Highway, a scene familiar to him. He added a note of sentiment with the inclusion of the horse and driver. An attention to minute detail gives the painting an incredibly focused realism, complemented by tiny sheep on the hillside and the tranquil river reflecting a clear summer sky. The sweep of the whole work, its spacious quality and breadth of handling, elevate it beyond a mere Ontario structure to "an epic of the soil."

For Watson, good art has its "roots in its native land and is a product of its soil." His aim was the study of nature: "To me nature speaks of a mighty region outside man, a great spirituality that vaguely flashes through space; and the wish to grasp this unfathomable mystery more firmly and have it repose on canvas became my greatest endeavour." Nor was it Nature alone that he sought, rather nature in action, "some story of the elements." Watson's work was so popular and successful by the 1880s that it was often shown to distinguished visitors from abroad. One of these was Oscar Wilde, who made a spectacular North American lecture tour in 1882; he declared that he had found a new "Canadian Constable" in Watson, and commissioned a painting. Perhaps Wilde's praise contributed to Watson's desire to travel; certainly, Watson realized the shortcomings of his training. In 1887 he travelled to England and Scotland, as well as making a brief visit to Paris, to study and meet contemporary artists abroad. He met Sir George Clausen and E. J. Gregory, and Wilde introduced him to Whistler. During his European trip Watson learned a new unity of movement and atmosphere, which culminated in his famous painting, *The Flood Gate* (National Gallery of Canada).

Watson listed Constable and other landscape painters like Turner and Daubigny of the Barbizon school in a frieze around two ceilings in his home at Doon. He clearly felt he had contributed to the landscape tradition. Certainly members of the Group of Seven would agree. Lawren Harris always found "something fine" about Watson's work, "something big and lasting." He added, "The deeper his insight, the clearer his expression."

Watson was Canada's earliest conservationist, lamenting the ruthless destruction of trees for hydro and telephone lines. In 1923 he wrote, "Trees are the first of all the beauties with which the Lord has embroidered the old earth.... They have a hard time. I must save some to show what a beast man is sometimes."

PLATE 66
Homer Watson   (1855-1936)
The Stone Road   1881
oil on canvas   91.4 x 130.2 cm
National Gallery of Canada

PLATE 66

PLATE 67

OZIAS LEDUC
Le Petit Liseur

Ozias Leduc was known to many as the "sage of St-Hilaire," a title that in many ways captures the spirit of the man. Born in the small village of St. Hilaire, at the foot of a once-volcanic mountain about forty kilometres from Montreal, Leduc lived there all his life. He built his own studio by hand and dedicated his life to painting and poetry. A man of great humility and wisdom, he devoted his secluded life to a profound inner search for meaning. Avoiding the distractions and manoeuvring of the art world, he painted church murals for his income, and easel paintings for his own personal pleasure. He chose as his subjects the simple everyday objects around him, and the people who were close to him.

For Le Petit Liseur (opposite) he asked his younger brother to serve as a model, wearing his high-school cap and uniform. The boy in fact is not reading, but copying an illustration from a textbook. An aura of serene calm pervades the painting. Each element, from the sleeves of the shirt to the books on the table and the boy's face, is treated with reverential care. It has an intensified reality that takes the viewer into another world, where time becomes frozen into an eternal moment. Like many other paintings by Leduc, it evokes a profound religious feeling—a dignity and humility reflecting the artist's own character.

Leduc worked slowly and meticulously, and with immense concentration. In his still-life paintings, such as the extraordinary Study by Candlelight (National Gallery of Canada), Leduc instills the work with an almost mystical light that illuminates a jug or a plate and the other objects on the table. Another painting, Les Trois Pommes (Collection Madame P. E. Borduas), was given to Leduc's disciple, Paul-Emile Borduas. Borduas saw him as a great master who showed him "the way from the spiritual and pictorial atmosphere of the Renaissance to the power of illusion which leads to the future. Leduc's whole life shines with this magic illusion."

Leduc made one trip to Europe—in 1897. He travelled to Paris with Suzor-Côté (Plate 69) and ended up spending eight months there. Little is known of what he saw or did during his stay, but the works done after his return indicate that he was not affected by the current Paris styles, for he continued to paint according to his own personal vision. In the years 1910–1920, Leduc painted a number of unusual landscapes of Mont St. Hilaire, such as Fin du jour (Montreal Museum of Fine Arts). These are all dark, atmospheric paintings, suggestive of deeper mysteries and symbolic meaning.

PLATE 67
Ozias Leduc   (1864-1955)
Le Petit Liseur   1894
oil on canvas   36.9 x 46.9 cm
National Gallery of Canada

MAURICE CULLEN
Cape Diamond

This view (opposite) of Wolfe's Cove, Quebec, shows the glow of sunset on snow-laden cliffs and on the roofs of fine old houses that edge the road beneath them. Snow-covered ice borders the river channel: beyond is Lévis. The ships at the wharf are carefully depicted, as are the houses (even to the lines of washing). Owned once by Robert Pilot, Cullen's son, this work has been variously dated between 1900 and 1910. Another version of the scene–in summer–is in the Musée du Québec.

In depicting the transitory play of light on the snow, Maurice Cullen followed the intricate laws of complementary colour; he used twenty different colours to create his "white" snow. Although he used the brighter palette of Impressionism and broken strokes of colour, as well as creating a vibrant painting texture to indicate the atmosphere, he showed only a minimal tendency towards the new style. He kept his colours separate, as far as possible, and wove them on the canvas, although often applying them in the pure state in small areas. By doing this, Cullen hoped to add "variety and brilliance to the completed work."

A native of St. John's, Newfoundland, Cullen began his art training in Montreal, studying sculpture at the Conseil des Arts et Manufactures, as well as with the prominent sculptor, Philippe Hébert, at the Monument National. Upon his arrival in Paris in 1889, he decided to change from sculpture to painting. By 1894, his work had achieved considerable attention in France. It was shown at the New Salon and was bought by the French government; he was also invited to join the prestigious Société Nationale des Beaux Arts.

In 1895 he returned to Montreal and made it his home, facing adverse criticism of his paintings and poor sales. His earliest works in this country, such as *Logging in Winter, Ste. Anne de Beaupré* (Art Gallery of Hamilton), broke with the past in their presentation of the Canadian winter.

Cullen painted from nature, out-of-doors. In counselling a young painter to strive for originality, he said, "Nature is a great book with most of the leaves uncut." Asked what material necessities he would need for an ideal life, he replied, "A studio of my own, a shack in the mountains, a garden for an acre of flowers, and a heavy snow-fall every winter."

The artist's significance for other Canadian artists can hardly be overestimated. Not only had he many students at the Art Association of Montreal, including Edwin Holgate (Plate 87), but he also influenced many painters in Ontario, through works shown in the Canadian Art Club. Two members of the Group of Seven spoke of his influence: Arthur Lismer (Plate 77), who saw his work when he arrived in Canada in 1911, and A. Y. Jackson (Plates 72, 73), who said, "To us he was a hero." Cullen's friend James Wilson Morrice (Plates 70, 71) felt that he was "the one man in Canada who gets at the guts of things."

PLATE 68
Maurice Cullen   (1866-1934)
Cape Diamond   c. 1910
oil on canvas   145.4 x 174.6 cm
Art Gallery of Hamilton

PLATE 68

PLATE 69

MARC-AURÈLE DE FOY SUZOR-CÔTÉ
Settlement on the Hillside

Born in Arthabaska, Quebec (often a subject of his work—as it probably is in this painting), Aurèle de Foy Suzor-Côté (1869-1937) trained in Paris at Julian's (where he won first prize for composition and figure painting), the Académie Colarossi, and under Léon Bonnat at the Ecole Nationale des Beaux-Arts . The first works he did in Paris—often still-life compositions—are examples of his academic training. Although by 1893 the influence of Impressionism showed in his brushwork, the full impact of the style did not affect him until 1908, the year he returned to Canada.

Suzor-Côté, like Cullen (Plate 68)—whom he must have considered a rival—was interested in studying the variables possible in the colours of snow. *Settlement on the Hillside* (opposite) has a rich, tapestry-like effect that captures the subtle play of light and shade. The artist emphasizes the effects of light and colour by carrying the eye through the shadows on the snow, along to the distant houses nestled into a hillside, giving only a tiny triangle of horizon to the picture.

This painter was also a well-known sculptor in bronze, favouring native or French-Canadian subjects.

PLATE 69
Marc-Aurèle de Foy Suzor-Côté   (1869-1937)
Settlement on the Hillside   1909
oil on canvas   58.4 x 73.0 cm
National Gallery of Canada

"Not Quebec only, but all of Canada, suffers a severe loss in the death of Marcus Aurèle de Foy Suzor-Côté, French Canada's greatest painter and one of her greatest sculptors. His fame was international, and for many years he had been recognized in the art capitals of the world as a brilliant artist. His training was French, but he worked out his own characteristic style, and he was never a copyist. His large canvases breathe the very atmosphere and colour of the woods of his beloved Quebec. He recorded on canvas many of the great historic moments and events in its storied past. And he gave to the world a series of studies of the French-Canadian habitant that have never been equalled and are not likely to be, for he dealt with some types that are fast dying out.... He was one of the most brilliant colourists North America has known, and his autumn scenes glowed with light, while as a painter of snow and the refractions of light in ice he was unequalled....

"Canadian art is the poorer for his passing, but he leaves a priceless legacy in paintings that are the property of the nation. He will not be soon forgotten."

—S. Morgan Powell, the Montreal *Daily Star*, 1937

JAMES WILSON MORRICE
The Ferry, Quebec

James Wilson Morrice, a Montrealer, attended the Académie Julian briefly in 1891, but left to study with the French Barbizon school artist, Henri Harpignies, whose tonal landscapes doubtless influenced him. He also admired the subtle colouring, smooth brushwork, high horizon, and pictorial design of the American expatriate, James McNeill Whistler.

Morrice settled in Europe, but returned to Canada every winter, where he would often join his friend, Maurice Cullen (Plate 68), on sketching trips down the St. Lawrence. Occasionally Morrice's early work closely parallels Cullen's, such as in *The Ferry, Quebec* (opposite), which was painted about two years after Cullen's *The Old Ferry, Louise Basin, Quebec* (National Gallery of Canada). Both artists were applying the techniques of European Impressionism to the Canadian landscape, but with their own personal styles.

The Ferry, Quebec is one of the great images of Canadian art. It is a view across the St. Lawrence River, with the dock at Lévis in the foreground and Quebec City across the river. The chugging ferry approaching the dock, the falling flakes of heavy wet snow, and the shifting smoke have an effect of spontaneity; but the result is an almost abstract pattern created by the classically balanced composition of four horizontal bands – wharf, river, distant shore, and sky. The distant table of land extends across two-thirds of the background and is balanced by the red-roofed building on the wharf. The central, icy blue band of the St. Lawrence River supplies the strongest colour in the work, and is framed in white by the snow-covered wharf and distant land, against an overall background of receding, twilight-grey sky. As Cullen once said of Morrice's art, "It looks as if it were painted from the recollection of a dream."

Artists like A.Y. Jackson (Plates 72, 73) acknowledged the part played by Morrice and Cullen in making the young painters of Montreal aware of the new art movements in the *avant-garde* art circles of France. Morrice also influenced younger Canadian artists, such as Clarence Gagnon and Robert Pilot, who followed him to Paris.

One of the first painters of international stature that Canada ever produced, Morrice always preferred living abroad, particularly after his parents died in 1914. A letter he wrote to Edmund Morris in 1910 suggests what the artist found of interest in Paris: "There is a very fine show of Cézanne's pictures on now. Fine work, almost unbelievably fine. I once disliked some of his pictures, but now I like them all. His is the savage work that one would expect to come from America—but it is always France that produces anything emphatic in art."

PLATE 70
James Wilson Morrice   (1865-1924)
The Ferry, Quebec   c. 1909
oil on canvas   61.0 x 81.3 cm
National Gallery of Canada

PLATE 70

PLATE 71

164

JAMES WILSON MORRICE
Environs of Tangiers

In *Environs of Tangiers* (opposite), Morrice has completely changed his pictorial space: now the background is flattened. The colour has altered, too, and is more brilliant and daring. The vantage point is far higher and more dramatic than in *The Ferry, Quebec* (Plate 70).

The change towards an emphasis on surface design, an increased range of colours, and lighter values was partly brought about by Morrice's friendship with Henri Matisse, whom he met in 1908 or 1909 in the halls of the Salon d'Automne in Paris, when they both exhibited there. Morrice, always a transient, followed Matisse to North Africa which he was to visit several times; he died in Tunis in 1924.

Matisse, who called Morrice "the artist with the delicate eye," recalled his drinking habits in a letter in 1925: "He had, everyone knows, an unfortunate passion for whisky. Despite that, we were, outside of our hours of work, always together. I used to go with him to a café where I drank as many glasses of mineral water as he took glasses of alcohol." In the café, Morrice often did his *pochades*, or sketches, following the French practice of painting *en plein air* (outdoors) on wooden panels (which he carried in a small paintbox in his pocket). He considered these gracefully brushed records of the changing scene to be complete works in themselves.

Through the café world, the artist met English novelists Arnold Bennett and Somerset Maugham, and art critic Clive Bell. Later, Bennett used Morrice as the model for Priam Farll in *Buried Alive*, and Maugham used him for Warren in *The Magician* and Cronshaw in *Of Human Bondage*.

" 'Well, look at that little bald man in the corner. That is Warren.'

"Arthur looked at the man she pointed out. He was a small person, with a pate as shining as a billiard-ball, and a pointed beard. He had protruding, brilliant eyes.

" 'Hasn't he had too much to drink?' asked Arthur frigidly.

" 'Much,' answered Susie promptly, 'but he's always in that condition, and the further he gets from sobriety the more charming he is. He's the only man in this room of whom you'll never hear a word of evil. The strange thing is that he's very nearly a great painter. He has the most fascinating sense of colour in the world, and the more intoxicated he is, the more delicate and beautiful is his painting. Sometimes, after more than the usual number of *apéritifs*, he will sit down in a café to do a sketch, with his hand so shaky that he can hardly hold a brush; he has to wait for a favourable moment, and then he makes a jab at the panel. And the immoral thing is that each of these little jabs is lovely. He's the most delightful interpreter of Paris I know, and when you've seen his sketches — he's done hundreds, of unimaginable grace and feeling and distinction — you can never see Paris in the same way again.' "

—W. Somerset Maugham, *The Magician*, 1908

PLATE 71
James Wilson Morrice (1865 -1924)
Environs of Tangiers   c. 1912
oil on canvas   63.5 x 81.3 cm
National Gallery of Canada

1910-1940

"Our art will never hold a commanding position ... until we are stirred by big emotions born of our landscape; braced to big, courageous efforts by our climate; and held to patient and persistent endeavour by that great pioneer spirit which animated the explorers and soldiers of early Canada."

Wyly Grier, 1913

A.Y. JACKSON
Terre Sauvage

A native of Montreal, A.Y. Jackson studied at the Art Institute of Chicago in his early twenties and later made two extended trips to Europe, where he established himself as a professional artist. In the spring of 1913, he held an exhibition in Montreal that had positive reviews, but no sales. He was about to move to New York and become a commercial artist when Lawren Harris (Plates 4, 76, 91) asked to buy his *Edge of the Maple Wood* (National Gallery of Canada). The offer drew him to Toronto, where he met some of the future members of the Group of Seven and became excited by their enthusiasm for the North. That fall he met Dr. James MacCallum, a Toronto ophthalmologist and avid art-collector, while sketching at Georgian Bay. The doctor liked Jackson's work and proposed to guarantee his expenses for a year. When Jackson returned to Toronto late in October, he "painted up" *Terre Sauvage* (opposite) in Lawren Harris's studio. With its boldly simplified shapes and garish colours, the painting was a radical breakthrough for Canadian art. It was one of the first paintings ever created in a style that was as rough and elemental as the landscape it portrayed. The rocks were painted with a heavily loaded brush that was dragged across the canvas; bright touches of pure green and red were used for the trees; and Jackson gave weight and mass to the heavy, cement-bag clouds—unlike the delicate tonal paintings of the Victorians. This work had an enormous influence on younger Toronto artists, especially Tom Thomson. Jackson himself considered the painting experimental and did not exhibit it until 1918.

"After painting in Europe where everything was mellowed by time and human association, I found it a problem to paint a country in outward appearance pretty much as it had been when Champlain passed through its thousands of rocky islands three hundred years before. It was a perfect autumn; there were a few snow flurries, but no cold weather. I did a lot of work, both canvases and sketches. The canvases were direct transcripts from nature....Paddling around the islands and exploring intricate channels and bays that cut into the mainland provided me with much material. I made studies for *Terre Sauvage*, the first large canvas of the new movement....In Toronto, Lawren Harris had a studio on the top floor of the branch of the Bank of Commerce at Bloor and Yonge Streets....I stayed there until the Studio Building was ready for occupation, working on the large canvas, *Terre Sauvage*, which MacDonald called Mount Ararat, because, he said, it looked like the first land that appeared after the Flood subsided."

– A.Y. Jackson, 1958

PLATE 72
A.Y. Jackson   (1882-1974)
Terre Sauvage   1913
oil on canvas   127.0 x 152.4 cm.
National Gallery of Canada

PLATE 72

PLATE 73

170

A.Y. JACKSON
First Snow, Algoma

A.Y. Jackson returned to Toronto in 1919, after serving as an artist in Europe during World War I. The war and the tragic death of Tom Thomson had deeply marked Jackson and the other Toronto painters. In an effort to rekindle their earlier enthusiasm, Lawren Harris rented a box car from the Algoma Central Railway and arranged to leave it on sidings as a base, while the artists sketched the magnificent Algoma landscape. During the second Algoma trip, in 1919, Jackson completed the sketch for *First Snow, Algoma* (opposite), which he later painted in his Toronto studio. This large painting is one of his most impressive, with its panoramic view of the Algoma countryside. The work's swirling snow patterns, vibrant colour, and rhythmic forms reflect the artist's lyrical perception of the land and his extraordinary painterly ability. In later years, Jackson always considered this his favourite work.

Shortly after its completion, the Group of Seven was officially formed, and their first exhibition was held in May, 1920. Aside from A.Y. Jackson, the original Group of Seven consisted of Lawren Harris, J. E. H. MacDonald, Arthur Lismer, Fred Varley, Frank Johnston, and Frank Carmichael, with Jackson eventually assuming the role of chief spokesman. A rugged individualist, he was never happier than when he was out in the bush, paddling a canoe, or exploring some new part of the country. His mission was to reveal Canada to Canadians, and over the years he painted canvases of nearly every corner of the country.

"In the autumn, Harris arranged a sketching party in Algoma and had a box car fitted up with bunks and a stove to accommodate us. In addition to a canoe, we had a three-wheel jigger, worked by hand, to go up and down the tracks....

The box car became a studio, and the party consisted of Harris, MacDonald, Frank Johnston and myself. Our car was hitched to the passenger train or the way freight. When we reached a place where we wished to paint it was left on a siding where the only inhabitants were the section men....

"The nights were frosty, but in the box car, with the fire in the stove, we were snug and warm. Discussions and arguments would last until late in the night, ranging from Plato to Picasso, to Madame Blavatsky and Mary Baker Eddy. Harris, a Baptist who later became a theosophist, and MacDonald, a Presbyterian who was interested in Christian Science, inspired many of the arguments. Outside, the aurora played antics in the sky, and the murmur of the rapids or a distant waterfall blended with the silence of the night. Every few days we would have our box car moved to another siding."

– A.Y. Jackson, 1958

PLATE 73
A.Y. Jackson   (1882-1974)
First Snow, Algoma   1919-1920
oil on canvas   106.7 x 127.0 cm
McMichael Canadian Collection

TOM THOMSON
The West Wind

Surely there are no greater landmarks in Canadian art than *The Jack Pine* (Plate 5) and *The West Wind* (opposite), both painted by Tom Thomson in the year of his death. These paintings have been described variously as representing the spirit of the North, the symbol of Canadian character, and the culmination of Canadian art. Reproduced countless times on stamps, posters, and in books, they have become the sacred icons of Canadian art, symbolizing the great legend of the lonely artist, inspired by the beauty of the northern landscape.

The sketches for both these works were probably painted in the spring of 1916, when Lawren Harris (Plates 4, 76, 91) and Dr. James MacCallum visited Thomson at Achray Station, on the eastern side of Algonquin Park. The three men travelled to Lake Cauchon, where they encountered a dramatic thunderstorm that became the subject of Thomson's *The West Wind*. According to Harris, Tom "became excited by the drama of the scene, grabbed his sketch box, ran out into the gale, squatted behind a big stump, and commenced to paint in a fury. He was one with the storm's fury save that his activity, while keyed to high pitch, was nonetheless controlled. In twenty minutes Tom had put down in living paint the power and drama of the storm in the North."

When Thomson returned to Toronto in the late fall of 1916, he settled in the shack behind the Studio Building, where he worked alone throughout the winter, painting at least eight major canvases. *The Jack Pine* and *The West Wind* were among the last works he completed before he returned to Algonquin Park that fateful summer of 1917.

"Thomson was a strange figure in Canadian Art–he drifted across the scene for a few years–lived his own life in the woods of Algonquin Park–pitched his tent on new trails–paddled and fished the lakes and streams–and when the mood took him he painted– putting all his experience and simple philosophy into his work. To many artists he was a myth, for he knew few people, but to those of us who have had the rare privilege of taking the trail with him and sharing a tent, or a studio in his brief city sojourns–he was more than an artist of ability,–he was one of those great types that a country produces sparingly and at times when they are needed.

"Tom Thomson is the manifestation of the Canadian character–thought of in terms of beauty. He reveals to us our own environment, changing the direction of our thoughts and aspirations from material and utilitarian considerations to contemplation of the beauty of Canada. A poet, but his language is not words,–a philosopher, but his philosophy is not to be read in books–a creator, an interpreter–an artist."

– Arthur Lismer, 1934

PLATE 74
Tom Thomson   (1877-1917)
The West Wind   1917
oil on canvas   120.7 x 137.5 cm
Art Gallery of Ontario

PLATE 74

173

PLATE 75

TOM THOMSON
Tea Lake Dam

The remarkable flowering of Tom Thomson's art during the last four years of his life has become legend. Every year, at the first sign of spring, he went to Algonquin Park and did not return until the snow fell. Between odd jobs as a guide and a forest ranger, Thomson sketched the changing seasons. His small oil sketches were painted on boards, which could easily be fitted into a sketching box and taken with him on canoe trips. For Thomson, they were finished works, not just studies for larger paintings. Far more than the paintings themselves, the sketches reveal Thomson's dazzling technique and his extraordinary colour sense. An intuitive artist, Thomson was at his best sketching outdoors.

Tea Lake Dam (opposite) is one of the finest of over four hundred sketches he completed. It includes all of Thomson's favourite motifs: the turbulent sky and clouds dominate three-quarters of the sketch; the spring landscape is painted in bold but delicate colours; and the rushing water is depicted in dabs of blue and white. There is freedom of form and a liveliness of brush strokes that come close to a pure spontaneity. Thomson possessed amazing powers of observation. He knew the landscape not as a tourist or summer visitor, but as a woodsman, lending authenticity to all his work.

In the summer of 1917, Thomson drowned in Algonquin Park, just before his fortieth birthday. With his death he became a mythical figure, capturing the imagination of all Canadians.

"Thomson came to life in the bush.... He saw a thousand things–animals and birds, and signs along the trail that others missed. He knew where to find subjects–a stretch of muskeg, a fine stand of pine with possibilities for the kind of thing he wanted to paint. He could drop a line in places, and catch a fish where other experienced fishermen had failed. He identified a bird song, and noted changes in the weather. He could find his way over open water to a portage or a camp on a night as black as ink. It was this sense of awareness and significance of simple sights and sounds, his uncanny sensitivity carried over into his painting and sketching that gave the authentic tang to his work."

– Arthur Lismer, 1954

PLATE 75
Tom Thomson   (1877-1917)
Tea Lake Dam   1915
oil on panel   21.6 x 26.7 cm
McMichael Canadian Collection

LAWREN HARRIS
Clouds, Lake Superior

In the 1920s, Lawren Harris abandoned his earlier decorative style and began painting boldly simplified works that were an expression of his deep spiritual beliefs. Harris was a theosophist who believed that "art is a realm of life between our mundane world and the world of the spirit," and his vision of art and nature was a mystical one. In *Clouds, Lake Superior* (opposite), Harris painted an infinite expanse of space, with heavy clouds floating over an open lake. The painting is bathed in light, symbolizing spirit. For Harris, the golden-white light of the sun was the life-essence that animated the soul. The soaring mountains were romantic symbols of his own search for spiritual heights.

Mt. Lefroy (Plate 4), depicting a pyramid-shaped peak thrusting dramatically into the sky, is one of his most aggressively powerful works. In portraying a space that no human being could inhabit, Harris has abstracted his shapes even more than he did in his Lake Superior paintings, and it is not difficult to foresee in it his progress towards abstraction (Plate 91).

As the unspoken leader of the Group of Seven, Harris was instrumental in formulating the group's philosophy. With his inexhaustible energy, he was a driving force, sweeping everyone along in a wave of enthusiasm. In contrast to his active nature, his paintings appear serene, for in them he sought to reveal the inner world of the spirit with precision and clarity.

PLATE 76
Lawren Harris   (1885-1970)
Clouds, Lake Superior   1923
oil on canvas   102.2 x 127.0 cm
Winnipeg Art Gallery

ARTHUR LISMER
A September Gale, Georgian Bay

Arthur Lismer received his early training at Sheffield's School of Art in England and at Antwerp's Académie Royale des Beaux-Arts. His work therefore had a more traditional base than that of some of the other members of the Group of Seven, from whom he gained a new excitement in handling colour as well as new subject matter. Lismer's first visit to Dr. James MacCallum's cottage on Georgian Bay was made in September of 1913, two years after he arrived in Canada from England. He visited the area again with Fred Varley in the fall of 1920, the year the Group of Seven was formed.

Lismer's A *September Gale, Georgian Bay* (p. 178) and Varley's *Stormy Weather, Georgian Bay* (p. 179) were developed from sketches done on the same day and practically side by side, and both works recall Thomson's *The West Wind* (Plate 74). Lismer's canvas, which shows a close-up view of the storm, is lower in tone and has a greater emphasis on design than Varley's, which surveys more of the panorama of the landscape itself, and shows a more Impressionistic response to the scene and an airier, looser handling.

A *September Gale, Georgian Bay* was part of an extremely productive period for Lismer. Later he was to have a decisive effect on Canadian art as a teacher and lecturer.

PLATE 77
Arthur Lismer   (1885-1969)
A *September Gale, Georgian Bay*   1921
oil on canvas   121.9 x 162.6 cm
National Gallery of Canada

PLATE 76

177

PLATE 77

PLATE 78

PLATE 79

FRED VARLEY
Stormy Weather, Georgian Bay
Vera

Fred Varley was an artist of immense passion and profound humanity. Born in Sheffield, England, he was four years older than Lismer (Plate 77), who came from the same town. Varley had already attended art school in Antwerp, where he had made quite a reputation for himself, when Lismer met him in Sheffield in 1912. "I can even remember my first impression of him. A man with a ruddy mop of hair–and it *was* red– which burned like a smouldering torch on top of a head that seemed to have been hacked out with a blunt hatchet. That colour was the symbol of a fire in his soul."

Varley came to Canada in 1912, with just a few dollars in his pocket. He worked at Grip, a commercial art firm, where he met Tom Thomson, who became a close friend. During the final offensive of World War I, Varley went overseas as a war artist and painted some of the most powerful statements ever made against the futility of war.

After the war, Varley returned to Toronto and began painting portraits of wealthy Toronto patrons, such as the Masseys. His moodiness, his bohemian ways, and his independent spirit set him apart from the other artists in Toronto at the time. However, he was close to the others in his rebellious spirit, and he became part of the original Group of Seven in 1920. Shortly afterwards, he painted one of the greatest landscapes in Canadian art: *Stormy Weather, Georgian Bay* (p. 179).

When Varley left for Vancouver in 1926, he broke his ties with the Group of Seven. The years that followed were the most fulfilling of his career. He was overwhelmed by the majestic beauty of the British Columbia landscape. He also met a beautiful student named Vera Weatherbie and fell deeply in love with her. His painting, *Vera* (opposite), is the most tender and moving of all the many portraits he did of her. With great assurance, he conveys a mood of relaxed sensuality; her slightly tilted head and sloping shoulders, the hint of a smile on her lips, and the forthright gaze, all suggest a feeling of intimacy. Varley was deeply involved in mysticism and claimed to see people's auras, or energy fields. He also believed that different colours expressed different spiritual states–blue and green represent high states of spirituality, whereas red is more terrestrial. In *Vera*, the colours green and blue dominate the painting. As Varley said, "Green is a more spiritual colour. That is why I use it so much. When you look at the painting [*Vera*] for a long time, other colours seem to weave their way into it, so the flesh and the dress and the setting gradually acquire more normal colouring– Perhaps the effect is purely imaginary–but then painting is an exercise of the imagination."

PLATE 78
Fred Varley   (1881-1969)
Stormy Weather, Georgian Bay   1920
oil on canvas   132.1 x 162.5 cm
National Gallery of Canada

PLATE 79
Fred Varley   (1881-1969)
Vera   c. 1930
oil on canvas   61.0 x 50.8 cm
National Gallery of Canada

J. E. H. MACDONALD
The Tangled Garden

J. E. H. MacDonald, the oldest member of the Group of Seven, and the one to whom the others brought their work for encouragement and advice, painted this powerful nature subject (opposite) in his own garden at Thornhill, north of Toronto. The bending golden sunflower that dominates the scene has the sinuous curve typical of the *art nouveau* style, with which MacDonald would have been familiar through his study of contemporary art magazines, and through his work as a commercial artist.

The painting is one of MacDonald's major works of this period. Recent critics have spoken of its tapestry-like qualities, relating them to a trip the artist made with Lawren Harris to see a Scandinavian art exhibition in Buffalo in 1913. The painting's flattened images, large bold forms, and emphasis on colour and sharp tonal contrasts come from the aesthetic of the artists who were to become the Group of Seven. The hot, lush colours are part of the artist's unique style that predominates in many of his paintings, as is the use of a strong diagonal line in the foreground. At the time the work appeared, one of the leading critics of the day, Hector Charlesworth of *Saturday Night* magazine, singled it out as a "quasi-futuristic" shock. MacDonald, although a shy man, was moved to reply, "If the function of the artist is to see, the first duty of the critic is to understand what the artist saw." Because of the debate, the work has become the single most discussed work in Canadian art.

"*Tangled Garden*, *Elements* and a host more, are but items in a big idea, the spirit of our native land. The artists hope to keep on striving to enlarge their own conception of that spirit."

– J. E. H. MacDonald, 1916

PLATE 80
J. E. H. MacDonald   (1873-1932)
The Tangled Garden   1916
oil on board   121.9 x 152.4 cm
National Gallery of Canada

PLATE 80

PLATE 81

J. E. H. MACDONALD
Falls, Montreal River

"I always think of Algoma as MacDonald's country. He was a quiet, unadventurous person, who could not swim, or paddle, or swing an axe, or find his way in the bush. He was awed and thrilled by the landscape of Algoma and he got the feel of it in his painting. He loved the big panorama."

– A.Y. Jackson, 1954

Jim MacDonald was forty-seven years old when the Group of Seven was formed in 1920, the same year *Falls, Montreal River* (opposite) was painted. MacDonald, who loved to be in the woods or the mountains, living close to nature, was an admirer of the American poet Walt Whitman and the American transcendental philosopher, Henry Thoreau. He believed that man could only rise above his physical self by contemplating nature, through which man reached a higher, more spiritual end.

    Falls, Montreal River is an expression of this philosophy. The sketch was made during the second trip to Algoma, the trip on which Jackson made his sketch for *First Snow, Algoma* (Plate 73). The extraordinary impression of three-dimensional space, created by the falls that lead down to a vanishing point in the centre of the painting, is heightened by the warm colours in the foreground and the cool blues of the distance. Everything is alive with movement and rich, vibrating colour, creating a feeling of infinite space and heightened vision.

"Every day advanced the passing of the leaf, and soon our painters had to go in quest of the desirable 'spot of red.' The hills that had been crimson and scarlet with maple were changed to purplish grey. The yellow leaves were following fast.... The sound of the bush changed with the lessening leaves—no softened rustle all about but the hollow soughing of a million trees from far heights and valleys. And there was a deeper note from the waterfalls, for the rains had filled the courses again after the drought of summer. There was an exhilaration for the sketchers in working by rapid and fall. Every rushing stream was a prompter of song, like the running of the tap to the house canary, and Lawren especially discovered that he had a singing voice when he could get a waterfall as accompanist. Two of the rare days of the trip were spent by the workers at the great Falls of the Montreal River, and they had many a good hour on smaller streams."

– J. E. H. MacDonald, 1919

PLATE 81
J. E. H. MacDonald   (1873-1932)
Falls, Montreal River   1920
oil on canvas   121.9 x 153.0 cm
Art Gallery of Ontario

EMILY CARR
Forest, British Columbia

"Oh, God, what have I seen? Where have I been? Something has spoken to the very soul of me, wonderful, mighty, not of this world. Chords way down in my being have been touched. Dumb notes have struck chords of wonderful tone. Something has called out of somewhere. Something in me is trying to answer."

This was the way Emily Carr responded to the Group of Seven—and Lawren Harris in particular—when she first met them in 1927. She had not painted for over fifteen years, while she struggled to support herself by running a boarding house and raising animals. Prior to that she had trained in Europe and became an accomplished artist, but had given up painting when her work was received with coolness and hostility.

Once she met Harris and the others, she started again, launching into the most productive period of her career. *Forest, British Columbia* (opposite) was painted early in this new phase, when she produced weighted, densely packed canvases of the deep forests, sculptural in feeling and large in scale. *Forest, British Columbia* conveys the forest's solemn splendour and towering strength. The eye is led past trees that seem to expand and grow into the sanctuary-like space beyond. For Carr, everything in nature was alive and a manifestation of a greater life-force. She perceived the forest as the Northwest Coast Indians did—as a brooding presence that was at once mysterious, sacred, and powerful. And she created deeply personal paintings that reflected her love of nature and her spiritual search.

"Sketching in the big woods is wonderful. You go, find a space wide enough to sit in and clear enough so that the undergrowth is not drowning you. Then, being elderly, you spread your camp stool and sit and look around. 'Don't see much here. Wait.' Out comes a cigarette. The mosquitoes back away from the smoke. Everything is green. Everything is waiting and still. Slowly things begin to move, to slip into their places. Groups and masses and lines tie themselves together. Colours you had not noticed come out, timidly or boldly. In and out, in and out your eye passes. Nothing is crowded; there is living space for all. Air moves between each leaf. Sunlight plays and dances. Nothing is still now. Life is sweeping through the spaces. Everything is alive. The air is alive. The silence is full of sound. The green is full of colour. Light and dark chase each other. Here is a picture, a complete thought, and there another and there. . . .

"There are themes everywhere, something sublime, something ridiculous, or joyous, or calm, or mysterious, tender youthfulness laughing at gnarled oldness. Moss and ferns, and leaves and twigs, light and air, depth and colour chattering, dancing a mad joy-dance, but only apparently tied up in stillness and silence. You must be still in order to hear and see."

– Emily Carr

PLATE 82
Emily Carr   (1871-1945)
Forest, British Columbia   c. 1932
oil on canvas   129.5 x 86.4 cm
Vancouver Art Gallery

PLATE 82

PLATE 83

PLATE 84

PLATE 85

DAVID MILNE
Painting Place No. 3
Across the Lake
Red Nasturtiums

David Milne grew up in Paisley, Ontario, and worked briefly as a teacher before deciding in 1904 to study art in New York, where he soon became a well-known painter. After eleven years there he moved to a little town called Boston Corners, in the rolling mountains of eastern New York state. The landscapes of this period, such as *The Mountain* (National Gallery of Canada), have an exquisite sense of pattern and design. Milne returned to Canada briefly in 1918, joined the army, and became a war artist in Europe. But when the war was over, he once again returned to Boston Corners, remaining in the United States for another nine years.

Painting Place No. 3 (p. 188) is a pivotal work, summarizing his early period and looking forward to the paintings of the thirties. The subject matter is a view across Big Moose Lake in the Adirondacks, but it was painted in Canada during the winter of 1929–1930. In this most successful work of the Painting Place series, Milne explores the problem of integrating the colours of black, white, and green on the canvas. It is a lyrical and poetic work that brings together Milne's two loves: landscape and still life. Here the subject matter is secondary to the visual kick achieved through the impact of line and colour on the senses. Milne considered this heightened aesthetic feeling to be the essence of his art.

Across the Lake (p. 189) was painted in 1921 at Dart's Lake in the Adirondacks, where Milne spent several summers working as a handyman at a resort. By this time his water-colour style had been pared down to the bare minimum; his works had become line drawings in colour, contrasting worked-over spaces with large areas of unpainted paper. It was a bold and vibrant use of the medium, arrived at by arduous self-analysis and self-criticism. Milne wrote extensively about his process of creative discovery, documenting the motivation for each work and the aesthetic problems it posed.

Red Nasturtiums (opposite) was painted during Milne's stay at Six Mile Lake on the Severn River in Ontario, where he lived during the 1930s, painting full-time with the aid of his patron, Vincent Massey. It represents a dramatic breakthrough in the use of colour; in his earlier works, Milne had emphasized the careful control of line, value, and hue, but here he chose intense colours brushed on with daring spontaneity.

PLATE 83
David Milne   (1882-1953)
Painting Place No. 3   1930
oil on canvas   51.4 x 66.7 cm
National Gallery of Canada

PLATE 84
David Milne   (1882-1953)
Across the Lake   1921
water colour over graphite, on paper   39.6 x 56.8 cm
National Gallery of Canada

PLATE 85
David Milne   (1882-1953)
Red Nasturtiums   1937
water colour over graphite, on paper   35.6 x 52.6 cm
National Gallery of Canada

LEMOINE FITZGERALD
Doc Snider's House

Born in Winnipeg, LeMoine FitzGerald remained loyal to his native region all his life. A fiercely independent artist, he slowly and methodically acquired the tools and the knowledge he needed to translate his intensely personal vision into paint. He studied nights, went to New York for five months to study at the Art Student's League, and painstakingly evolved his technique. To support himself he taught art at the Winnipeg School of Art where he became principal in 1929, a position he held for twenty years. At this time, through his friends Bertram Brooker (Plate 90) and Lawren Harris, (Plates 4, 76, 91), he came into contact with the Group of Seven. He exhibited in their last show and was asked to become a member in 1931.

One of the works in the 1931 exhibition, *Doc Snider's House* (opposite), was painted over a period of two years. The subject was the house of a dentist who lived next door to FitzGerald in Winnipeg. The artist delights in the contrast between the thin limbs of the trees and the solid cubic shapes of the houses. Pale, delicate colours express the frozen quality of the winter landscape. Here, as in his other works, FitzGerald concerned himself with the beauty of his immediate surroundings – the shimmering light, the feeling of space, the beauty of nature. Although his subjects were simple ones and his goals were modest, he created a lasting statement that penetrated "a little deeper into the meaning of things."

PLATE 86
LeMoine FitzGerald   (1890-1956)
Doc Snider's House   1931
oil on canvas   74.9 x 85.1 cm
National Gallery of Canada

EDWIN HOLGATE
Ludovine

Her body tense, *Ludovine* (p. 194) faces the viewer, as though wondering when to flee. The eldest of a large family sustained by the local cod fishery in Natashquan on the Gulf of St. Lawrence, Ludovine is wearing mourning clothes; her mother has just died. One of the great Canadian portraits, this painting shows an adolescent with resolve, fortitude, and resignation. The artist has painted her sympathetically, using intense, strong colours suitable to the stern mood of the work, and stripping bare all unnecessary elements to portray the inner character of the young girl.

When Edwin Holgate was asked to join the Group of Seven in 1930, he was the first non-Torontonian member. As a Montreal artist, he studied at the Art Association of Montreal under William Brymner, (Plate 3) and Maurice Cullen (Plate 68). He also made several trips to Paris, where he travelled and studied art.

Holgate's work reflects the rural settings of small Quebec villages and the Laurentian landscape. He was one of the first Canadian artists to paint the nude, especially in a natural, outdoor setting.

Under the impact of Holgate, Montreal developed a strong figurative school which, although it was regional in character, looked abroad for stimulus and support.

PLATE 87
Edwin Holgate   (1892-1977)
Ludovine   c. 1930
oil on canvas   76.2 x 63.5 cm
National Gallery of Canada

PLATE 86

PLATE 87

PLATE 88

PLATE 89

CHARLES COMFORT
Young Canadian

Charles Comfort was born near Edinburgh, Scotland, but grew up in Winnipeg. His first encouragement as an artist was from Fred Brigden, the head of a commercial art firm in that city. The early stimulus for his career was a visit to the first exhibition of the Group of Seven in Toronto in 1920: "The first impact of the exhibition on me as a young student was one of burgeoning colour. The second was the dynamic, almost ruthless energy employed in the use of oil paint. The third was the shift in the nature of subject-matter. ... The overwhelming theme was the vigorous beautiful challenge of the little-known wilderness of the north." Comfort returned to Winnipeg determined to pursue a career as a creative artist. From 1923 to 1925 he studied at New York's Art Student's League.

In 1925, Comfort moved to Toronto, where he became part of the art scene, supporting himself by working at the Toronto branch of Brigden's firm. *Young Canadian* (p. 195), one of the greatest portraits ever painted in Canada, shows Comfort's close friend Carl Schaefer—also an artist—against a background scene of rural Ontario. At the time of this work (1932), Schaefer was Comfort's assistant in painting murals in the North American Life Assurance Company. In *Young Canadian*, Schaefer's disillusioned eyes and empty hanging hands form a haunting image of despair, a symbol of the Depression.

PLATE 88
Charles Comfort   (1900-   )
Young Canadian   1932
water colour on paper   90.2 x 105.4 cm
Hart House, University of Toronto

JOHN LYMAN
Woman with White Collar

In the 1930s and 1940s, Canadian art changed dramatically. The man most responsible for this transformation was John Lyman. Lyman had received his early art training in Paris, and did not return to Canada to live until 1931, after an absence of almost twenty-four years.

Once in Montreal, Lyman met other artists who were sympathetic to his approach, and he began to hold a weekly *salon* in his apartment. He established a school called the Atelier, he lectured on art, wrote for the *Montrealer*, and eventually founded the Contemporary Arts Society in 1939. All of these efforts were directed towards the encouragement of an art based on the European concept of modernism. It was a cool and classical approach that stressed the idea of "pure" painting, in direct opposition to the romantic subject-matter of the national-landscape school.

Lyman's portrait of a *Woman with White Collar* (opposite) illustrates this philosophy of art. Although it is a portrait of Mrs. Helen Marsh, the identity—and personality—of the sitter is secondary to the formal arrangement of line and colour. Lyman stresses the verticals of the neck and costume, and blends the skin tones in with the background. The figure has a strong architectonic quality, but is also part of the flat surface of the canvas. The painting is at once a restrained and elegant portrait of a human being and a formal arrangement of lines and colours on a flat surface.

PLATE 89
John Lyman   (1886-1967)
Woman with White Collar   1936
oil on canvas   61.3 x 44.1 cm
National Gallery of Canada

BERTRAM BROOKER
Sounds Assembling

Bertram Brooker was a journalist, writer of nine books (one of which, *Think of the Earth*, won the 1936 Governor General's Award), advertising executive, and pioneer of abstract painting in Canada.

Born in England, Brooker grew up in Winnipeg and began to paint without prior training in 1924, after meeting members of the Group of Seven at Toronto's prestigious Arts and Letters Club. With Lawren Harris he discussed the relationship of music, especially that of Bach, to painting. The works in Brooker's first exhibition – held at the same club in January 1927 – were described by the artist as "expressions of musical feeling; one a direct interpretation of a mood suggested by ... Dvorak's New World Symphony."

Sounds Assembling (opposite), an example of this synesthesia, also reflects Brooker's knowledge of contemporary events in French art, particularly of Cubism and Futurism, as well as careful study of Wassily Kandinsky's *Concerning the Spiritual in Art.* However, the image itself derives purely from his own imagination and reflects his belief in the mystery of all life.

Brooker's abstract works were greeted with a mixture of astonishment and hostility. Painted during the height of public controversy over the "radical" Group of Seven paintings, they were even more radical than those by the group. For a variety of reasons, Brooker returned to figurative art shortly after painting *Sounds Assembling.* With his phenomenal energy, he continued to involve himself in many other activities besides painting, and the significant breakthrough of these early abstracts was soon forgotten.

"The artist should be aware of present tendencies, but not immersed in them to the extent of destroying his backward and forward perspective. Art and literature on the grand scale is never narrowly contemporary. It gathers its energies from the heroic exemplars of a past time and leaps forward at such a pace and with such herculean stride that it over-shoots the present, and to succeeding futures ever seems to recede, inevitably ahead of oncoming generations. Its essential grandeur is in this tremendous arch from past to future which swings high over the dwarfed concerns of the 'present' of each generation that catches up to it.

"There is a spirit here, a response to the new, the natural, the open, the massive – as contrasted with the old, artificial, enclosed littlenesses of Europe – that should eventually, when we rely on it less timidly, become actively creative. And this creativeness, recognized as our own, and proceeding from the awakened consciousness of a new people with a new future, will itself become a quickening power ... so that religion – and hence art – becomes vital and fresh; an hourly response to life's exultations!"

– Bertram Brooker, 1929

PLATE 90
Bertram Brooker   (1885-1955)
Sounds Assembling   1928
oil on canvas   113.0 x 91.4 cm
Winnipeg Art Gallery

PLATE 90

PLATE 91

LAWREN HARRIS
Composition No. 1

In the fall of 1934, Lawren Harris (Plates 4, 76) left Toronto for Hanover, New Hampshire, where he and his second wife lived for several years. During this period he went beyond representational art and began experimenting with abstraction. This shift forms part of a logical development from his boldly simplified paintings of the Rockies to works of pure colour and form, with no recognizable image.

While in New Hampshire, Harris did several abstractions. Some, exemplified by *Equations in Space* (National Gallery of Canada), used clearly defined geometric forms; others incorporated direct references to nature and the colour symbolism of Kandinsky. This symbolism was based on the theosophical beliefs to which both Kandinsky and Harris subscribed. They felt art must express spiritual values as well as the visible world, and that each colour had symbolic significance: blue expressed a desire for transcendence; white represented purity and the divine white light; and yellow was an earthy colour.

From Hanover, Harris went to Sante Fe, New Mexico, for just over a year, and then to Vancouver, BC, in 1940, where he settled permanently. *Composition No. 1* (opposite) is the first work he did after returning to Canada, and reveals an assured and individual approach to non-representational art. It is still possible to discern the triangular mountain shape, but here the mountain also represents the theosophical triangle, symbolizing the three principles of spirit, force, and matter. The colours yellow and blue also have symbolic value, relating to "man's participation in eternal cosmic motion."

"Art at its highest is not only a creative adventure into a realm beyond that of our everyday concerns, pointing toward a greater and more inclusive reality, but also a power at work in mankind, a power making for greater understanding of universal values, of the hidden meaning of life, thus directing man nearer to a sensible and just solution of his problems. But, for this, each age and each people must rediscover in terms of first-hand, direct experience its entrance into the greater and enduring life that overshadows our mundane existence and puts us *en rapport* with the timeless expressions of the summit of the spirit of man in all ages and places.

"This is done by creative adventure in the arts – a process of turning ourselves inside out. That is, total environment evokes in us the need to discover living values that increase the depth of our awareness; it leads us both to find ourselves in our environment and to give that environment new and more far-reaching meaning."

–Lawren Harris, 1943

PLATE 91
Lawren Harris   (1885–1970)
Composition No. 1   1940
oil on canvas   156.2 x 156.2 cm
Vancouver Art Gallery

1940-1978

"The great duty, the unique duty is spontaneously to organize a new world, where the most noble passions can develop beautifully, collectively. Humanity belongs to man alone. Every individual is responsible for his brothers... for their miseries, material and psychological, and for their misfortunes."

Paul-Emile Borduas, 1948

PAUL-EMILE BORDUAS
Sous le vent de l'île

Early in 1947, Paul-Emile Borduas and several friends held an exhibition in Pierre Gauvreau's apartment on Sherbrooke Street in Montreal. Borduas' painting *Sous le vent de l'île* (opposite), which was the main attraction of the show, was at the time known by the title *Automatism 1:47*. After seeing this work, critic Tancrède Marsil became the first to refer to Borduas and his group as *automatistes*.

For several years Borduas had been exploring the automatic technique of the Surrealists; he began his pictures with no preconceived ideas, and let his unconscious mind dictate the forms and the colours. With *Sous le vent de l'île* he created a new concept of space, with organic forms floating over a deep void that extends to infinity. These intensely coloured *taches*, or dabs, made with a palette knife, float over a background that resembles an island seen from the air. The sweeping horizontal brushstrokes evoke the wind, but Borduas was not painting a representational landscape; it is rather a dream-world of the artist's own imagination.

Borduas painted *Le chant de la pierre* (Plate 8) shortly after his move to Paris in 1955. By this time he had assimilated many of the advances made by the abstract expressionists; his paintings moved towards greater whiteness and a more shallow space between figure and ground. Working almost exclusively with a palette knife, he layered the pure colours over a black background. In his later works he eliminated even more colours, until he was working purely in black and white.

"Borduas opens up to us an infinite universe of poetry, and that is what is important and what delights us. What a marvellous dreamer! He is a more vibrant poet than any we have had in our literature, and is, moreover, a powerful and free poet, a tormented poet who carries us to the very heart of the enigmas, of the dream, and there imposes the irradiating beauty of the beings which he catches in his sombre and vigorous emotion. His sensibility, so profoundly individualistic, is truly pictorial and of an indescribable richness. The past painting whispered light airs and hummed modulations in a low voice. Borduas fills the present with a song of such voluminous resonances, of such breadth, that it will reverberate untiringly. Borduas is the poet."

– Maurice Gagnon, 1945

PLATE 92
Paul-Emile Borduas   (1905-1960)
Sous le vent de l'île   1948
oil on canvas   114.3 x 147.3 cm
National Gallery of Canada

PLATE 92

205

PLATE 93

ALFRED PELLAN
Citrons ultra-violets

The return of Alfred Pellan to Canada in 1940 was a momentous event in the history of Canadian art. He had spent the previous fourteen years in Europe, where he had assimilated the recent developments of Cubism and Surrealism and become an established artist, winning first prize in the Salon de l'Art Mural de Paris in 1935. Then, in 1939, came the war and the German occupation of France. By June, 1940, Pellan was back in Quebec, with over four hundred works created during his years in Europe. Some of these were shown in a retrospective exhibition in Quebec and Montreal, provoking shock waves throughout the art community. A group of loyal supporters gathered around Pellan, impressed by his work, his immense energy, and his commitment to modern art.

Pellan continued to paint, drawing on past traditions and his fecund imagination to explore the inner world of dream and fantasy. In *Citrons ultra-violets* (opposite) he weaves an imaginary vision, drawing many of his forms from nature. In the bottom right is a figure with distorted hands and face. Other shapes evoke a wide range of associations: atoms, cells, eyes, snakes, insects, and sexual imagery. The work, with its brilliant draftsmanship and a unique sense of colour, reflects Pellan's admiration for the great European artists – Picasso, Paul Klee, and de Chirico – and at the same time bears the stamp of his own personal style.

A prolific artist, Pellan has produced an almost unending succession of paintings that appear to burst forth with energy and life. All are brilliantly coloured, highly decorative, and filled with an exuberant *joie de vivre*.

"It was impossible, here and elsewhere, to present an art as unpopular as that of Pellan.... At this moment of celebration, Pellan held his public at the foot of the wall, the walls of the gallery of art. For the first time, one of our painters pressed the indolence of the spirit and made it necessary to reflect on pictorial art. He hurt the public, hurt it a great deal.... It's true that the public grew afraid of him. A man who has power, a sorcerer, gives rise to fear. He has power, this is conceded, and he uses it frenetically, with passion, a heart and an intelligence which are crushing.... Pellan is a man of his century. Sooner or later, we will become aware of it.... His painting satisfies all his being, and he delivers himself in it of oppression, truth, his interior truth. He spares nothing to express it.... We rediscover Pellan alive, bewitching as always, crying with joy or with pain in colours which belong to him alone, electrified colours which come alive in your view and in your spirit, which haunt you like a cry of anguish. After having seen these paintings, nothing seems to be happening elsewhere."

–Jacques de Tonnacour, 1943

PLATE 93
Alfred Pellan   (1906-   )
Citrons ultra-violets   1947
oil on canvas with gold leaf appliqués   208 x 167 cm
Musée du Québec, Québec

JEAN-PAUL RIOPELLE
Pavane (triptych)

Since 1948 Jean-Paul Riopelle has lived in Paris, where he has established a reputation as one of Canada's most celebrated international artists. Born in Montreal, Riopelle was a young student of nineteen when he first met Borduas (Plates 8, 92), who introduced him to radical new directions in art, politics, psychoanalysis, and Surrealist literature.

In Europe, he developed his characteristic technique of applying paint with a palette knife loaded with pure colour. The culmination of this approach is found in Pavane (opposite), a huge painting that captures the feeling of the pavane, a slow and majestic Spanish dance. The whole surface of the painting vibrates with colour, like a rich tapestry or mosaic. Not only does each swipe of the palette knife contain lush, pure colour, but the entire work is carefully orchestrated so that the bright reds of the upper section are balanced by the darker colours in the lower part. It is alive with movement as the patterns shift and change like a giant kaleidoscope.

A prodigious worker, Riopelle has produced literally thousands of works: paintings, drawings, prints, assemblages, and sculptures. His work is not entirely non-objective; it draws on nature for its main source. As Riopelle once said in a rare statement about his art, "For me, nature is the sole reference. Liberty exists only in the acknowledgement of that fact, which at the same time involves the strongest commitment to it. A tree grows only one way; there is no such thing as a tragic, joyful or elegaic way of growing. There is only the right way." The work itself is like a living organism, with its own internal structure and energy.

"Colours and forms of an always-evocative landscape which reflects his temperament, dominate Riopelle's pictorial imagination and are the basic elements in his work. He finds them together in his feelings and memory; he senses them as figurative symbols of his various moods. The man is so overpowered and permeated by colour and form that he uses them with passionate ferocity in his painting, like a flow of words which alternately reveals all that is both violent and gentle in his being.

"There is a constant relationship between the spiritual moods of the painter and his interpretation of the most uninhibited and primitive characteristics of seasons and of natural forms; his paintings seem to capture the mood of impenetrable woods, of lands without horizons and without sky. There is a sudden explosion when water and plant life, frozen throughout a very long winter, suddenly blossoms into a myriad-coloured profusion where the light is alternately dazzling bright or tenderly and softly transparent.... The picture is not composed according to the traditional rules of art, but rather in accordance with the organic changes of nature."

– Franco Russoli, 1963

PLATE 94
Jean-Paul Riopelle   (1923-   )
Pavane (triptych)   1954
oil on canvas   2.99 x 5.49 m
National Gallery of Canada

PLATE 94

PLATE 95

JOCK MACDONALD
Fleeting Breath

Born in Scotland, Jock Macdonald arrived in Canada in 1926 at the age of twenty-nine, after being appointed Head of Design at the School of Decorative and Applied Arts in Vancouver. He became a close friend of Fred Varley (Plates 78, 79), another teacher at the school, and the two made many sketching trips together. Varley was an important influence, encouraging him to "stop drawing and start painting." Macdonald also became involved in Vancouver's small artistic community and, through friends such as Harry Täuber, developed an interest in mystical concepts and their relationship to art. In 1934, he produced his first abstract or automatic painting, called *Formative Colour Theory* (National Gallery of Canada), which was created in one sitting with no pre-conceived planning.

During the Depression years, Macdonald, Varley and Täuber started a new art school, which lasted only two winters. The next years were filled with terrible hardships and poor health, but Macdonald began to emerge as an artist.

In 1946, he moved first to Calgary, then to Toronto, where he began teaching at the Ontario College of Art, exerting tremendous influence on younger artists and reaching a new creative plateau. The canvases he painted in the last two years before he died were the culmination of his life's work. *Fleeting Breath* (opposite) is an outstanding example of these late works. In it, the forms have become softer and more suggestive of spiritual energies, and carefully blended colours create a veil-like space that appears to fluctuate and "breathe." Macdonald wanted to communicate the unseen forces behind all matter, hoping each viewer would experience the work on a personal level.

"Never have I entirely deserted objective painting. I believe it absolutely necessary to associate myself with the visual world. It is from the visual world that an artist derives his vocabulary of form and colour. It is necessary to observe continually, to memorize, and attune oneself to the forces in nature.... Artists must discover idioms which interpret man's new concepts about nature, especially about the interrelationship of all things, the energies of motion, new spatial concepts.... I believe that every true artist desires to interpret the consciousness of the time in which he lives. A change in consciousness brings into being new forms. This is exciting. But there must be the same order in the painting as in the superb works of past centuries. The order in art remains constant."

– Jock Macdonald, 1957

PLATE 95
Jock Macdonald   (1897-1960)
Fleeting Breath   1959
oil on canvas 122.3 x 149.2 cm
Art Gallery of Ontario

WILLIAM RONALD
J'accuse

William Ronald, the founding member of Painters Eleven and a student of Jock Macdonald (Plate 95) at the Ontario College of Art, was one of the few Canadian artists to partake fully of the American mainstream – in his case, Abstract Expressionism. He was friendly with Mark Rothko, Franz Kline, William Baziotes, Darby Bannard, and Frank Stella, and he admired Jackson Pollock and Bradley Walker Tomlin. He was also carried by one of the most prestigious galleries in the world, Kootz Gallery in New York, from 1957 to 1963. By 1965 he was back in Canada.

While in New York, Ronald painted works that were non-objective, uninhibited, exuberant, and spontaneous–full of vibrant, strongly contrasting colours. What distinguished his painting from that of other artists was his large, dominating central images, as opposed to contemporary works that had no focal point, such as the all-over composition of Jackson Pollock. His canvases occasionally hint surrealistically at the form of a human head or animal hides, suggesting enormous portraits or figurative paintings. Ronald usually applied his thick paint with a palette knife in a highly expressionistic *tachist* manner; but he also used a brush flatly. *J'accuse* (opposite) is perhaps the finest work from his New York period, and is one of his first central-image paintings. The title reflects Ronald's interest in the writing of Jean Cocteau, Jean-Paul Sartre, and Samuel Beckett in its emblematic feeling.

PLATE 96
William Ronald   (1926-   )
J'accuse   1956
oil on canvas   152.4 x 175.2 cm
Robert McLaughlin Gallery, Oshawa

GRAHAM COUGHTRY
Two Figure Series XIX

Graham Coughtry, along with his close friends Michael Snow (Plates 101, 129) and Gordon Rayner (Plate 98), was part of a new generation of artists in Toronto–younger than the Painters Eleven–who came onto the scene in the late 1950s. They shared the same interests, particularly a passion for jazz. Coughtry has often said that the greatest influence on his art was jazz saxophonist John Coltrane.

From the beginning, Coughtry's main preoccupation was the human figure. His early works are deeply moving visions of isolation and despair. In 1961, he painted the first work in the Two Figure Series, in which he attempted to depict a sexual confrontation between two figures. This theme provided the imagery for over twenty different works painted in Toronto and Ibiza over the next few years. Some were violent and aggressive; others were idyllic and calm. They were all painted rapidly and their intensity is highly charged. In *Two Figure Series* XIX (p. 214) the explosive energy of the earlier paintings has given way to a more harmonious feeling. The figures are fused, and it is impossible to tell which is male or female. The work is not simply a representation of two figures, but instead depicts the merging process through colour as well as form, in the union of the hot red-orange with the warm yellow-green.

PLATE 97
Graham Coughtry   (1931-   )
Two Figure Series XIX   1964
oil on canvas   182.8 x 152.4 cm
Private collection

PLATE 96

213

PLATE 97

PLATE 98

PLATE 99

GORDON RAYNER
Magnetawan No. 2

Unlike his good friend Graham Coughtry (Plate 97), Gordon Rayner did not go through the art-school system. A fantastic manipulator of paint and of unlikely painting materials, Rayner has always experimented with the canvas's shape and with various collage elements; he was also one of Canada's first masters of the acrylics medium. His works ricochet from one concern to another in consecutive canvases. As Rayner has said, "My paintings are really things, individual objects that have nothing to do with each other. The only thing they have in common is that I do them – my colour, my touch."

What all Rayner's work does have in common is a love affair with the land and the elements, "living on the edge of the bush, the sound of rain on the roof and all that." *Magnetawan No. 2* (p. 215), done at an isolated north-woods cabin on the Magnetawan River in northern Ontario, was inspired by a terrifying lightning storm; he did five works on the subject, one of his few series efforts.

If Rayner's role in the Artists' Jazz Band has influenced him, it may have given his work a certain staccato and bounce. Rayner adds, "It's like all the little jingle-jangle noisemakers I have around my drum set; in the paintings, too, I try to fit in all the little bits and pieces around me."

PLATE 98
Gordon Rayner   (1935-   )
Magnetawan No. 2   1965
acrylic on canvas   225.4 x 225.4 cm
National Gallery of Canada

HAROLD TOWN
Banners

Like the Group of Seven, Painters Eleven, a group that emerged in the 1950s, came together primarily for the purpose of exhibiting *avant-garde* art, in this case abstract art. Unlike the Group of Seven, however, Painters Eleven had no proselytizing stance.

Harold Town was not only a founding member, he also gave the group its title and wrote all the forewords to their catalogues.

A painter of immense dynamism and boundless energy, Town's role as a draftsman and print-maker distinguished him from other members of the group. His historical orientation often profoundly influenced his choice of subjects. *Banners* (opposite) is one of a series of works that have large, heraldic shapes intended to strike the viewer as joyful, like a banner in a parade, or as fearful, like a banner in a battle.

When it was shown at the Fourth Biennial Exhibition of Canadian Art at the National Gallery of Canada in 1961, *Banners* was described by critic Robert Fulford as "a majestic composition [which] distils the essence of the heroic approach." Town's work in this period is essentially dramatic and gestural, with intricate oriental shapes, eccentric patterns, glowing colour, and an idiosyncratic use of line.

Although in many ways a romantic, Town has, through his writing, interviews, and acerbic comments, come close to being the conscience of the contemporary Canadian art scene.

PLATE 99
Harold Town   (1924-   )
Banners   1959-1960
oil and lucite on canvas   182.9 x 182.9 cm
Norman MacKenzie Art Gallery, Regina

JACK BUSH
Orange Centre

Jack Bush has been internationally recognized as one of the most important painters of the modernist school. His long evolution as an artist reflects his dedication and commitment. He was one of the founding members of Painters Eleven, and spent many years exploring the parameters of Abstract Expressionism in his work. At the time of the momentous visit of New York critic Clement Greenberg to Toronto in 1957, Bush was already forty-eight years old. Following Greenberg's suggestions, Bush gave up the heavy impasto surface of Abstract Expressionism and began to explore the realm of pure colour, applying his paint thinly in broad, simple areas.

In the early sixties, Bush painted the first of his "sash" paintings, which were partly inspired by seeing a shop-window manikin wearing a horizontally striped dress. *Orange Centre* (opposite), one of the great works in the series, is structured around a central colour-column, with broader fields of colour on either side. For Bush, the essence of painting was flatness, and in this painting he attempts to make the central column and the areas on either side of it appear as flat as the canvas they are painted upon.

In 1968 Bush gave up commercial art to paint full time, and launched into the most productive period of his career. By "tapping the intuitive," Bush explored new relationships of form and colour, producing canvases that place him among the most important painters of today. Like the work of Matisse, whom Bush admired intensely, his paintings are meant to be experienced and enjoyed. They are a celebration of colour—vibrant, intense, and joyful.

"My Art—what is it? What's it all about?...

"Something beautiful to the eye...something to look at, just with the eye, and react. Looking at something causes the whole being to react, like it or not. And mostly not, but that doesn't matter, that's good. It's when one reacts with an inexplicable wonder that the magic begins. When one reacts against, that is testing one's own judgment as to values and qualities. That's good. A second and third look will teach us something—we may gain an insight we did not have, or we can cross it off....

"My Art—Well, I've been lucky. A slow learner, I think the milieu of my early and middle period was exciting, but somewhat a waste of time, plus working commercially for a living. Two big breaks: a psychiatric therapeutic session of many years freed me from the oppression of local rules; then I saw the outside world —and contact with dedicated artists in other countries gave me the courage and encouragement to go on my own way—for broke.

"Why not? I have a song to sing—the best way I know how. If only six people listen—that's enough. I'm lucky—the six who listened and liked it are pretty keen on quality, and nothing short of top quality at that."

– Jack Bush, 1967

PLATE 100
Jack Bush   (1909-1977)
Orange Centre   c. 1964
acrylic on canvas   205.7 x 174.0 cm
Edmonton Art Gallery

PLATE 100

PLATE 101

MICHAEL SNOW
Venus Simultaneous

Born in Toronto, Michael Snow charted new regions of sensibility in Canada. His early work, influenced by Paul Klee, showed an element of wit and romantic fantasy; it was followed by a period of abstract painting, and a much-heralded return to the figure in 1961, with his Walking Woman series. The Walking Woman has received a remarkable variety of interpretations. Its profile became his trademark, which he explored in sculpture, painting, drawing, environmental happenings, and films.

In *Venus Simultaneous* (opposite), there are eight Walking Women, each with a different relationship to the canvas or ground: one is set out from the canvas on a piece of plywood; two are in silhouettes that protrude from the sides. Like the title, the work presents a paradox: it is half-sculpture, half-painting. All of the artist's Walking Women have the same silhouette cut-out, positive or negative shape. Here, they are beginning to come off the canvas. The theme, which related the figure to the environment in every material and method, was to continue until 1967.

Late in 1963, Snow and his wife, artist Joyce Wieland (Plate 123), moved to New York. There Snow produced films, which he had begun to experiment with in 1956. *Wavelength*, "a time monument" made by the artist in 1967, won the Grand Prize at the Fourth Brussels International Experimental Film Festival. In all of his films, he aspires to reveal and elaborate on the fundamental character and the essence of the medium. Today Snow is probably the best-known Canadian artist in the world, and has been described by critics as "the inventor of the film art."

"From 1961 to 1967 all my work used the same image, The Walking Woman. I worked in every material and method I could think of. It was a huge theme-and-variations composition. In painting, for example, I used water colour, ink, tempera, oil, enamels, spray enamels, acrylics, etc. on various grounds. I stenciled ties, sweatshirts, match books, made rubber stamp compositions; had things printed, mass-made; used printed stickers and rubber stamp to make dispersed and lost compositions. Some of these had a time aspect: that one might see a part (printed sticker) in the Sheridan Square subway stop, find another on the stairs, then find another in the 8th Street Bookstore."

"I am interested in doing something that can't be explained."

–Michael Snow, 1967

PLATE 101
Michael Snow (1929-   )
Venus Simultaneous 1962
oil on canvas and wood   200.7 x 299.7 cm
Art Gallery of Ontario

JOHN MEREDITH
Seeker (triptych)

John Meredith was born in Fergus, a small town in southern Ontario, and studied under Jock Macdonald (Plate 95) at the Ontario College of Art. Meredith's early works were explorations of flattened vertical bands of central images within a calligraphic linear framework–sometimes with a semi-figurative reference–in a shallow spatial depth. They were done in a variety of colours, with built-up and textured paint surfaces. Later, Meredith began to use loud colours, and the effect was powerful.

Still working in the abstract-expressionist area, in 1964 Meredith began smudging the still-wet lines in his paintings, a technique borrowed from his drawings. In these works, his use of line is lyrical and electric; the forms are sometimes visceral and organic in character.

Seeker (opposite) was painted with the artist's parents in mind, and was later dedicated to them. A triptych, the first the artist ever did, the work took four months to complete and represented a major breakthrough in applying his drawing techniques to his paintings. Based on a number of studies, the large work is typical of Meredith's output in its smudged lines and bright, high-keyed colours. The meaning of this and all Meredith's work is ambiguous. Meredith is an introspective person, and his paintings are an expression of his complex and obsessive personality. The forms he creates are highly original and compelling in their dramatic presence.

"It is my intention, through the medium of paint, to express and portray, give substance to, the subconscious reactions to form, beauty, power, etc., as they relate to myself and as they react upon and affect me emotionally. I try to give a visual existence to my thoughts, feelings and intellectual reactions to things within and outside of me. I want to develop new ideas within myself and expand them through experimentation with colours and their relationship to each other. It is essential that I explore myself as an artist."

– John Meredith, 1967

PLATE 102
John Meredith   (1933-   )
Seeker (triptych)   1966
oil on canvas   177.8 x 366.4 cm
Art Gallery of Ontario

PLATE 102

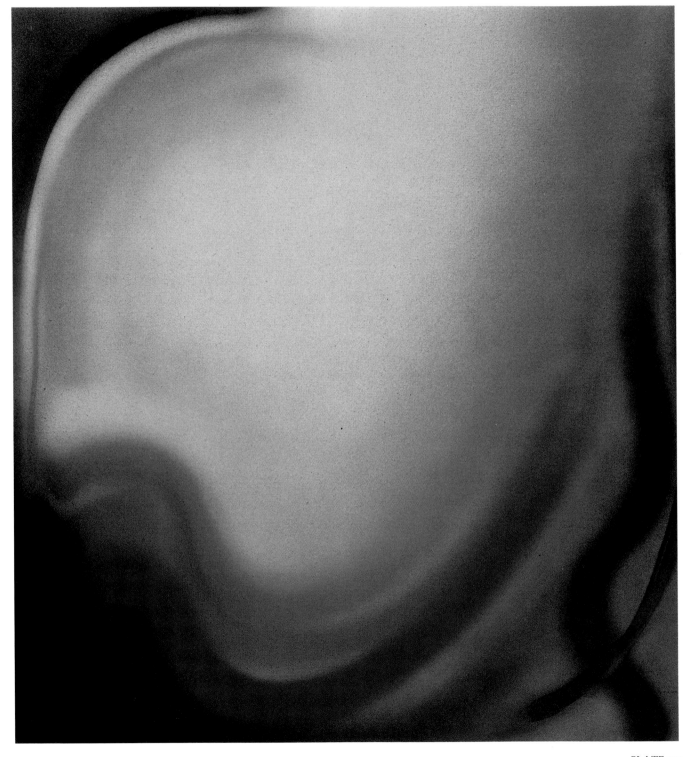

PLATE 103

KENNETH LOCHHEAD
Inner Release

In 1950, when he was only twenty-four, Kenneth Lochhead moved from Ottawa to Regina, where he became director of the School of Art at Regina College. A few years later, along with Arthur McKay, he initiated the summer workshops for professional artists at Emma Lake. At this point Lochhead was painting works with strange statuesque figures in a vast, empty landscape. However, after the influential visits of Kenneth Noland, Jules Olitsky, and Clement Greenberg to Emma Lake in the early 1960s, Lochhead adopted many of the ideas of modernist painting. This approach stressed the primacy of colour and the essential qualities of paint as a medium. His first abstract paintings such as *Dark Green Centre* (Art Gallery of Ontario) were highly praised by Greenberg, and were included in Greenberg's famous Post-Painterly Abstraction exhibition of 1964. The following year Lochhead created large canvases, using a stain technique to make several L-shaped bands of colour. These works soon established Lochhead's reputation as an important Colour-Field painter.

Many critics were surprised when Lochhead suddenly abandoned geometric shapes in 1970 and began a series of highly romantic works involving great, fluid areas of pure colour. *Inner Release* (opposite) was one of these new works, in which Lochhead found his own personal idiom. Painting with a spray gun, and with the canvas lying flat on the floor, Lochhead varied his colour application by adjusting the nozzle opening of the gun and the distance between the gun and the canvas. The act of painting became a kind of dance, with the artist drawing and painting at the same time with the sweep of the gun.

"I like to look at paintings that reflect man's conviction, his grace, his sensuousness, his play, his delight, his creativeness, his coherence, his nobility, his spirit, and his feeling.

"I believe in the celebration of life. Through painting I find some love and joy."

–Kenneth Lochhead, 1972

PLATE 103
Kenneth Lochhead   (1926-   )
Inner Release   1971
acrylic on canvas   118.1 x 106.7 cm
Collection of Mr. Jack Orr, Toronto

RONALD BLOORE
Painting 1961

Ronald Bloore has been an assertive presence in Canadian art over the past twenty years, through both his art and his intellect. In 1958, when he arrived in Regina to direct the Norman MacKenzie Art Gallery, he immediately began to make his influence felt by setting up controversial exhibitions and by inviting Barnett Newman and Clement Greenberg to the Emma Lake workshops. He was also an important catalyst for the Regina Five, stressing an individual approach to art and an uncompromising concern for quality. In 1965, he left Regina for Toronto where he has been influential as an artist, teacher and critic.

The evolution of his own work has been a long and deliberate process of refining his art down to a distilled essence. *Painting 1961* (opposite) was a radical work at the time it was painted, when most other artists were involved in Abstract Expressionism or Colour-Field painting. In this work, he allows the crimson undercoating to appear beneath an all-white surface, creating a broken linear design in the shape of two spoked wheels, which are just slightly off centre. Bloore built up the surface on a masonite panel with layers of paint, which were then scraped or sanded to create a hard and durable surface. Bloore's paintings are, above all, about light. And like a Byzantine mosaic or an Egyptian hieroglyph, they must be experienced physically, with the light moving across them, caressing the surfaces. Even though Bloore himself says there are no secrets or no messages in his works, they do suggest symbols from ancient times.

"A statement by me about my work would be valueless in the general sense of the word because, for myself, the meaning of any work of art is determined entirely by the individual experiencing it. All that I am able to offer is a brief suggestion concerning how I think my paintings have originated during the last couple of years or so.

"I am not aware of any intention while painting with the exception of making a preconceived image function formally as a painting. By this I mean that the appearance of each work has been consciously determined in my mind before executing it, and the general concept is not significantly altered by the requirements of material limitations.

"The paintings fall into distinct series which are usually composed of four or five large works which were preceded by smaller ones in which some formal and technical problems have been examined."

– Ronald Bloore, 1961

PLATE 104
Ronald Bloore   (1925-   )
Painting 1961   1961
oil on masonite   120.7 x 197.5 cm
Art Gallery of Ontario

PLATE 104

PLATE 105

GUIDO MOLINARI
Mutation sérielle verte-rouge

A contemporary of Tousignant (Plate 106), Guido Molinari is one of the great innovators and theoreticians of Canadian art. A man of towering intellect, Molinari challenged the very act of painting from his earliest works, some of which were painted in darkness or while blindfolded. His intention was to show that if the paintings of the *automatistes* were to be truly "automatic," then they must be done without the kind of self-censorship that accompanies traditional visual perception. Conscious of the impact of Paul-Emile Borduas (Plates 8, 92) on the Montreal art community, he sought new alternatives by exploring the Surrealist writings of André Breton, and the work of Piet Mondrian and Jackson Pollock.

Molinari progressively eliminated surface texture and colour from his work, until he was working with basic, hard-edged geometric forms in black and white. When he re-introduced colour in 1958, it was in simple vertical bands of pure colour, which he used exclusively for the next six years. Deceptively simple, a painting such as *Mutation sérielle verte-rouge* (opposite) appears to be little more than twenty-four vertical stripes of green, red, yellow, and blue. However, as the eye moves back and forth across them, the colours start to fluctuate and "breathe." What started as simple geometric shapes becomes a pulsating energy field—an entirely new space, no longer in the painting, but located somewhere between the viewer and the object. In this sense Molinari has succeeded in destroying the canvas as object, creating a purely sensory experience.

"My own position regarding the problem of colour is that it is through a redefinition of the colour phenomena and dynamism that painting can realize its full potentialities.

"I have tried to do this through the use of the complex hypothesis of seriality. To summarize it briefly, we can say that seriality is the only structured pictorial process which:
a) rejects entirely the substantialization of one colour as the pole of expressivity of the artist or of identification in the perception process.
b) shows that it is only through recurrence, or repetition, or relocalization, that a certain colour can acquire a dialectic function in the painting.
c) it is based on a constance of form and through the phenomena of recurrence rejects any dual system of expression based on the opposition of *qualities* of colours (dark and clear, etc.) or *quantities* of colours through contrasts between big and smaller forms, or linear and mass confrontations.
d) I have also tried to eliminate the secondary oppositions in textures, soft and hard limitations, etc. which always allow for a restriction of the colour message and a loss in dynamism and expression."

– Guido Molinari, 1972

PLATE 105
Guido Molinari   (1933-   )
Mutation sérielle verte-rouge   1966
acrylic on canvas   205.7 x 248.9 cm
Art Gallery of Ontario

CLAUDE TOUSIGNANT
Gong 88, No. 1

Claude Tousignant belongs to a generation of artists who grew up in Montreal when Borduas and the *automatistes* were making their great breakthroughs in painting. He saw the seminal exhibitions of 1954 and 1955, La Matière chante, Espace 55, and Les Plasticiens, which showed the work of local artists who were searching for new alternatives to *automatisme*.

In 1956 the Galerie l'Actuelle, run by the artist Guido Molinari (Plate 105), held a showing of Tousignant's paintings. In these radical works he pushed the limits of Abstraction even further than the other Montreal artists, by reducing painting to simplified colour panels with flawless, shining surfaces. It was an attempt to create an art of pure sensation, with no references to subject matter.

From this basic minimal statement of geometric shapes and simple primary colours, Tousignant gradually let his intuitive feelings emerge again. He began to explore the dynamic relationships between colours, and moved towards a circular format in the "target paintings" of 1964. In a series of Chromatic Transformers, he created concentric circles that rhythmically pulsate as the colours interact. *Gong 88, No. 1* (opposite) is part of a second series, which carried his exploration of optical perception even further. He has reduced the number of colours and used wide concentric bands containing narrower bands; the wide bands are divided into two equal bands by the superimposition of different coloured circles. It is a complex and rigorous structure, but the effect is one of great immediacy, expressing the pure sensation of colour.

"What I wish to do is to make painting objective, to bring it back to its source – where only painting remains, emptied of all extraneous matter – to the point at which painting is pure sensation . . . to say as much as possible with as few elements as possible."

– Claude Tousignant, 1959

PLATE 106
Claude Tousignant   (1932-   )
Gong 88, No. 1   1966
acrylic on canvas   223.5 cm (diameter)
National Gallery of Canada

PLATE 106

PLATE 107

JEAN-PAUL LEMIEUX
Le visiteur du soir

Jean-Paul Lemieux has long created an art that is both lyrical and gentle, penetrating and bold. In 1941, he painted his famous *Lazare* (Art Gallery of Ontario), which shows Lazarus rising from the grave while German paratroopers land on Quebec soil, shooting innocent victims, and people in a church placidly listen to a sermon. Other works make a strong statement about man's loneliness and isolation in contemporary society. *Le visiteur du soir* (opposite), one of the most powerful statements on this theme, shows the solitary figure of a priest approaching at dusk across a snow-covered landscape. The priest, who evidently was coming to administer the eucharist to the dying, is a haunting, faceless figure — the image of death in an empty landscape.

Le visiteur du soir was a turning point in his work. It was painted after a trip to Europe, when he realized how unique his own environment was, with its sense of infinite space and broad horizons. Lemieux set out to paint it, but not as a landscape painter; people are what interest him, solitary people in the vast landscape, frozen in time.

Lemieux himself witnessed this scene in his youth in Quebec; and like many of his other paintings, it recalls childhood memories. Lemieux has lived in Quebec all but a few years of his life, spending the winters in Quebec City and the summers on beautiful Iles-aux-Coudres. Steeped in the traditions of Quebec, he paints the familiar world around him, pursuing his own independent vision.

"What fascinates me most is the dimension of time; time which passes on and man before this passage of time. I am not in tune with the Paris fashion. I am not part of the general current. The trends of contemporary art do not stir me. I look at these works, I read what is said about them but I feel nothing in common with them even though I am sure they have a good deal of merit.

"I paint because I like to paint. I have no theories. In landscape and figures, I try to express the solitude in which we live. In each painting, I try to recall my inner memories. The milieu which surrounds me interests me only because it allows me to depict my inner world."

– Jean-Paul Lemieux, 1967

PLATE 107
Jean-Paul Lemieux (1904-   )
Le visiteur du soir 1956
oil on canvas 80.0 x 109.9 cm
National Gallery of Canada

JACK SHADBOLT
To Old Gardens

Jack Shadbolt is what he paints—the magic metamorphosis of the butterfly, the all-seeing wisdom of the owl; the burgeoning growth of the forest; the ritualistic splendour of the Northwest Coast Indian. Many writers have alluded to the shaman-like qualities of Shadbolt: a creator of images and words, a balancer, a bringer of equilibrium, a specialist in ecstasy.

Over the past thirty years, Shadbolt has been a catalyst for West Coast art, as a dynamic teacher, a spell-binding lecturer, a brilliant writer, and friend of many artists. Always a prolific worker, he has turned out an astonishing number of paintings, poems, drawings, murals, and collages, even while teaching. When he finally retired in 1966, his art went through an extraordinary renaissance, culminating in works such as To Old Gardens (opposite), which epitomizes Shadbolt's amazing energy.

To Old Gardens is an exuberant expression of life-energy. The two female figures indulge in a frenzied, erotic dance, while in the centre panel an urn of late-summer flowers evokes a joyous celebration of life. On another level, the androgynous figures appear to be crucified on the wall, wrapped in serpent-like vines—a horrid nightmare vision. It is an image from the depths of a potent imagination, a ritual transformation that is mysterious, haunting, and seductive.

PLATE 108
Jack Shadbolt   (1909-   )
To Old Gardens   1971-1972
ink, latex, crayon, acrylic   152.0 x 304.0 cm
Collection of Beverly and Boris Zerafa, Toronto

CHRISTOPHER PRATT
March Night

Christopher Pratt lives in the country near St. Mary's Bay, Newfoundland. The Salmonier River runs close-by, and a wooded hillside stands opposite the house. On a cool March night, when the fog from the nearby ocean rolls in, the view from the window might present a scene identical to that of March Night (p. 236).

Ever since childhood, Pratt has spent countless hours walking over Newfoundland's barrens and tundra, and sailing around the rugged coastline, absorbing it into his being. March Night is a distillation of these experiences. It does not represent a specific wall or a specific landscape. It began conceptually, as an idea in the artist's mind. Pratt began by making postage-stamp-sized sketches in which he gradually gave the idea some physical reality, building on it until the object had its own existence and its own intensified reality. In March Night he created a stark and ominous world that hints at deeper meanings. It is a world suffused with a clear and mysterious light that does not come from any outside source, but is in the painting. The precise horizontals of the wooden wall form a perfect rectangle, viewed with absolute frontality. The wall is a direct confrontation, blocking the view beyond. Dramatic tension is built up at the critical edge between the closed and the open space. It becomes the fine edge between the known and the unknown, between order and chaos, sanity and insanity, life and death.

PLATE 109
Christopher Pratt   (1935-   )
March Night   1976
oil on masonite   101.4 x 228.6 cm
Art Gallery of Ontario

PLATE 108

PLATE 109

PLATE 110

237

PLATE 111

ALEX COLVILLE
Truck Stop

The year after he painted *Truck Stop* (p. 237), Alex Colville addressed a group of high school students in Amherst, Nova Scotia: "Sooner or later, but inevitably, you will die. Between now and that final moment, what will you do? How will you live?" Colville has long been preoccupied with the idea of death, and the way death can enhance life, ever since he was a young war artist in Europe, sketching the dead at a concentration camp in Belsen. All his works possess a sense of gravity, a sense of waiting or suspended time. But they are also a celebration of existence and the concrete world.

Truck Stop epitomizes Colville's perception of reality. It is a picture compiled from many different events, and painted from memory during a stay in England. Detail by detail, the whole scene was built up so that it felt totally authentic—even to the number of bolts on the hub. The composition was structured with mathematical precision, using well-defined verticals and horizontals, and a perfect isosceles triangle between the hubs and the lamp post.

On one level, the painting represents a familiar scene that everyone recognizes; on another, its details become disconcerting, almost like a dream image. The eerie morning light, the man with his arm in a cast, and the alert pose of the dog combine to produce an enigmatic and obsessive image.

PLATE 110
Alex Colville   (1920-   )
Truck Stop   1966
acrylic polymer emulsion   91.5 x 91.5 cm
Museum Ludwig, Köln

WILLIAM KURELEK
In the Autumn of Life

William Kurelek was raised in Stonewall, Manitoba, a small farming community north of Winnipeg. He grew up during the Depression, and much of his imagery is based on the Prairies during the thirties, as well as Roman Catholicism, which he converted to in 1957. Kurelek was a moralist and missionary who felt that the main role of painting was to deliver a message. To do so, he felt he had to "dress it up in the clothing of a pleasant pastoral scene." *In the Autumn of Life* (opposite) is an expansive landscape: its open sky and panoramic view show Kurelek's genuine gifts as a landscape artist. Based on Kurelek's parents' farm on Hamilton Mountain, it makes a statement about world events and the present-day role of Christianity. Because of the almost photographic reality to the scene, the viewer doesn't at first notice the atomic explosion in the background. A note on the back of the painting reads as follows: "After a life of hard work, my parents approach retirement....Their family...love to visit on their farm near Hamilton. I have pictured such a family reunion among material possessions, but I hope that visitors to this exhibition will pardon me for looking beyond race and national boundary to the world-wide struggle looming threateningly on the horizon....We may ask—what is the ultimate meaning of man's struggle for a place in the sun? As I see it, this is a religious question."

PLATE 111
William Kurelek   (1927–1977)
In the Autumn of Life   1964
oil on masonite   59.1 x 120.3 cm
Art Gallery of Ontario

GERSHON ISKOWITZ
Uplands H

Gershon Iskowitz was only eighteen in 1939 when the Germans invaded Poland. He spent the next three years in forced-labour camps before he was sent to Auschwitz in 1942. There he bribed the guards for art materials by painting their portraits. In secret, he sketched his friends and life at camp. For Iskowitz, painting was necessary for survival. After being transferred to Buchenwald, he tried to escape, but was shot in the leg and left for dead. Shortly afterwards, the Americans liberated Germany.

After Iskowitz came to Canada in 1949 and began painting portraits to support himself, he made many visits to the area around Parry Sound, where he became deeply involved in the beauty of the northern landscape. For the next twenty years, he continued to evolve his own personal style with amazing persistence. His paintings did not sell, but he refused to teach or do anything that would interfere with his art.

Recognition finally came when he was asked to represent Canada in the 1972 Venice Biennale. Viewers rejoiced in the shimmering colours of work such as *Uplands* H (opposite), which was included in the exhibition. The painting was inspired by a helicopter trip Iskowitz once took in northern Manitoba. Several years later, he drew on these impressions to create *Uplands* H, which shows a large red shape floating over the landscape. Applying layer upon layer of colour, Iskowitz built up the surface until it became luminous, iridescent, and vibrating with energy. *Uplands* H celebrates life, the joy of colour, and the miracle of existence.

"You reflect your own vision. That's what it's all about. You put in your own intelligence, your own expression, your own ability. You put yourself in any form of art.

"People say, oh, Gershon Iskowitz is an abstract artist. I hear that a lot of times. But it's a whole realistic world. It lives, moves . . . it has to move, or it's dead! I see those things . . . the experience, out in the field, of looking up in the trees or in the sky, of looking down from the height of a helicopter. So what you do is try to make a composition of all those things, make some kind of reality: like the trees should belong to the sky, and the ground should belong to the trees, and the ground should belong to the sky. Everything has to be united. That's painting.

"Now, most of my work comes visually from memories, and the colour also is self-invented. I reflect things I've seen before up north, but you've got to look for a while to see the fact. If it becomes too obvious, it's no use, it's just a decoration. And the Uplands series, this is a new evolution for me of flying shapes . . . the whole landscape. But it's nothing to do with documentary. It's above that, it's something you invent on your own."

– Gershon Iskowitz, 1975

PLATE 112
Gershon Iskowitz   (1921-   )
Uplands H (diptych)   1972
oil on canvas   241.3 x 365.8 cm
Art Gallery of Ontario

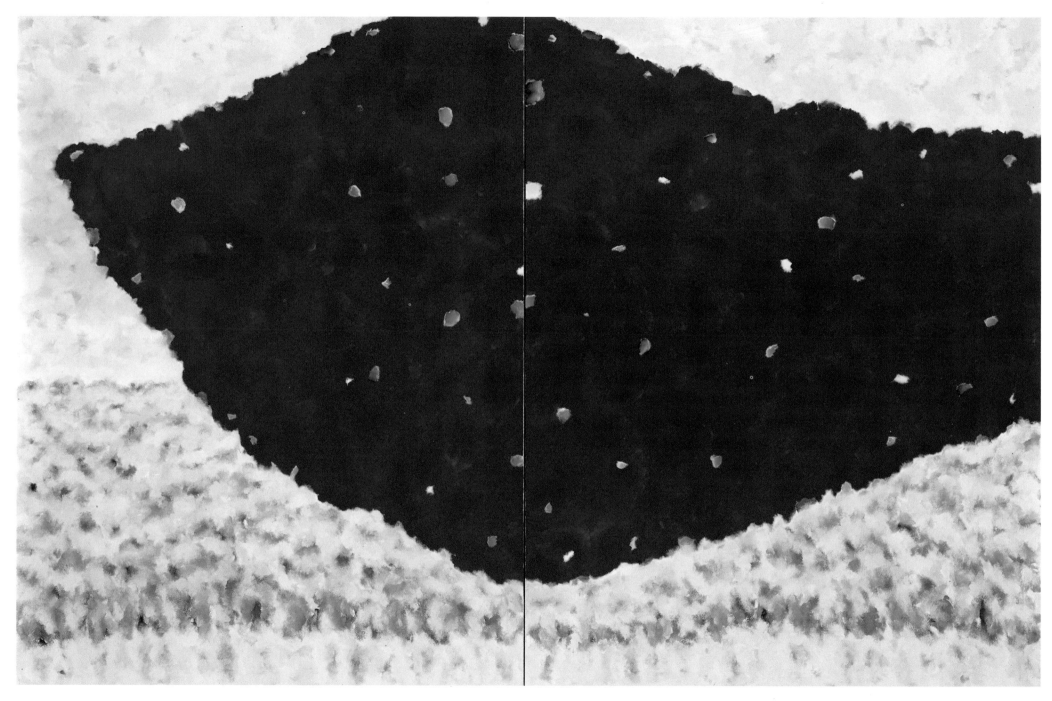

PLATE 112

PLATE 113

JACK CHAMBERS
Sunday Morning No. 2

One Sunday morning, Jack Chambers came downstairs and looked into his livingroom, where his two children were watching television. Suddenly, in a moment of heightened reality, the scene became an instant of revelation. Chambers was concerned with capturing that shock of recognition in his paintings, first by recording the essential information of the event by taking photographs, then by painstakingly reconstructing the scene in paint. His aim was to recreate the intensity of that original moment, and to instill that energy into the work. *Sunday Morning No. 2* (opposite), a brilliant piece of photographic realism, on a deeper level is a religious work, celebrating life and the miracle of existence.

His painting of *Lake Huron No. 4* (Plate 7) captures the same heightened reality. It represents a view up a steep embankment towards the sky, from the beach on Lake Huron. By photographing the sky separately, while looking straight up, Chambers created an unusual perspective in which the viewer is looking at the painting and up into the sky at the same time. Within the context of Chambers' ideas on art, the solitary tree and the steps leading up to the top of the embankment take on special significance. The steps become a symbolic link — a Jacob's ladder — between earth and sky, the material and the immaterial world. The tree in the centre of the painting becomes a cosmic Tree of Life, mediating between this world and that of the spirit–a manifestation of pure energy. Chambers wrote extensively about his theories on perception and developed a style he called Perceptual Realism. He believed that nature was a mysterious and unique expression of creative energy. In a moment of

"white light," it was possible to see beyond the object itself and to experience another aspect of reality. It was this reality that Chambers wanted to communicate through his art.

Chambers spent many years acquiring the special skills and self-discipline needed to translate these ideas into his art. Born in London, Ontario, he left for Europe at the age of twenty-two, and enrolled in the Academy of Fine Arts in Madrid, where he was given a rigorous technical training. With the help of scholarships and other outside work, he managed to stay in Spain eight years. When he returned to London in 1961, he began to paint the familiar environment around him in a new way. In 1968, at the height of his career, Chambers discovered that he had leukemia. He battled against the illness for the next ten years with amazing courage, painting his best-known works and formulating his Perceptual Realist style. To those who knew him, he was warm, humane, unassuming, and down-to-earth. But he was also a visionary, with a unique perception of reality.

"I am not interested in art, I am interested in life. When you are interested in life more than you are in painting, then your paintings can come to life."

–Jack Chambers, 1972

PLATE 113
Jack Chambers   (1931–1978)
Sunday Morning No. 2   1969–1970
oil on wood   121.9 x 121.9 cm
Private Collection

GREG CURNOE
Corner

The work of Greg Curnoe has always focused on his immediate environment, and his studio in particular. His art is an extension of his life, and the studio is where he works and spends a major part of each day. It is filled with objects that are meaningful to him, from his collection of rare pop bottles to newspapers, magazines, his record player, radio, and his ten-speed bicycle.

Corner (opposite) shows the inside of the studio in one of the largest and most extraordinary water colours ever created in Canadian art. Enormous in scale, this work is to Curnoe what the famous *Interior of My Studio* was to the French painter Gustave Courbet. It is an allegory of the life of Greg Curnoe: hockey cards of his favourite stars, plans for the great dirigible, a patched bicycle tube, a simple pencil sharpener, a *Wilf Carter Request* album, two clocks with two different times, and two large hi-fi speakers. Like all other great images of the artist's studio, it contains a painting within a painting, in this case an unfinished work of Curnoe and a friend playing golf. It also includes a magnificent landscape seen through the studio window.

In *Corner*, Curnoe opens up a new way of seeing, in which ordinary objects become extraordinary. He is like a map-maker or a surveyor, charting, mapping, measuring, timing his environment. He documents the everyday things around him, viewing the world with a kind of innocence, as if he were seeing everything for the first time. His work is a celebration of the real, of his cultural roots, and the beauty of the commonplace. It is a joyous celebration, painted in Curnoe's own rainbow colours.

Curnoe's work is close to conceptual art, with its emphasis on documentation and the process of making art. Curnoe, however, consciously rejects any attempts to be categorized according to the international style of the "Imperial Centre," New York City. As far as he is concerned, his art is regional (he sometimes stamps REGION on his paintings), made in London, Ontario, where he was born, brought up, and has spent all his life. For Curnoe, London, his studio, and his own backyard, are both macrocosm and microcosm, where he can see Egypt on TV, listen to Cuba on the radio, and talk to Edinburgh on the phone. He firmly believes in Canadian culture and is highly critical of those who look to the United States for ideas or approval. Curnoe's concept of culture is not the opera, the ballet or art galleries; it is folk music, old comic books, and maps of the country.

As a co-founder (in 1972) of the Association for the Documentation of Neglected Aspects of Culture in Canada, Curnoe has collected slides and other material on folk culture in Canada. All these activities form part of a rich and integrated existence, where art and life are one. "Art doesn't change me, it's what I'm doing. It's rarely that an influence from my art determines the way I live, it's usually the other way around. The way I live determines what I do in my art — if they can be distinguised, and I don't think they can really be distinguished."

PLATE 114
Greg Curnoe   (1936-   )
Corner   1975-1976
water colour and graphite on paper   149.2 x 364.5 cm
National Gallery of Canada

244

PLATE 114

PLATE 115

PLATE 116

YVES GAUCHER
Triptych

Yves Gaucher has over a period of many years relentlessly pursued his own personal artistic vision. Although he has explored the language of colour, Gaucher's work is radically different from that of Molinari and Tousignant; instead it is, like the work of Charles Gagnon, an art of the colours and the sounds of silence, an art of contemplation.

Gaucher's art is about music and mathematics. Born into a musical family where everyone played an instrument, he was playing in professional jazz bands at night and working during the day by the age of seventeen. Music continues to be a central part of his life and has provided the inspiration for much of his work. On hearing a concert of Anton Webern's music in Paris, he recalled that "the music seemed to send little cells of sound out into space, where they expanded and took on a whole new quality and dimension of their own."

His *Triptych* (opposite, top) forms part of his Signals and Silences series, and was originally painted as three separate works. Each of them has an individual title: the red panel is *Signals, Another Summer*, the yellow one is *Signals, Very Softly*, and the blue one is *Silences/Silence*. As with all his other work since the early 1960s, they explore problems of expanse, rhythm, and duration. They are like high frequency sound impulses or signals, communicating a mysterious energy that is beyond time and place.

PLATE 115
Yves Gaucher   (1934-   )
Triptych   1966
acrylic on canvas   203.2 x 262.6 cm
Art Gallery of Ontario

CHARLES GAGNON
November Steps (For Toru Takemitsu)

Although he grew up in Montreal at the same time as Molinari (Plate 105) and Tousignant (Plate 106), Charles Gagnon did not share their interest in international art trends. He remained more of a philosopher, concerned with expressing his vision of the world in whatever medium seemed most appropriate.

November Steps (opposite, bottom) was painted shortly after returning from a trip to Japan, where he became a close friend of Japanese composer Toru Takemitsu, who had written a musical composition called *November Steps*. Gagnon's painting was created for Toru Takemitsu and evokes the same mood as the music – one of quiet contemplation. The black borders are a centring device, and the area within them is an infinite space or field for meditation. Like a movie screen, the painting is a window on reality, where space is behind the canvas rather than in front of it. At first nothing appears to be happening, until the viewer stops, reflects, and sees; he discovers that both nothing and everything are happening.

This work served as the inspiration for Gagnon's second film, *The Sound of Space*, which, like the painting, was an attempt to find inner peace in a world of total conflict. It is a contemplative religious experience that reveals how unreal conventional reality is. All of Gagnon's work has a profound relationship to Zen thought, where "to be enlightened by all things is to free one's body and mind and those of others."

PLATE 116
Charles Gagnon   (1934-   )
November Steps (For Toru Takemitsu)   1966
oil on canvas   182.9 x 365.8 cm
National Gallery of Canada

NEW WAYS OF SEEING

The contemporary era has been one of lightning change, encompassing awesome technological feats such as computers, colour television, space travel, global communications, nuclear warfare, and placing man on the moon, as well as hallucinogenic drugs, ecological disasters, and mushrooming urbanization. The old art forms were no longer adequate to reflect the dynamics of a changing society, and artists turned to new forms of expression – photography, film, video, holography, earthworks – as well as new perceptions of the traditional media of painting and sculpture. As the antennae of society, contemporary artists have attempted to come to terms with the changing environment. They continue to fulfil the traditional role of the artist – to explore human values, to find meaning in the universe, and to examine the individual's relationship with his environment – while breaking new ground and opening up new ways of seeing. Some of the following works may be the artistic landmarks of the future.

ROBERT MURRAY *Swing* Plate 117

In the 1950s and 1960s, sculpture went through an extraordinary renaissance. Sculptors broke from the traditional concept of forms based on a central core and experimented with forms that moved outward into space. Their works achieved a new expansiveness of scale, which demanded public spaces and public commissions to support their huge size and cost. One of the leading international exponents of this new direction in art is Robert Murray. Murray's *Swing* (p. 251), made of aluminum plate, is one of his most elegant and accomplished pieces. It appears so light that it is almost ready to float into the air. Murray is an experienced pilot, and it is easy to see the parallels between this work and the sensation of flying. There is a dynamic relationship between the curved and angular planes, and a sensuous feeling for colour.

PATERSON EWEN *Rain Over Water* Plate 118

In *Rain Over Water* (p. 251) Paterson Ewen appears to be working within the traditional painting format. However, this huge work was made by joining together three four-foot by eight-foot sheets of thick plywood, lying them flat, and gouging out the wood with a router. Once the surface has been worked, acrylic paint is applied in the grooves and rolled on the flat surfaces with a printer's roller.

The work reflects Ewen's fascination with natural phenomena, especially rain – the way it falls, its velocity, its density. Ewen's painting makes the viewer "feel rain" and communicates a new perception of the landscape.

JOHN BOYLE *Midnight Oil* Plate 119

One of the great traditions in art is historical painting, celebrating the legends and great events of a culture. In recent years, John Boyle has revived this tradition and given it new relevance with his works dedicated to Canada's great national heroes, such as Louis Riel, Gabriel Dumont, Chief Poundmaker, Stephen Leacock, and Tom Thomson. *Midnight Oil* (p. 251) is a major landmark, bringing together many diverse elements in a monument to Tom Thomson. In this painted sculpture, Boyle shows Thomson in several familiar poses, based on the few known photographs of the artist. He has combined elements of the past and present, from Thomson's life and his own.

For Boyle, art is a process of self-discovery, which can lead to greater self-understanding. He is passionately concerned with individual freedom and with celebrating the great achievements of Canadian culture.

COLETTE WHITEN   *Family*   Plate 120

When Colette Whiten first exhibited her sculptures in Toronto in 1972, many viewers reacted with astonishment. In place of a finished sculpture was a strange apparatus made of wood, concrete blocks, and rope, which was originally used to support the person being cast. Exhibited along with the structure were a few isolated castings of arms, legs, and torsos, as well as photographs, films, and videotape documenting the process of casting. The structures resembled medieval torture instruments, and these associations were heightened by the fact that all the casts were of men. The effect of the work was at once disturbing, enigmatic, and erotic.

Family (p. 252) is a recent group of sculptures representing her two daughters and Gernot Dick. As with most of her work, the figures themselves are literally air, surrounded by mass. What appears to be a rounded frontal view is a concave surface or a negative space, which jars conventional perceptions. Once again, she has encased her subjects in plaster and mercifully set them free.

TONY URQUHART   *Rocamadour I*   Plate 121

Tony Urquhart who began as a painter, gradually turned to sculpture in the 1960s. His early sculptures were tiny six-sided canvases with landscapes on each side. Later, he created wooden boxes mounted on pedestals, with small hinged doors that opened to reveal fantastic interior scenes. *Rocamadour I* (p. 252) is one of the most impressive of these boxes. A mysterious landscape of the imagination, it is almost a representational sculpture, inspired by a visit to the small medieval town of Rocamadour in southern France. While walking up the narrow streets, Urquhart noticed a caged garden, or gazebo, behind a house with bits of grape vine clinging to it, and scraps of cloth hanging out to dry. In *Rocamadour I*, with its wooden framework, painted plastic wings, and mysterious objects, the caged garden becomes at once real and imaginary, man and landscape, sacred and profane. It is a world in miniature, rich in associations – an icon of our time.

IRENE WHITTOME   *White Museum No. 1*   Plate 122

The work of Irene Whittome is made by the deliberate accumulation of materials. *White Museum No. 1* (p. 252) is a virtual "museum" made out of objects that we normally throw away. She has taken long pieces of wood, wrapped and bound them in canvas and twine, and placed them in glass-fronted wood cases. These vertical images, isolated behind glass, become evocative, mummified shapes, suggestive of ritual and magic. By using cast-off materials, Whittome has bestowed importance on what is normally considered insignificant. *White Museum No. 1* is archetypal imagery, composed of powerful fetishes suggestive of kings and queens, and connecting on a deep, instinctual level.

JOYCE WIELAND   *I Love Canada*   Plate 123

Joyce Wieland has established a solid reputation as a painter, filmmaker, sculptor, and printmaker. She has also revived quilting, an art form traditionally associated with women, and given it new credibility. A firm believer in the collaborative effort required to fabricate her large quilts, she involves relatives and friends in their production. She also uses the medium to express her spirited nationalism and her love of nature.

I Love Canada/J'aime le Canada (p. 253) is a statement about the need for dialogue between French and English Canada. Wieland feels that they are chained together through a contract called "federalism." The insert hidden under the flap in this quilt states "Down with U.S. Imperialist Technology."

As a cultural activist, Joyce Wieland believes that art can be responsible to society. She also wants her art to nurture and be an extension of nature. Works like *The Water Quilt* (Art Gallery of Ontario) make a direct comment on ecological problems. In it she has stitched sixty-four delicately beautiful Arctic wildflowers on flaps, which lift up to reveal grim ecological warnings from James Laxer's book, *The Energy Poker Game*. The same kind of directness and honesty pervades all her art, expressing her personal vision.

LOUIS DE NIVERVILLE *Funk* Plate 124

Louis de Niverville draws his imagery from the depth of his psyche. Many of his images relate to his early childhood in Ottawa. At age six, he entered the hospital with spinal tuberculosis and spent the next four and a half years there. This period instilled in the artist a sense of survival, a rich world of fantasy, and a deep underlying loneliness. While in the hospital he began doing drawings, which were enthusiastically praised, and he decided then that he wanted to become a painter.

De Niverville never had any formal art training, teaching himself by studying other artists. *Funk* (p. 253) is one of his major works, painted over an earlier work that he had abandoned in sheer frustration. On impulse, he combined two dissimilar photographs, and the result was *Funk*. In commenting on it, the artist said, "The painting is about texture and smell, a yellowing satin dress and Christmas tree lights in July." The bizarre perspective, the phosphorescent colour, and the incredible expressions of the children's faces—not to mention the dog—all are intensely personal and hauntingly beautiful. The work provides a psychic escape from the regimentation of society, and a bridge into the world of dreams.

DON PROCH *Rainbow Mask* Plate 125

Don Proch grew up on a farm in Grandview, Manitoba, where his grandfather drove him to school in a horse and buggy and he lived in a log cabin with no electricity. At age eight he moved to the tiny town of Inglis, Manitoba, two miles from the abandoned settlement of Asessippi. This town later became the subject of Proch's famous Asessippi Exhibition at the Winnipeg Art Gallery in 1972. For this show, he formed the Ophthalmia Company, which was dedicated to the expression of the Prairie farmer's experience of the land. He involved a diverse group of talented people in the production of works for the exhibition, a mixed-media show involving photographs, videotape, printing, sculpture, and Proch's remarkable Prairie drawings.

In the mid-seventies Proch began a series of masks. The *Rainbow Mask* (p. 253), one of the most startling of them all, is made of fibreglass and contains a heat-sensitive neon light in rainbow colours. The entire outer surface is covered with an intricate graphite landscape drawing that has no vanishing point, suggesting a feeling of endless space. The viewer can imagine himself viewing the entire landscape with full 360° peripheral vision, as if he were inside the mask. *Rainbow Mask* is not only a statement about man's relationship to the land, but it has deeper associations of magic, ritual, and mystery. Proch creates a new perception of the Prairie landscape, combining man and landscape in a unique visual experience. It is not only a contemporary mask, similar to a motorcyclist's or a goalie's, but it also evokes the artist-shaman's mask of prehistoric times.

IVAN EYRE *Manitou* Plate 126

When Don Proch studied at the University of Manitoba School of Art, one teacher who had a great influence on him was Ivan Eyre. Eyre was born and brought up on the Prairies and has been deeply influenced by that environment. In paintings such as *Manitou* (p. 253), Eyre challenges the reality of everyday experience. The work is a Prairie landscape, but not a traditional one; it is a magical, dream-like vision in which darkness moves into light and light into darkness. There is an aura of mystery, suggested by the dark cave-like area in the foreground, and the open space of the grassy Prairie, bathed in a luminous pink light. It is an image that has its origins in Eyre's own experience and feelings: "clear spaces, air rich with dreaming, the sensuality of a shaded dark prairie grove, a black bank of exposed roots in an empty stream bed, a windless summer evening sky luminous with a pink light." He is reaching for a higher level of reality, revealing the "crack between the worlds." The title *Manitou* is the word for Spirit or Being, and in this painting Eyre provides a window into all that is awesome, stupendous, mysterious, and unfathomable. It is both this world and that of the imagination, containing the past, the future, and the present.

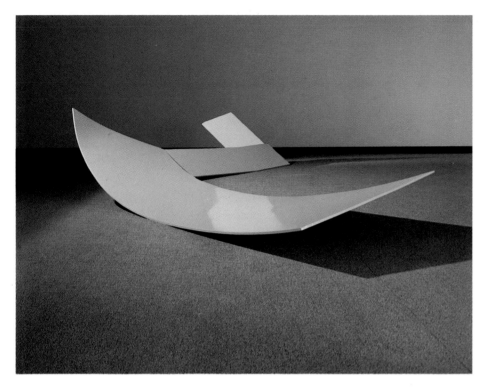

PLATE 117

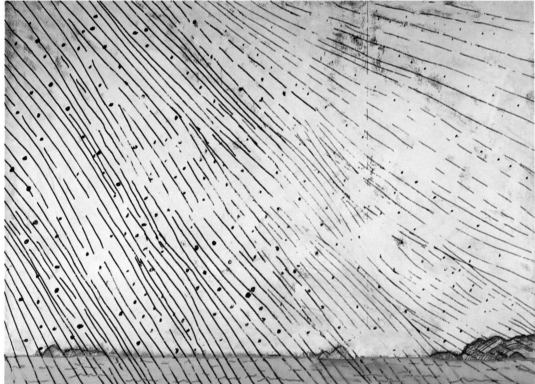

PLATE 118

PLATE 119

PLATE 120

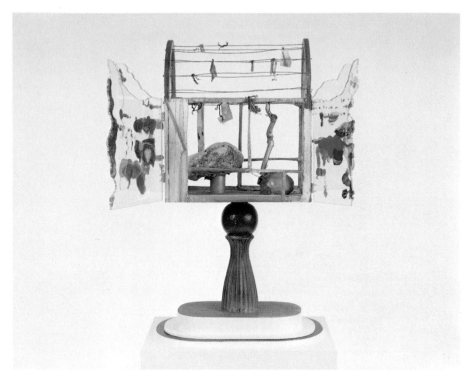

PLATE 121

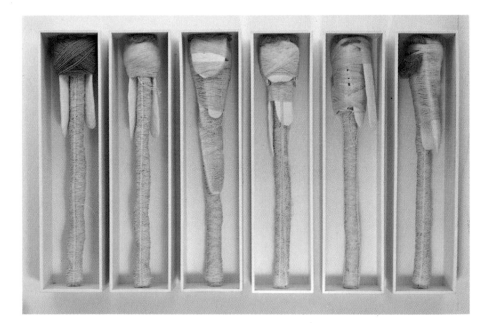

PLATE 122

PLATE 123

PLATE 125

PLATE 124

PLATE 126

PLATE 127

PLATE 128

PLATE 129

ROY KIYOOKA   *StoneDGloves*   Plate 127

Roy Kiyooka is an artist, writer, poet, painter, sculptor, photographer, and filmmaker, but he is above all a highly refined and sensitive receiver/transmitter – an individual whose presence and spirit runs through Canadian art like an electric current. In his life, he has been an inspiration, friend, and teacher of artists from one end of the country to the other. He achieved prominence in painting and sculpture, then abandoned both to explore a new world of visual perception through film and photography. Few people have recognized the originality of this recent work, which is disarming in its simplicity. As one friend commented, it is not about Zen, it *is* Zen. While at Expo 70 in Osaka, Japan, he took over three thousand photographs of gloves that had been abandoned at the construction site: torn gloves, buried gloves, cotton, leather, and rubber gloves. He selected about forty photos, blew them up, and exhibited them in an exhibition called StoneDGloves. These works are at once sculpture, painting, photography, and visual poetry. In this photograph (p. 254) and in the poems, the empty, discarded glove becomes a rich and profound metaphor for the frailty of existence; it is about time and timelessness, art and artlessness.

N.E. THING CO. LTD.
Reflected Landscape: The Arctic Sunset   Plate 128

When N.E. Thing Co. Ltd. undertook its first experimental projects in Vancouver in the 1960s, many similar conceptual investigations were being carried out simultaneously by the leading artists in New York. For a brief but important period, the company was on the leading edge of art experiments throughout the globe. Founded in 1966 by co-presidents Iain and Ingrid Baxter, it is a legal company involved in the business of art.

In 1969, the N.E. Thing Co. Ltd. visited Inuvik in the Canadian Arctic, where they created a number of works. One of them was *Reflected Landscape: The Arctic Sunset* (p. 254), in which they set up a mirror on the tundra so that it would reflect the entire Arctic sun on the mirror's surface as the sun set. The work can be viewed as a conventional "landscape," or as a portrait of the sun, or as a "painting within a painting," or as a document of an event. It exists in several different forms–a 35mm original slide, a series of colour offset lithographic prints, and several large backlighted transparencies. Like most N.E. Thing projects, it breaks down familiar patterns of seeing art and the natural environment. It emphasizes the artist's role as a perceiver, rather than a maker of objects. In the company's view, the environment is a work of art, and there is no difference between life and art.

MICHAEL SNOW   *La Region Centrale*   Plate 129

Michael Snow is undoubtedly one of the giants of contemporary art, whose importance has been universally recognized by major critics in Canada, the United States, and Europe. Like all great innovators, Snow challenges traditional modes of perception. Snow is one of those rare visionaries who has the ability to translate his vision into an amazingly simple and concentrated artistic statement.

Many of his recent works are films, and Snow is one of the inventors of film art. His films explore the intrinsic properties of the medium: light, duration, movement, and sound.

La Region Centrale (p. 254) is a three-hour landscape film that Snow made by placing a camera on a specially designed machine, capable of moving in all directions. The machine was set up on a remote mountain top, where it filmed the landscape as the camera moved over it. It is a film that could only have been made in the age of space travel; it deals with the concept of a primeval landscape, as it was before man set foot on it. As one critic said, "he catapults us to the heart of the world before speech, before arbitrarily imposed meanings, even subject. He forces us to rethink not only cinema but our universe." On one level, *La Region Centrale* can be seen as a breakthrough in the union of technology and art: on another, it can be experienced as a profound meditation on nature.

NEW WAYS OF SEEING: CAPTIONS

PAGE 251:

PLATE 117
Robert Murray   (1936-   )
Swing   1973
aluminum painted yellow   84.4 x 571.5 x 284.4 cm
Art Gallery of Ontario

PLATE 118
Paterson Ewen   (1925-   )
Rain over Water   1974
acrylic on plywood   243.8 x 335.9 cm
Artist's collection, courtesy of
Carmen Lamanna Gallery, Toronto

PLATE 119
John Boyle   (1941-   )
Midnight Oil   1969
oil on wood with flashing light and wheel-shaped panel
233.6 cm square
London Regional Art Gallery

PAGE 252:

PLATE 120
Colette Whiten   (1945-   )
Family   1977-1978
plaster, wood, burlap, and metal

	Gernot	*Shauna*	*Megan*
height	190.5 cm	168.2 cm	149.2 cm
width	93.9 cm	80.6 cm	64.7 cm
depth	66.0 cm	61.6 cm	48.2 cm

Collection of the artist, courtesy of
Carmen Lamanna Gallery, Toronto

PLATE 121
Tony Urquhart   (1934-   )
Rocamadour I   1970
wood, oil, plexiglass, found objects
162.6 (height) x 50.8 (width) x 40.6 cm (depth)
National Gallery of Canada

PLATE 122
Irene Whittome   (1942-   )
White Museum No. 1   1975
wood, liquid liquitex, moulded paper, string, plexiglass
6 pieces, each 106.7 x 25.4 x 20.3 cm
Vancouver Art Gallery

PAGE 253:

PLATE 123
Joyce Wieland   (1931-   )
I Love Canada   1969
quilted and embroidered cotton assemblage, metal chain
160.0 x 167.6 cm
Norman MacKenzie Art Gallery, Regina

PLATE 124
Louis de Niverville   (1933-   )
Funk   1973
acrylic airbrush on canvas   183.2 x 183.2 cm
Musée d'Art Contemporaire, Montreal

PLATE 125
Don Proch   (1944-   )
Rainbow Mask   1976
silverpoint and graphite on fibreglass and neon construction
33.8 x 21.4 x 29.0 cm
Glenbow-Alberta Institute, Calgary

PLATE 126
Ivan Eyre   (1935-   )
Manitou   1973
oil and acrylic on canvas   162.5 x 142.2 cm
Government of Manitoba

PAGE 254:

PLATE 127
Roy Kiyooka   (1926-   )
StoneDGloves   1970
photographic print   68.6 x 101.3 cm
Vancouver Art Gallery

PLATE 128
N.E. Thing Company Ltd.
Reflected Landscape: The Arctic Sunset   1969
mirror, sun, camera, twilight, 35mm colour film
3.5 x 3.5 cm
Artists' collection

PLATE 129
Michael Snow   (1929-   )
La Region Centrale   1970-1971
16mm colour film, sound   180 minutes
Artist's Collection; print in
National Gallery of Canada

BIBLIOGRAPHY

For anyone wanting to read further on Canadian art, Russell Harper's *Painting in Canada: A History* is undoubtedly the most important book on the subject. Dennis Reid's *A Concise History of Canadian Painting* is also an invaluable and informative source, especially on twentieth-century art. In the native arts, Nancy-Lou Patterson's *Canadian Native Art*, and George Swinton's *Sculpture of the Eskimo* provide excellent introductions to this important field. Those interested in contemporary art should refer to the three major art periodicals in Canada – *artscanada*, *Vie des Arts*, and *Art Magazine*.

GENERAL

Fulford, Robert. *An Introduction to the Arts in Canada*. Toronto: Copp Clark Publishing, 1977.

Harper, J. Russell. *Early Painters and Engravers in Canada*. Toronto: University of Toronto Press, 1970.

———. *Painting in Canada: A History*. 2nd ed. Toronto: University of Toronto Press, 1977.

———. *A People's Art: Primitive, Naive, Provincial and Folk Painting in Canada*. Toronto: University of Toronto Press, 1974.

Hubbard, R.H. *Canadian Landscape Painting 1670-1930*. With essay by Northrop Frye. Madison: University of Wisconsin Press, 1973.

———. *The Development of Canadian Art*. Ottawa: National Gallery of Canada, 1963.

Lord, Barry. *The History of Painting in Canada: Toward a People's Art*. Toronto: NC Press, 1974.

National Gallery of Canada. *Three Hundred Years of Canadian Art*. Catalogue by R.H. Hubbard and J.R. Ostiguy. Ottawa, 1967.

Reid, Dennis. *A Concise History of Canadian Painting*. Toronto: Oxford University Press, 1973.

CHAPTER 1

Carpenter, Edmund. *Eskimo Realities*. New York: Holt, Rinehart and Winston Inc., 1973.

Dickason, Olive Patricia. *Indian Arts in Canada*. Ottawa: Department of Indian Affairs and Northern Development, 1972.

Duff, Wilson. *Images Stone B.C.* Toronto: Oxford University Press, 1975.

Houston, James. *Eskimo Prints*. Toronto: Longman Canada Ltd., 1971.

McLuhan, T.C. *Touch the Earth: A Self-Portrait of Indian Existence*. London: Sphere Books Ltd., Abacus Edition, 1973.

Musée de l'Homme. *Chefs-d'oeuvres des arts indiens et esquimaux du Canada*. Paris: Société des Amis du Musée de l'Homme, 1969.

National Museum of Man, National Museums of Canada. *"Bo'jou, Neejee!": Profiles of Canadian Indian Art*. Catalogue text by Ted J. Brasser. Ottawa, 1976.

———. *The Inuit Print*. Text by Helga Goetz. Ottawa, 1977.

Patterson, Nancy-Lou. *Canadian Native Art: Arts and Crafts of Canadian Indians and Eskimos*. Toronto: Collier MacMillan Canada Ltd., 1973.

Reid, William. *Out of the Silence*. Fort Worth: Amon Carter Museum of Western Art, 1971.

Swinton, George. *Sculpture of the Eskimo*. Toronto: McClelland & Stewart Ltd., 1972.

Taylor, William E., Jr., Swinton, George, and Houston, James. *Sculpture of the Inuit: Masterworks of the Canadian Arctic*. Canadian Eskimo Arts Council/University of Toronto Press, 1971.

Vancouver Art Gallery. *Arts of the Raven: Masterworks of the Northwest Coast Indian*. Text by Wilson Duff with contributory articles by Bill Holm and Bill Reid. Vancouver, 1967.

Woodcock, George. *Peoples of the Coast: The Indians of the Pacific Northwest*. Edmonton: Hurtig Publishers, 1977.

CHAPTER 2

Morriset, Gérard. *La peinture traditionnelle au Canada français*. L'encyclopedie du Canada Français. Ottawa: Le Cercle du Livre de France, 1960.

Trudel, Jean. *Un chef-d'oeuvre de l'art ancien du Québec: La Chapelle des Ursulines*. Québec: Les Presses de l'université Laval, 1972.

CHAPTER 3

Bell, Michael. *Painters in a New Land*. Toronto: McClelland & Stewart Ltd., 1973.

CHAPTER 4

Murray, Joan. "Painting in Canada." *Canadian Collector* 10 No. 5 (Sept.-Oct. 1975) 52-57.

Reid, Dennis. "Painting in Canada." *Canadian Collector* 13 No. 1 (Jan.-Feb. 1978) 44-54.

CHAPTER 5

Duval, Paul. *Four Decades: The Canadian Group of Painters and Their Contemporaries*. Toronto: Clarke, Irwin & Co. Ltd., 1972.

Hill, Charles C. *Canadian Painting in the Thirties*. Ottawa: The National Gallery of Canada, 1975.

Jackson, A.Y. *A Painter's Country*. Toronto: Clarke, Irwin & Co. Ltd., 1958.

Mellen, Peter. *The Group of Seven*. Toronto: McClelland & Stewart, 1970.

National Gallery of Canada. *The Group of Seven*. Catalogue by Dennis Reid. Ottawa, 1970.

CHAPTER 6

Duval, Paul. *High Realism in Canada*. Toronto: Clarke, Irwin & Co. Ltd., 1974.

Robert, Guy. *L'art au Québec: depuis 1940*. Ottawa: Les Éditions La Presse, 1973.

Townsend, William, ed. *Canadian Art Today*. London: Studio International, 1970.

Withrow, William J. *Contemporary Canadian Painting*. Toronto: McClelland & Stewart, 1972.

ACKNOWLEDGEMENTS

The following information constitutes an extension of the captions accompanying each plate. All photography was supplied by the museums credited in the captions, except where indicated below in parentheses, or by one of the following: (M.N.) - Michael Neill; (J. deV.) - John deVisser; (E.O.) - Eberhard Otto for *artscanada* magazine. Every reasonable effort has been made to ascertain the ownership of illustrations used. Information would be welcomed that would enable the publisher to rectify any error. Plates are indicated by number.

Page 19. National Museum of Man; *Page 21.* (E.O.); *Page 22.* Rothman's Permanent Collection of Eskimo Sculpture (Ernest Mayer, Winnipeg Art Gallery); *Page 25.* Courtesy of the Trustees of the British Museum; *Page 29.* National Gallery of Canada; *Page 30.* McCord Museum, Montreal; *Page 34.* National Gallery of Canada; *Page 35.* National Gallery of Canada; *Page 39.* McMichael Canadian Collection, Kleinburg, Ontario; *Page 46.* National Gallery of Canada; *Page 49.* Artist's Collection.

1. Coll: Beaverbrook Canadian Foundation, Beaverbrook Art Gallery, Fredericton, N.B., Canada; *2.* Art Gallery of Ontario, Toronto - Gift of the Government of the Province of Ontario, 1972; *3.* The Royal Canadian Academy of Arts, Diploma Work, deposited 1886 (M.N.); *4.* Courtesy of the McMichael Canadian Collection, Kleinburg, Ontario (M.N.); *5.* (M.N.); *6.* Art Gallery of Ontario, Toronto - purchase, 1976; *7.* (Nancy Poole's Studio); *8.* Toronto Dominion Bank Collection of Canadian Art; *9. – 11.* Collection: The National Museum of Man, The National Museums of Canada (M.N.); *12.* (M.N.); *13.* Courtesy of Museum of the American Indian, Heye Foundation, N.Y.; *14. – 16.* Collection: The National Museum of Man, The National Museums of Canada (M.N.); *17.* (M.N.); *18.* Courtesy of the Royal Ontario Museum, Toronto, Canada; *19.* (M.N.); *20.* Courtesy of the Royal Ontario Museum, Toronto, Canada; *21.* (E.O.) August, 1970; *22.* The Metropolitan Museum of Art, Gift of James A. Houston, 1969; *23.* (J. deV.); *24.* (M.N.); *25.* (M.N.);

26. – 27. Collection: The National Museum of Man, The National Museums of Canada (M.N.); *28.* (M.N.); *29.* (E.O.) June, 1975; *30.* Reproduced by permission of *The Huntington Library, San Marino, California*; *31.* The Ursulines of the Quebec Monastery (National Gallery of Canada); *32. – 34.* (J. deV.); *35.* The Ursulines of The Quebec Monastery (J. deV.); *36.* (National Gallery of Canada); *37.* The Ursulines of the Quebec Monastery (J. deV.); *40.* (M.N.); *41.* Gift of Major Edgar C. Woolsey, Ottawa, 1952; *45.* Art Gallery of Ontario, Toronto; lent by Mr. & Mrs. J. B. Robinson, 1944; *48.* Gift of the Estate of the Honorable W. C. Edwards, Ottawa, 1928; *51.* Collection of the Art Gallery of Hamilton, Gift of Mrs. R.N. Steiner in memory of her mother, Mrs. L.C. Dillon, 1965 (M.N.); *56.* (Natural Science Library); *58.* The Royal Canadian Academy of Arts, diploma work, deposited 1891 (M.N.); *60.* Collection of the Art Gallery of Hamilton, Bruce Memorial, 1914 (M.N.); *62.* The Royal Canadian Academy, diploma work, deposited 1881; *63.* (M.N.); *64.* The Royal Canadian Academy, diploma work, deposited 1880; *67.* (M.N.); *68.* Collection of the Art Gallery of Hamilton, Bequest of H.L. Rinn, 1955 (M.N.); *69.* (M.N.); *71.* (M.N.); *73.* Courtesy of the McMichael Canadian Collection, Kleinburg, Ont. (M.N.); *74.* Art Gallery of Ontario, Toronto - Gift of the Canadian Club of Toronto, 1926 (M.N.); *75.* Courtesy of the McMichael Canadian Collection, Kleinburg, Ontario (M.N.); *76.* Donated by Mr. John A. MacAulay, Q.C., Collection of the Winnipeg Art Gallery; *77.* Reproduced with the permission of Marjorie Lismer Bridges; *79.* Vincent Massey Bequest, 1968 (M.N.); *80.* Presented in memory of Richard Southam by his brothers, 1939; *81.* Art Gallery of Ontario, Toronto - purchase, 1933; *82.* (M.N.); *83.* The Vincent Massey Bequest, 1968; *84.* Gift from the Douglas M. Duncan Collection, Toronto, 1970 (M.N.); *85.* Gift from the Douglas M. Duncan Collection, Toronto, 1970 (M.N.); *86.* Gift of Dr. P. D. Ross, Ottawa, 1932 (M.N.); *87.* The Vincent Massey Bequest, 1968; *88.* Hart House Permanent Collection, University of Toronto (Art Gallery of Ontario); *90. – 91.* (M.N.); *95.* Art Gallery of Ontario, Toronto; Canada Council Joint Purchase Award, 1959; *96.* The Robert McLaughlin Gallery, Oshawa - purchase, 1971 (1971.RW.94); *97.* (Isaacs Gallery); *98. – 99.* (M.N.); *100.* From the Vincent Melzac Collection, on extended loan to the Edmonton Art Gallery (M.N.); *101.* Art Gallery of Ontario, Toronto - purchase, 1964; *102.* Art Gallery of Ontario, Toronto - purchase, 1967; *103.* From the Collection of Jack Orr, Toronto - (E.O.) October/November, 1971; *104.* Art Gallery of Ontario,

Toronto - purchase, 1976; *105.* Art Gallery of Ontario, Toronto - purchase, Corporations' Subscription Endowment, 1967; *107.* (M.N.); *108.* (Vancouver Art Gallery); *109.* Art Gallery of Ontario, Toronto - purchase, 1977; *110.* (Cologne Art and Museum Library); *111.* Art Gallery of Ontario, Toronto; Gift from the McLean Foundation, 1964; *112.* Art Gallery of Ontario, Toronto; purchase, 1977; *113.* (E.O.); *114. – 115.* (M.N.); *116.* Art Gallery of Ontario, Toronto - purchase, with the assistance of the Canada Council Special Purchase Assistance Program, 1977; *117.* Art Gallery of Ontario, Toronto (Mirvish Gallery, Jane Corkin); *118.* Courtesy: Carmen Lamanna Gallery (M.N.); *119.* Courtesy of the London Public Library Board (M.N.); *120.* (E.O.) May, 1978; *121. – 123.* (M.N.); *124.* (E.O.) May, 1973; *125.* (M.N.); *126.* From the Collection of the Department of Public Works, Manitoba Provincial Government (Ernest Mayer); *127.* (M.N.); *128.* (Iain Baxter); *129.* (National Gallery of Canada).

The text on the following pages was prepared by Joan Murray: 115, 136, 139, 140, 143, 144, 147, 148, 153, 154, 158, 161, 162, 165, 176(B), 182, 192(B), 197(A), 198, 212, 217, 221, 222, 239.

INDEX

Page numbers in italic refer to illustrations.

Across the Lake, 40, *189, 191*
After the Bath, *6*, 143
Altar Wall, 25, *96, 97*
Angel of the Last Judgment, 25, *98, 99*
Ashevak, Karoo, 21; *Spirit, 22*
Assiniboin Hunting Buffalo, 17, *130, 131*
Assumption of the Virgin, 26, *90, 91*
Atlas, Nicholas Vallard's, 23, *86, 87*
Automatism 1:47, (Sous le vent d'île), 44, *204, 205*
Banners, *216, 217*
Bear, *18, 19*
Bear on Ice, *74, 75*
Beaucourt, François Malepart de, 28; *Marguerite Mailhot, 110, 111*
Behind Bonsecours Market, Montreal, 31, *132, 133*
Bell-Smith, F.M., 32, 153; *Portrait of Queen Victoria; 34; Lights of a City Street, 136, 137*
Berczy, William, 28; *The Woolsey Family, 108, 109*
Berthon, George Théodore, 31; *The Three Robinson Sisters, 114, 115*
Birrell, Ebenezer, *Good Friends, 124, 125*
Bloore, Ronald, 48; *Painting 1961, 226, 227*
Bookwus Mask: Wild Man of the Woods, *65, 67*
Borduas, Paul-Emile, 35, 42, 43, 44, 46, 157, 203, 207, 208, 229, 230; *Le chant de la pierre, 12; Sous le vent de l'île, 204, 205*
Boyle, John, 150, 175; *Midnight Oil, 248, 251*
Box: Haida Myth of Bear Mother, *82, 83*
Breeze, Claude, 50; *Sunday Afternoon: From an Old American Photograph, 46*
British Naval Squadron off Nova Scotia, *126, 127*
Brooker, Bertram, 41, 192, 201; *Sounds Assembling, 198, 199*
Bruce, William Blair, 33; *The Phantom Hunter, 144, 145*
Brymner, William, 33, 139, 192; *A Wreath of Flowers, 7*
Bush, Jack, 45, 217, 233; *Orange Centre, 218, 219*

Canada Southern Railway at Niagara, The, 32, *35*
Cape Diamond, *158, 159*
Captain Bulger at Red Lake, *30*
Carmichael, Franklin, 37, 40, 140, 171; *Northern Silver Mine, 39*
Carr, Emily, 40, 48, 211; *Forest, British Columbia, 186, 187*
Ceremonial Frontlet, 62, *64*
Ceremonial Headdress, *68, 69*
Chambers, Jack, 11, 48, 49, 50; *Sunday Morning No. 2, 242, 243*
Chant de la pierre, Le, *12, 204*
Chilkat Blanket, 62, *63*
Chutes de Saint-Ferréol, Les, *116, 117*
Citrons ultra-violets, *206, 207*
Clouds, Lake Superior, *176, 177*
Colville, Alex, 48; *Truck Stop, 237, 239*
Comb with Face/Shaman's Tube, *56, 57*
Comfort, Charles, 40, 45; *Young Canadian, 195, 197*
Composition No. 1, *200, 201*
Corner, *244, 245*
Coughtry, Graham, 46, 217; *Two Figure Series XIX, 212, 214*
Crooked Nose Mask, *18, 68, 69*
Cullen, Maurice, 36, 153, 161, 162, 192; *Cape Diamond, 158, 159*
Curnoe, Greg, 48, 49, 50, 175; *Corner, 244, 245*

Davies, Thomas, 28; *A View of the Lower Part of the Falls of St. Anne, 104, 105*
Death Bringer Club, The, 17, 58, *59*
Death of General Wolfe, The, 27, *29*
Doc Snider's House, *192, 193*
Dorset, *Dragline Handle, 56, 57; Shaman's Mask, 54, 55; Shaman's Tube/Comb with Face, 56, 57*
Dragline Handle, *56, 57*

Edson, Allan; 153; *Mount Orford and the Owl's Head from Lake Memphremagog, 148, 150*
Environs of Tangiers, *164, 165*
Ewen, Paterson, *Rain over Water, 248, 251*
Ex-Voto of the Three Castaways, 26, *94, 95*

Eyre, Ivan, *Manitou, 250, 253*
Fallen Birch, *146, 147*
Falls, Montreal River, *184, 185*
Family 1977-78, *252, 255*
Ferry, Quebec, The, *162, 163*
First Snow, Algoma, *170, 171*
FitzGerald, LeMoine, 40; *Doc Snider's House, 192, 193*
Fleeting Breath, *210, 211*
Forest, British Columbia, *186, 187*
Fowler, Daniel, 143; *Fallen Birch, 146, 147*
France Bringing Faith to the Indians of New France, *88, 89*
Fraser, J. A., 34, 35; *Laurentian Splendour, 151, 153*
Funk, *253, 255*
Gagnon, Charles, *November Steps, 246, 247*
Gaucher, Yves, *Triptych, 246, 247*
Giant, Half Human, Half Animal, Attacks, A, *78, 79*
Gong 88, No. 1, *230, 231*
Good Friends, *124, 125*
Habitant Farm, The, *120, 121*
Haida Myth of the Bear Mother, Box, *82, 83*
Hamel, Théophile, 30; *Madame Renaud and Her Daughters Wilhelmine and Emma, 114, 115*
Harris, Lawren, 37, 38, 39, 41, 42, 154, 168, 171, 172; 182, 186, 192, 198, 211,; *Mt. Lefroy, 8; Clouds, Lake Superior, 176, 177, Composition No. 1, 200, 201*
Harris, Robert, 32, 33, 135, 140, 255; *A Meeting of the School Trustees, 138, 139*
Heriot, George, 28; *Lake St. Charles near Quebec, 105, 107*
Hind, William, 31; *Self-Portrait, 128, 129*
Hoesem-hliyawn, *Hole-in-the-Sky, 20, 21*
Hole-in-the-Sky, *20, 21*
Holgate, Edwin, 40, 158; *Ludovine, 192, 194*
Holy Father, The, 25, *100, 101*
Ice Cone, Montmorency Falls, The, *120, 122*
I Love Canada, *253, 255*
In the Autumn of Life, *238, 239*
L'incendie du Quartier Saint-Jean, *10, 28*
Indians Portaging Furs, *118, 119*
Inner Release, *224, 225*

Iroquois, *Crooked Mouth Mask, 68, 69*
Iskowitz, Gershon, *Uplands H. (diptych), 240, 241*
J'accuse, *212, 213*
Jack Pine, The, *5, 14, 172*
Jackson, A.Y., 36, 37, 38, 39, 40, 45, 158, 162, 176, 185; *Terre Sauvage, 168, 169; First Snow Algoma, 170, 171*
Jacques Cartier Landing with Colonists, *86, 87*
Kane, Paul, 19, 31, 103; *Assiniboin Hunting Buffalo, 130, 131*
Kenojuak, 22; *Sun Owl, 78, 79*
Kigusiuq, Janet, 76; *A Giant Half Human, Half Animal, Attacks, 78, 79*
Kiyooka, Roy, *StoneDGloves, 254, 255*
Krieghoff, Cornelius, 30; *Merrymaking, 5; Indians Portaging Furs, 118, 119; The Habitant Farm, 120, 121*
Kurelek, William, 50; *In the Autumn of Life, 238, 239*
Kwakiutl, *Bookwus Mask, 65, 67*
Lake Huron No. 4, *11, 243*
Lake St. Charles near Quebec, *106, 107*
Laurentian Splendour, *151, 153*
Le Ber, Pierre, 26; *Marguerite Bourgeoys, 92, 93*
Leduc, Ozias, 35, 36; *Le Petit Liseur, 156, 157*
Légaré, Joseph, 23, 29, 31, 112, 255; *L'incendie du Quartier Saint-Jean, 10; Les chutes de Saint-Ferreol, 116, 117*
Lemieux, Jean-Paul, *Le visiteur du soir, 232, 233*
Levasseur, Pierre-Noël, 25, 90; *Altar Wall, 96, 97; Angel of the Last Judgment, 98, 99, The Holy Father, 100, 101*
Lights of a City Street, 32, *136, 137*
Lindner, Ernest, 48, *Walking Through the Woods, 49*
Lismer, Arthur, 37, 38, 39, 40, 120, 158, 171, 172, 175, 181, 182; *A September Gale, Georgian Bay, 176, 178*
Lochhead, Kenneth, 47, 48; *Inner Release, 224, 225*
Luc, Frère, 26, 89; *Assumption of the Virgin, 90, 91*
Ludovine, *192, 194*

Lyman, John, 42, 44; *Woman with White Collar*, 196, 197
MacDonald, J.E.H., 37, 38, 39, 45, 140, 168, 171, 176; *The Tangled Garden*, 182, 183; *Falls, Montreal River*, 184, 185
Macdonald, Jock, 45, 186, 212, 222; *Fleeting Breath*, 210, 211
Madame Renaud and Her Daughters Wilhelmine and Emma, 114, 115
Magnetawan No. 2, 215, 217
Manitou, 253, 255
Manno, *Bear on Ice*, 74, 75
March Night, 234, 236
Marguerite Bourgeoys, 26, 92, 93
Marguerite Mailhot, 110, 111
Mask, Crooked Nose, 68, 69
Meeting of the School Trustees, A, 138, 139
Meredith, John, *Seeker (triptych)*, 222, 223
Merrymaking, 5, 119
Micmac Indians, 123, 125
Midnight Oil, 251, 255
Milne, David, 40; *Painting Place No. 3*, 188, 191; *Across the Lake*, 189, 191; *Red Nasturtiums*, 190, 191
Mishipeshu Rock Painting, 18, 70, 71, 80
Molinari, Guido, 47, 230, 247; *Mutation sérielle verte-rouge*, 228, 229
Mortgaging the Homestead, 140, 141
Morrice, James Wilson, 36, 41, 153, 158, 192, 197; *The Ferry, Quebec*, 162, 163, *Environs of Tangiers*, 164, 165
Morriseau, Norval, 20, 71; *Warrior with Thunderbirds*, 80, 81
Mother and Child (Oshaweetuk-A), 72, 73
Mother and Child (Tiktak), 74, 75
Mt. Lefroy, 8, 176
Mount Orford and the Owl's Head from Lake Memphremagog, 148, 150
Murray, Robert, *Swing*, 248, 251
Mutation sérielle verte-rouge, 228, 229
Myeengun, 80; *Mishipeshu Rock Painting*, 70, 71
N. E. Thing Company Ltd., 50, 51; *Reflected Landscape: The Arctic Sunset*, 254, 255
Niverville, Louis de, *Funk*, 250, 253
Northwest Coast Indian, 19, 20, *Sechelt*

Image, 58, 59; *The Death Bringer Club*, 58, 59; *The Twin Mask*, 60, 61
November Steps, 246, 247
Nude, 41
O'Brien, John, *British Naval Squadron off Nova Scotia*, 126, 127
O'Brien, Lucius R., 35, 135, 153; *Sunrise on the Saguenay*, 148, 149
Oonark, Jessie, 21, 79; *Untitled Wall Hanging*, 76, 77
Orange Centre, 218, 219
Oshaweetuk-A, *Mother and Child*, 72, 73
Oxen Drinking, 152, 153
Painting 1961, 226, 227
Painting Place No. 3, 188, 191
Pavane (triptych), 208, 209
Peel, Paul, 33, 142, 143; *After the Bath*, 6
Pellan, Alfred, 43, 44, *Citrons ultra-violets*, 206, 207
Petit Liseur, Le, 156, 157
Phantom Hunter, The, 144, 145
Plamondon, Antoine, 29, 30, 115; *Soeur Saint Alphonse*, 112, 113
Portrait of Queen Victoria, 34
Pratt, Christopher, 48, *March Night*, 234, 236
Proch, Don, *Rainbow Mask*, 250, 253
Rain Over Water, 251, 255
Rainbow Mask, 253, 255
Raphael, William, 31; *Behind Bonsecours Market, Montreal*, 132, 133
Rayner, Gordon, 47, 212, *Magnetawan No. 2*, 215, 217
Red Nasturtiums, 190, 191
Reflected Landscape: The Arctic Sunset, 254, 255
Region Centrale, La, 221, 254, 255
Reid, Bill, 17, 18, 20, 53, 62, 67; *Box: Haida Myth of Bear Mother*, 82, 83
Reid, G. A., 140; *Mortgaging the Homestead*, 141, 143
Rindisbacher, Peter, 31, *Captain Bulger at Red Lake*, 30
Riopelle, Jean-Paul, 44, 46; *Pavane (triptych)*, 208, 209
Rising Sun, The, 201
Roberts, Goodridge, *Nude*, 41, 42

Rocamadour I, 252, 255
Rock Painting, 71, 70
Ronald, William, 45, 46; *J'accuse*, 212, 213
St. Lawrence, 25, 98, 99
Sea Monster Headdress, 18, 66, 67
Sechelt Image, The, 17, 58, 59
Seeker, The, 222, 223
Self-Portrait, 128, 129
September Gale, Georgian Bay, A. 176, 178
Settlement on the Hillside, 160, 161
Shadbolt, Jack, 47, 48; *To Old Gardens*, 234, 235
Shaman's Mask, 18, 54, 55
Shaman's Tube, 56, 57
Skirmish with Eskimo, 25
Snow, Michael, 46, 47, 51, 212; *Venus Simultaneous*, 220, 221; *La Region Centrale*, 254, 255
Soeur Saint-Alphonse, 112, 113
Sounds Assembling, 198, 199
Sous le vent de l'ile, 44, 204, 205
Spirit, 21, 22
Stone Road, The, 35, 154, 155
StoneDGloves, 254, 255
Stoney, *Ceremonial Headdress*, 68, 69
Stormy Weather, Georgian Bay, 176, 179, 181
Sunday Afternoon: From an Old American Photograph, 46, 50
Sunday Morning No. 2, 48, 242, 243
Sun Owl, 78, 79
Sunrise on the Saguenay, 148, 149
Suzor-Côté, Marc Aurèle de Foy, 36, 157; *Settlement on the Hillside*, 160, 161
Swing, 251, 255
Tangled Garden, The, 39, 182, 183
Tea Lake Dam, 174, 175
Terre Sauvage, 38, 168, 169
Thomson, Tom, 9, 37, 38, 39, 40, 50, 168, 171, 181, 255; *The West Wind*, 172, 173; *Tea Lake Dam*, 174, 175
Three Robinson Sisters, The, 31, 114, 115
Tiktak, *Mother and Child*, 74, 75
Todd, Robert, *The Ice Cone, Montmorency Falls*, 120, 122
To Old Gardens, 234, 235
Tousignant, Claude, 47, 229, 247; *Gong 88*,

No. 1, 230, 231
Town, Harold, 45, 46, 175; *Banners*, 216, 217
Triptych, 246, 247
Truck Stop, 237, 239
Tsimshian, *Ceremonial Frontlet*, 62, 64; *Chilkat Blanket*, 62, 63; *Sea Monster Headdress*, 66, 67
Two Figure Series XIX, 212, 214
Twin Mask, The, 17, 61, 60
Untitled Wall Hanging, 76, 77
Uplands H (diptych), 240, 241
Urquhart, Tony, 50; *Rocamadour I*, 249, 252
Vallard, Nicholas, 23; *Jacques Cartier Landing with Colonists*, 86, 87
Varley, Fred, 37, 38, 39, 40, 171, 176, 211; *Stormy Weather, Georgian Bay*, 179, 181; *Vera*, 180, 181
Venetian Bather, A, 142, 143
Venus Simultaneous, 220, 221
Vera, 180, 181
View of the Lower Part of the Falls of St. Anne, A, 104, 105
Visiteur du soir, Le, 232, 233
Walker, Horatio, 35; *Oxen Drinking*, 152, 153
Walking Through the Woods, 49
Wall Hanging, Untitled, 76, 77
Warrior with Thunderbirds, 80, 81
Watson, Homer, 35, 36; *The Stone Road*, 154, 155
West, Benjamin, 27; *The Death of General Wolfe*, 29
West Wind, The, 172, 173, 176
Whale, Robert, 32; *The Canadian Southern Railway at Niagara*, 35
White, John, *Skirmish with Eskimo*, 25
White Museum No. 1, 252, 255
Whiten, Colette, *Family*, 249, 252
Whittome, Irene, *White Museum No. 1*, 249, 252
Wieland, Joyce, 46, 47, 50; *I Love Canada*, 249, 253
Wild Man of the Woods, Bookwus Mask, 65, 67
Woman with White Collar, 196, 197
Woolsey Family, The, 108, 109
Wreath of Flowers, A, 7, 33
Young Canadian, 195, 197

Designed by Bob Young
Assembly by Wally Augustowitsch
Typesetting by Mono Lino Typesetting Company Limited
Film separations and colour lithography by Herzig Somerville Limited
Text lithography and binding by Hunter Rose Company Limited